*f*P

Sundays Will Never Be the Same

Racing, Tragedy, and Redemption—

My Life in America's Fastest Sport

DARRELL WALTRIP

with Nate Larkin

FREE PRESS

New York   London   Toronto   Sydney   New Delhi

FREE PRESS
A Division of Simon & Schuster, Inc.
1230 Avenue of the Americas
New York, NY 10020

First Free Press hardcover edition February 2012

FREE PRESS and colophon are trademarks of Simon & Schuster, Inc.

For information about special discounts for bulk purchases,
please contact Simon & Schuster Special Sales at 1-866-506-1949
or business@simonandschuster.com.

The Simon & Schuster Speakers Bureau can bring authors to your live event.
For more information or to book an event, contact the Simon & Schuster Speakers
Bureau at 1-866-248-3049 or visit our website at www.simonspeakers.com.

Manufactured in the United States of America

1   3   5   7   9   10   8   6   4   2

Library of Congress Cataloging-in-Publication Data
Waltrip, Darrell.
Sundays will never be the same : racing, tragedy, and redemption—
my life in America's fastest sport / Darrell Waltrip with Nate Larkin.
p. cm.
1. Waltrip, Darrell. 2. Automobile racing drivers—United States—Biography.
3. Stock car drivers—United States—Biography. 4. Earnhardt, Dale, 1951–2001.
5. Stock car racing—Accidents—United States. I. Larkin,
Nate. II. Title.
GV1032.W37A3 2012
796.72092—dc23
[B]
2011045569

ISBN: 978-1-4516-4489-0
ISBN: 978-1-4516-4491-3 (ebook)

For my wife,

Stephanie Rader Waltrip

The real hero of this story

CONTENTS

1   My New Life   1

2   The Road to Daytona   13

3   Rebel without a Clue   25

4   The Redhead   35

5   Escape from Owensboro   45

6   Shaking Things Up   57

7   The Rookie Is a Brat   69

8   Playing Hardball in the Big Leagues   87

9   Driving for Junior   107

10   Leap of Faith   117

11   Chasing Dale   131

12   No Pain, No Naproxen   151

13   The Owner-Driver Years   169

14   Toward the Finish Line   187

15   The Unthinkable   201

    Epilogue   225

    Acknowledgments   229

    Index   231

Sundays Will Never
Be the Same

CHAPTER ONE

MY NEW LIFE

Have you ever gotten out of bed in the morning, walked into the bathroom, looked at yourself in the mirror, and said, "Today things are going to change"? Me neither. I don't talk to myself in mirrors. But I have gotten out of bed *knowing* that things were going to be different, and that's exactly how I felt on the morning of February 18, 2001.

Big-time changes were happening for me, and I knew it. People around me knew it too, and they had been saying so all week, speculating and joking with me the way race people do. Still, none of us—certainly not me, and not anybody I talked to in the days afterward—suspected that the Sudden Change, the lightning-quick pivotal event that would burn that Sunday into our collective memory and alter the course of our lives forever, was only hours away.

On that morning the air around the Daytona International Speedway was heavy with the familiar smells of fuel and burning rubber. The track had been busy for two weeks in the run-up to the first big race of the season, the Daytona 500.

In case you're not familiar with NASCAR, let me explain. Typical events in NASCAR's top series are three-day weekends, with practice laps and qualifying heats on Friday and Saturday, followed by the big race on Sunday. The Daytona 500, however, is different. NASCAR holds its "Super Bowl" at the beginning of its season rather than the end, and this race, its richest and most prestigious, is the final act in an extended drama of speed and suspense known as "Speedweeks." This year major spectator events during Speedweeks had included a 70-lap all-star race called the Budweiser Shootout and the season-opening races for NASCAR's two lower-tier series, the Busch Grand National series and the Craftsman Truck series—plus the preliminaries for the Daytona 500.

Unlike other races, the qualifying laps for the Daytona 500 are run a week before the race, and only the first two starting positions are awarded when those timed solo laps are over. Four days later all drivers compete in one of two heart-stopping races known as the Twin 125s (nowadays their official name is the Gatorade Duels), battling for starting position in the Sunday race that will be watched by a quarter-million fans in the stands and millions more on television.

I knew the drama of Speedweeks well, but up until this morning I had always experienced the Daytona 500 as a driver. And I can tell you this: for a driver, going to the track on Sunday is like going to war. Other drivers may be your friends and colleagues on any other day, but on Sunday you are going out there against 42 other guys, and every one of them is a threat. Every one of them threatens your livelihood, just as you threaten his. When the announcer calling the race tells the television audience that drivers are "battling for position" on the track, that's no metaphor.

And there is a thrill in that battle that no other experience can match. The feel of the wheel in your hands, the power of 750 horses under your feet, the roar, the blur, the bump, the difficult pass, together trigger an adrenaline rush that you will never capture anywhere else. Racing is a peak experience, and the feeling only intensifies when you win.

I knew the feeling of winning the Daytona 500; I'd won the race in 1989. I'd won plenty of other races too, a total of 84 during my Winston Cup career. I'd won the Cup Championship three times. On NASCAR's list of All-Time Winningest Drivers, I was tied with Bobby Allison for third. (In the modern era of NASCAR, after 1972, I was in the lead.) But all of that was history now, because I had retired. On this Sunday I would not be walking to pit row for the start of the race. Instead I'd be climbing up to the broadcast booth in my new capacity as lead analyst for Fox Sports.

My kid brother Michael would be in the race, though. Sixteen years my junior, Michael had been driving in the Winston Cup series since 1985. He had started the Daytona 500 14 times, finishing five times in the top ten, but he had never won the race. In fact Michael now held the NASCAR record for consecutive starts without a win. In 462 Winston Cup races, he had never finished better than second.

This season, seven-time Winston Cup champion Dale Earnhardt had expanded his racing team to three cars, and he'd hired Michael to drive one of them. Earnhardt had an awful lot of confidence in his cars, and he liked Michael, so when people made comments about his selection of a driver who'd never won a race, Dale just brushed the criticism aside. His son, 26-year-old Dale Earnhardt Jr., who had been named NASCAR's Rookie of the Year in 2000, would be driving the #8 car for Dale Earnhardt, Inc., and Steve Park would be driving Earnhardt's other car, the #1 Chevy. Earnhardt would be in the race too, piloting the signature black #3 Chevy for owner Richard Childress.

I'd talked with my brother on Saturday, discussing the day ahead and its storybook possibilities. It was entirely possible, I told Michael, that he would win this race. He might very well get his first Winston Cup victory on my first day in the broadcast booth! If so, we would be like Ned and Dale Jarrett. Ned, the retired driver turned broadcaster, had been calling the Championship 400 at the Michigan Speedway in 1991 when his son Dale took his first checkered flag. Two years later the younger Jarrett had narrowly edged out Dale Earnhardt for the win in the Daytona 500 as his father openly rooted for him and coached him to victory from the broadcast booth. (Ned was embarrassed by his partisanship in that race and had tried to apologize to Earnhardt afterward, but Earnhardt had waved the apology away with a smile. "I'm a father too," he said.)

Earnhardt had been busy during Speedweeks, as he always was at Daytona, and I had worked hard to schedule a single on-camera interview with him before the big race. Our glamorous roving reporter Jeannie Zelasko, however, spoke with him multiple times. It seemed like whenever Jeannie came around the garage, Dale suddenly wasn't that busy anymore. On Friday I was scanning the monitors in the broadcast booth when I noticed that Jeannie was interviewing Earnhardt yet again. When she finished, I broke in. "Hey Jeannie," I said, "give those earphones to Dale, will you?" Jeannie quickly obliged, telling Earnhardt that I had a couple of questions for him.

"Hey Dale," I said, "how come you always have time for Jeannie but you never have time for me?"

Dale gave me a cockeyed grin, as though I'd just asked the stupidest question in the world. "She's prettier," he answered.

"So tell me, Dale," I said, "when are *you* going to retire?"

Dale pretended to be mystified by the suggestion. "Why should *I* retire?" he replied. "*I'm* still competitive!"

The jab was good-natured. Dale and I were now friends, but our relationship had not always been cordial. We were rivals on the racetrack for years. Our rivalry had spilled into public view in the early 1980s after a flippant remark I'd made in an interview; I'd told a print reporter that I could say anything I wanted about Dale and his team because "they wouldn't be able to read it anyway." Dale hadn't found that comment nearly as funny as I had.

My career had peaked in 1992, but there was no denying that Earnhardt was still competitive, especially at Daytona. Throughout the 1990s he had won every Twin 125 in which he had competed, an incredible ten consecutive victories. In 1998 he had finally taken the checkered flag in the Daytona 500, a win that announcer Mike Joy had called "the most anticipated victory in NASCAR history." After the race, as Earnhardt slowly rolled toward Victory Circle, every crew member from every team had lined up on pit road to shake his hand. It was an unprecedented show of respect, a moment that solidified Earnhardt's place in the pantheon of NASCAR's greatest drivers.

In the Twin 125s earlier this week, Earnhardt had finished

third, earning the seventh starting position for the race on Sunday. He would be starting on the inside in the fourth row when the flag dropped on the 2001 Daytona 500. Dale Jr. had earned the sixth position, so he'd be starting on the outside in the third row. My brother Michael, behind the wheel of the #15 car, had qualified for the 19th starting position, so he'd be starting in the tenth row. Steve Park would be starting in the 13th row, in the 25th position.

The race was scheduled to start at one o'clock, but the pre-race broadcast began at noon. As noon approached, I took my place at the studio desk opposite Chris Myers, who would be hosting the pre-race show. Jeff Hammond, my friend and former crew chief, sat between us. Jeff would be working as a roving reporter during the race, but he seemed to think his main job during Speedweeks was to talk me through the broadcasts in much the same way he'd talked me through countless trips around the track. After some light-hearted banter, the three of us introduced the television audience to the issues we had identified as the potential themes of the day.

The car manufacturer Dodge was making its return to NASCAR this year, after a 16-year absence. Most people hadn't expected much from Dodge after such a long layoff, but by now it was clear to everyone that the Dodge team, led by Ray Evernham, had really done its homework. Bill Elliot had won the pole for the big race by posting the fastest average lap speed during qualifying—187.715 miles per hour—in a Dodge. Stacy Compton, also in a Dodge, had finished second in qualifying. Sterling Marlin had earned the third starting spot for the big race by winning the first of the Twin 125s in a Dodge.

The blistering speed of the Dodge cars had fueled speculation about the reasons for their dominance. Were they aerodynamically superior? Wind tunnel tests conducted by NASCAR in Atlanta on Monday seemed to indicate they were. Were their engines better? Driver Jimmy Spencer, quoted that morning in the Charleston, South Carolina, *Post and Courier*, said, "The Dodge is about 40 horsepower more than a Ford or a Chevrolet. . . . Maybe the good

Lord above will make them all blow up on Sunday. I'd love it."

Dodge's rumored advantages had pushed the other teams into a frenzy of last-minute tweaking, finessing, and second-guessing. On Saturday Jeff Gordon blew the engine of his Chevrolet during the final hour of practice. Gordon's team replaced the engine overnight, and other teams, suddenly dissatisfied with the performance of their engines, nervously followed suit. On the night before the Daytona 500 ten cars received engine transplants.

In addition to speed, drivers and owners were concerned about safety. The tragic memories of 1994—Neil Bonnett's fatal crash in turn 4 during practice, and Rodney Orr's death during practice three days later—still haunted Speedweeks, and more recent fatalities on the circuit had revived the concern. On May 12, 2000, Adam Petty, the 19-year-old grandson of NASCAR legend Richard Petty, was killed when he lost control of his car and crashed into the wall in turn 3 in Loudon, New Hampshire, while practicing for a Busch series race the next day. Exactly eight weeks later Winston Cup driver Kenny Irwin lost his life in a crash on the same track, in the same turn, also during practice.

Beginning in 1988 NASCAR had tried to improve safety by requiring the use of restrictor plates at the two tracks with the longest straightaways, the superspeedways in Daytona and Talladega. (By reducing airflow into the carburetor, a restrictor plate starves the engine of oxygen, effectively slowing the car down.) Driver reaction to the restrictor plates was mixed. While lower speeds reduced the risks to drivers and spectators in the event of a crash, the limitations also made the cars increasingly identical. Like other NASCAR initiatives intended to create parity on the track, the restrictor plates tended to produce races in which cars traveled around the track in huge bunches. With dozens of cars racing only inches apart at more than 180 miles per hour, even a small mistake by one driver could easily trigger a massive pileup. Since the introduction of restrictor plates, Daytona and Talladega had become notorious for awe-inspiring multicar crashes. And the fans loved 'em—as long as the drivers were able to walk away afterward.

Outside one of the entrances to the stands this year, NASCAR had set up a special "show car." It was painted like Earnhardt's #3 Chevy, but this car was cut away to reveal the safety features NASCAR had made mandatory. A plaque beside the car pointed out the window netting, the welded tubular steel roll cage, the four-point shoulder harness, the foam-and-rubber fuel cell, the roof flaps designed to deploy when a car started spinning in order to prevent it from flipping or going airborne, and other features intended to protect the driver. This was state-of-the-art stuff, and it helped drivers and fans maintain the belief that NASCAR racing could be dangerous without being lethal. That belief was essential to the sport. In order to drive all-out, drivers needed to believe they could walk away from any crash. Fans, on the other hand, were well aware that a spectacular accident could happen at any moment; that prospect was a big part of what made motor racing so exciting. Nobody came to Daytona to watch badminton. This was NASCAR, and it was not a sport for sissies.

Back when I was driving, I'd become accustomed to working with tunnel vision; my field of view had been restricted to what was happening right in front of me at any given moment during a race. I'd been forced to rely on my crew chief and a team of spotters, communicating by radio, to let me know what was going on behind me and elsewhere on the track. Now, however, my vantage point in the broadcast booth offered me a whole new perspective, and I was still adjusting to it. Now I could take in the entire field all at once. What an impressive spectacle it was! With the crowd on its feet, the cars, two by two, followed the pace car around the track. As the column swept through turn 4 and the pace car ducked into pit road, the field surged toward the start/finish line, where a jubilant Terry Bradshaw stood above the track waving the green flag. The cars thundered down the front stretch, the pitch of their engines rising in a deafening crescendo, and poured into the first turn with 250,000 voices urging them on. I heard myself cheering too.

Right from the start it was clear that this race would be one for the ages. The field flashed around the entire two-and-a-half-mile tri-oval every 48 seconds, and by the 26th lap, when Dale Earnhardt powered briefly to the front of the pack, the lead had already changed six times. By the 57th lap the lead had changed 12 times, and Earnhardt was back in 20th place. By the 95th lap the lead had changed 20 times.

The cars were battling a tremendous headwind on the back straightaway, and the Dodge cars seemed to be faring better than most; Dodges led 18 of the first 19 laps. Bill Elliot, the pole sitter, started to fall out of contention early, but the Dodges of Sterling Marlin and Ward Burton continued to dominate, Marlin holding the lead for 40 laps, Burton for 53.

On the 99th lap my brother Michael moved into tenth place, and by the 171st lap he had fought his way to the front. On lap 173, however, disaster struck.

The Big One happened during a commercial break. When the television audience rejoined the broadcast we were showing replays of the colossal accident, which was triggered when Robby Gordon nudged the back of Ward Burton's car on the back straightaway, sending it drifting up the track toward the wall. Tony Stewart tried, unsuccessfully, to get out of Burton's way, but his #20 Pontiac started to spin, and, as the air got under it, the car suddenly sailed skyward, twisting and flipping in mid-air for what seemed like an eternity, then tumbled back into the torrent of oncoming traffic, pieces flying and flames blossoming, as other drivers careened and collided in a futile effort to avoid making contact with it.

When the smoke cleared, Stewart's car was virtually unrecognizable, and 17 others were in ruins. Miraculously Stewart walked to the ambulance under his own power, and nobody else was seriously injured either, but the pileup left even NASCAR veterans shaking their heads in amazement.

The race was red-flagged while the track was cleared. Since the running order was frozen, cars that were still drivable slipped into the pits to survey the damage. Then, when there were 22 laps left to go, the race was officially restarted—with my brother at the front of the pack! Michael was now racing toe-to-toe with Dale Earnhardt (his owner), Dale Jr. (his teammate), and Sterling Marlin, whose #40 Dodge Intrepid still seemed to be the fastest car on the track.

Thinking aloud, I spoke to my brother from the broadcast booth. "Mikey," I said, "that's two Earnhardts up there. I think you're odd man out, buddy." My concern escalated on lap 182, when it looked like Earnhardt was trying to pass Michael to take the lead. "Michael's in a bind," I said to the television audience. "If he lets Earnhardt by, I'm gonna kick his butt, and if he don't let Earnhardt by, *Earnhardt's* going to kick his butt. So he's in trouble!"

As the final laps unwound, however, it gradually dawned on me that Earnhardt was scripting the race—*and he wanted one of his cars to win.* Michael and Dale Jr. were running first and second, and Earnhardt was running interference behind them, blocking every effort by Marlin and the other pursuers to reach the front.

Since a bump from behind can make a car lose traction momentarily, causing it to slide up the track in a turn, Marlin bumped Earnhardt several times as the finish line approached, but the maneuver didn't work. "Sterling has beat the front off that old Dodge trying to get by Dale," I observed. But Earnhardt, wily and stubborn as ever, held his line in the turns and wouldn't let Marlin by.

The victory that our family had dreamed about was within Michael's grasp, and I could hardly believe it. The tension became unbearable. "I can't watch," I said. "This is what we've all prayed for."

My partners in the broadcast booth fell silent, and I found myself talking to my brother as though I were in the car beside him.

Michael, you're in the best place you've ever been. Hold 'er there.

Just don't get overconfident, Mikey.

Seven laps to go in the biggest race in the world!

My poor momma, she's gonna be havin' a fit!

C'mon, buddy. One to go!

Keep it low, Mikey. Keep it low. Don't let 'em under ya. Take that back straightaway wide, buddy. Get all over the place! Don't let 'em run up on ya! C'mon man! Watch that mirror, watch 'im! He's going to make a run inside. Block him! Block him! Attaboy! You got 'im, Mikey! You got 'im!

And that's when it happened, right there in the final turn of the final lap. Sterling Marlin finally got his nose under Earnhardt, but as he did, their cars grazed. Earnhardt's car slipped sideways, dropping momentarily toward the apron, then suddenly careened up the 31-degree turn and into the concrete retaining wall. A moment later Michael took the checkered flag, flashing across the finish line a scant 0.124 seconds ahead of Dale Jr.

I was overcome with emotion, almost too choked to speak. I was thrilled by my brother's victory, but beneath my elation I could feel a nagging sense of dread. Those around me didn't seem too worried about Dale. He was Dale Earnhardt, after all, an indestructible figure driving the safest race car in the world. To most people who'd seen it, Earnhardt's wreck hadn't looked that bad, but I knew better. The fans were leaving the stands, and the television production people were preparing to wrap up the broadcast. "I hope Dale's okay," I said to the television audience. "I guess he's all right, isn't he?"

The cameras went to Michael in Victory Circle, then came back to me for reaction to my brother's win. "As proud as I am of Michael, and as excited as I am for him," I said, "I'm still prayin' for Dale. They're still workin' on him."

In the final seconds of the broadcast, my partners and I reviewed a slow-motion video of Dale's crash. By now it was clear that Dale was seriously injured—he'd been loaded into an ambulance and rushed to the hospital—but we still had no details about his condition. I watched the replay of the accident with dismay. Dale had hit the wall head-on at more than 160 miles per hour. "Those kinda licks are the worst kind," I said. "They're sudden.

That's the kind of crash that hurts you. That sudden stop, that's a driver's worst nightmare."

After the broadcast ended, I turned to Big Andy, the sheriff's deputy assigned to escort me to Victory Circle for the celebration. I'd known Big Andy for years—he was a fixture at Daytona—and I knew that his wife worked as a nurse in the emergency room at Halifax Hospital. Andy was white as a ghost, and there were tears running down his face.

"What's wrong?"

"We've got to go to the hospital right now," Andy said. "I just got off the phone with Maryann. Dale isn't going to make it."

Andy's news stunned me. I stood there for a moment, my mind reeling. Dale Earnhardt was not going to make it? Dale was dying? The very thought was almost incomprehensible, its ramifications unthinkable. Michael's victory and my new career suddenly seemed inconsequential by comparison. Dale was dying? In the blink of an eye the world had changed, and we were completely unprepared for it.

My mind was racing as I followed Big Andy down the stairs. If Dale Earnhardt was dying, then race day in America had just been altered forever, not just for Dale's family and friends, but for everyone who had ever come to the track or watched a Sunday race on television. If Dale was dying, then everything had changed.

Sundays would never be the same.

CHAPTER TWO

THE ROAD TO DAYTONA

The events of February 18, 2001, marked a turning point in the evolution of stock car racing in America. It was fitting, I suppose, that the fateful day would unfold in Daytona Beach, the city that had been hosting motor races for nearly a century, the city where NASCAR was born. Daytona figures heavily in Dale Earnhardt's life story, and in my own as well.

When I made my first trip to Daytona, in 1965, I was sure I was going to meet my destiny. I'd been dreaming about competing at America's greatest racetrack since I was 12 years old, flying around the go-kart track in my hometown of Owensboro, Kentucky. At 16, as I blasted around our local paved tracks in a modified '58 Ford, I imagined I was David Pearson, chasing the checkered flag at Daytona. Now, at the exalted age of 18, I was finally ready. I could hear the Beach calling my name.

I had already made the 100-mile trip to Salem, Indiana, where I'd proven myself on that half-mile oval in the countryside, and I'd traveled 140 miles to compete at the Music City Motorplex in Nashville, Tennessee. But the Daytona International Speedway was another world. The fabled track was four states and 800 miles away, drenched in sun and surrounded by glory. Junior Johnson would be there, along with Bobby Allison and Ned Jarrett, competing with 40 other drivers in the Daytona 500 on Valentine's Day. I would not be in that race—*not yet.* My mission on this trip was to win the Sportsman series race that would be held on the Saturday before the Daytona 500.

All through that cold Kentucky winter, several of my friends and I had been working on my ride, a car owned by Paul Freels. My friend Ed Sanders had a buddy named Slick Owens who worked over at Holman-Moody, the company that was making custom racing engines. Ed worked a deal with Slick and got us a brand-new Holman-Moody engine to go in Paul's '58 Ford. Ray Skillman, whose family owned Skillman Auto Sales, helped us install it. Ray liked to drag race and fool with cars, and he was as enthusiastic about the project as I was, but neither of us really knew what we were doing. Putting that engine in that car was kind of like dropping a 650-horsepower turbocharged engine into a Volkswagen. The car was never intended to go 170 miles per hour at Daytona Beach. We didn't care, though. We painted it orange and plastered a big number 98 on the side (which we would have to change to 88 when we reached the track), dreaming of victory in Daytona.

Jim Yeiser, a local farmer who was a friend of the family, agreed to haul the car to Daytona on his flatbed farm truck. The truck didn't have a tilt bed on it, so we backed it out into a ditch, then got some planks and, with the help of a bunch of my friends, rolled the car across the ditch onto the bed of the truck. The car almost didn't fit, but we pushed it tight against the back of the cab and lashed it into place. Then Jim, Ray, and I loaded up the rest of our stuff, climbed into the cab, and took off down the highway toward Daytona Beach.

Drivers have been bringing their cars to Daytona for more than a century. According to legend, the whole business started in 1903, when the owners of two horseless carriages encountered each other on what was then Ormond Beach. The beach was a natural place for them to meet, since the hard-packed sands along the ocean provided a smoother and more stable driving surface than any inland road. In the words of a popular magazine, the beach was "smooth as a billiard table, hard as marble, 100 feet wide and 27 miles long, straight as an African spear."

After bragging for a while about the merits of their machines, the two gentlemen shook hands on a friendly wager. That was all it took. A small crowd gathered for the race, and a spectator sport was born. Other races quickly followed. Within two years the first film crew showed up. Soon drivers from around the world were hauling their glistening machines to Daytona in pursuit of the World Land Speed Record.

In 1927 Major H. O. D. Segrave, a dashing 30-year-old British military hero, broke the 200 miles per hour barrier in his Golden Arrow, crossing a mile of Daytona sand in less than 17 seconds. The following year, 26-year-old Frank Lockhart lost control of his Stutz Blackhawk while trying to break Segrave's record, tumbling into the surf in a spectacular crash. Lockhart survived the crash and started planning his next run from his hospital bed. Six weeks later, the car repaired, he was back on the beach for a second try. The second crash killed him.

Segrave's record was broken later that same year by Ray Keech in a rolling monstrosity called the White Triplex. Owned by a Philadelphia millionaire named J. M. White, the Triplex was designed without any serious regard for driver safety. Three 12-cylinder Liberty Aircraft engines were mounted on a truck chassis, one in front and two side-by-side in the rear, with the driver in an open cockpit in the middle. There was no gearbox and no clutch. With Keech at the wheel, the Triplex reached a top speed of 207.55 miles per hour.

Not to be outdone, Major Segrave returned to Daytona the following year and broke the record set by the Triplex, pounding down the beach in the Golden Arrow at 231.44 miles per hour. Two days later J. M. White wheeled his three-engine machine back out onto the sand, determined to reclaim the record. White's first challenge was to find someone to drive the behemoth. Ray Keech, who had driven the car on its first successful run, refused to drive it again. "There is not enough money to get me back in that hot seat," he said.

White soon found another driver, a well-liked local garage operator named Lee Bible. Amiable but inexperienced, Bible climbed aboard the Triplex, waved to the photographers, and roared down the beach, topping out at 202 miles per hour. At the end of the strip, however, something went wrong. (Later, the general consensus was that Bible had taken his foot off the accelerator too quickly.) The car swerved suddenly, then rolled, then somersaulted into the faraway dunes, finally coming to rest in a spray of sand and smoke. Bible was thrown from the car and died instantly, but he was not the only casualty. A Pathé newsreel photographer named Charles Traub panicked when he saw the car coming in his direction, abandoned his camera, and ran the wrong way: directly into the path of the tumbling car. Traub was killed on the spot.

The death of a spectator forced the organizers of the Daytona Land Speed Trials to face the fact that the size of the crowds and the speed of the cars had made their venue unsafe, and they began looking for a safer one. The last speed record at Daytona was set in March 1935, when Sir Malcolm Campbell reached 276 miles per hour in his famous Bluebird V. The following year the trials were moved to Bonneville Salt Flats in Utah.

The loss of the time trials posed a serious threat to the economy of Daytona Beach, and the civic leaders wasted no time in devising a plan to keep the crowds coming. Their future, they agreed, still lay in racing. Daytona, after all, had become synonymous with motor racing; it was "the birthplace of speed." Even though the nation was still in the grip of the Great Depression, Americans were obsessed with the automobile, and they were driving south in record numbers. The City Fathers quickly mapped out a racetrack near the center of town, close to the shops, restaurants, and hotels. The track actually ran 1.5 miles along the beach, then returned 1.5 miles along a paved public road, the two sections connected by banked sand turns.

The first race on the Daytona Beach Road Course was held in March 1936. Sponsored by the city and sanctioned by the American Automobile Association, the 250-mile race was restricted to street-legal family sedans manufactured in 1935 and 1936. The race drew a huge crowd, but most of the spectators never paid admission because they reached the dunes before the ticket-takers arrived. As it turned out, the track could not withstand the churning tires of 27 cars slewing through the banked turns. On lap 75, with the track virtually impassable, the AAA officials stopped the race and declared Milt Marion of Long Island the winner. When the money was counted, the city had lost $22,000 on the event. It was the last time the city would sponsor a race.

The fifth-place finisher in 1936 was a local filling station owner named Bill France. In the years that followed it was France who, by default, wound up organizing and eventually sponsoring other stock car races in Daytona. Racing was suspended during World War II, but in 1947 France convened a meeting of drivers, owners, and mechanics at the Streamline Hotel in Daytona Beach, initiating the talks that would lead to the formation of the National Association of Stock Car Auto Racing—NASCAR—in 1948.

NASCAR, with Bill France firmly in control, standardized the rules for stock car racing. Beginning in 1949, all cars were required to be "strictly stock." Drivers were allowed to remove headlights and install seat belts, but in every other respect the car that took the checkered flag on Sunday afternoon was identical to the car any workingman might drive off the showroom floor on Monday morning. As the years passed, NASCAR gradually allowed other modifications that improved the performance and safety of the cars, while still insisting that the racing machines look like family sedans.

By 1956 it was clear that stock car racing in Daytona had outgrown the beach course. Crowds regularly exceeded 30,000. The races could be run only during low tide, and marking out a course and clearing that many people from the beach during a six-hour window had become a daunting task. France began making plans for a superspeedway in Daytona, one even grander than Harold Brasington's wildly successful Darlington Raceway in South Carolina, which had opened in 1950 and played host to NASCAR's annual Labor Day event, the Southern 500.

When the Daytona International Speedway opened on February 22, 1959, more than 41,000 spectators overflowed the stands for the first running of the Daytona 500. There were 59 cars in the field that day, competing for a total purse of $67,760. The track was an awe-inspiring sight, a 2.5 mile tri-oval circuit with achingly long straightaways and Himalayan 31-degree banked turns. A modern superspeedway with an integrated 3.56-mile road course, the new facility was so vast that powerboat races could be held on its infield lake.

In a sobering premonition, however, one driver had already died by the time the track officially opened. Marshall Teague was a hero in Daytona, known as "the king of the Beach" for his exploits on the Daytona Beach Road Course. Behind the wheel of his lightweight Fabulous Hudson Hornet, Teague won 27 of the 34 major stock car events in which he competed during 1952 and 1953. He left NASCAR in 1953, however, after a dispute with Bill France. In 1959, 11 days before the track opened to the public, Teague was behind the wheel of an Indy-style roadster, trying to break a closed-track speed record he had set the day before, when the car spun and flipped through the third turn, killing him.

Before the track's first year was over, two more drivers had suffered fatal injuries at the Daytona International Speedway. On April 4, 1959, George Amick was killed during a 100-mile U.S. Auto Club race. On June 14, 1959, Dr. Bernie Taylor lost his life during a powerboat race on the infield lake.

By the time I arrived at the track with my friends in 1965, the track had claimed the lives of five drivers. Of all the tracks I would compete on in the years ahead, the Daytona International Speedway was the only one that scared me.

It was growing dark when Ray, Jim, and I reached the interstate, but we didn't even consider stopping. Our plan was to drive straight through to Florida, taking turns sleeping. As it turned out, however, nobody got any sleep that night, because every time the truck hit a bump, the car jolted against the back of the cab—BOOM! It was like riding inside a drum, except the rhythm wasn't consistent enough to put you to sleep. We rode that way all night—boom, boom, ba-BOOM!—knowing that if the car ever *stopped* beating on the cab, we would *really* have a problem.

When we arrived in Daytona early the next morning, the sky was a dazzling blue and the wind that rustled the palm trees carried the scent of the ocean. In the lee of the grandstand, a security guard directed us to the tunnel that would take us to the infield. A few minutes later we rumbled up out of the tunnel and caught our first glimpse of the enormous track.

The sight was absolutely breathtaking. Turn 4 rose behind us, blocking the morning sun, and the front straightaway stretched past the diminishing stands, toward the horizon. Turn 1 and turn 2 seemed to be five miles away. The backstretch shimmered in the distance, beyond the sparkling waters of Lake Lloyd. Trucks and campers dotted the infield like Conestoga wagons parked on a prairie. We could see some activity around a distant line of one-story buildings, which we surmised were the garages, and we headed in that direction.

Our first challenge was to unload the car. There simply was no place on the infield where you could back the truck off into a ditch and unload the stupid thing. We rode around for a while, looking everywhere for a suitable place, and finally settled on a low spot in the grass. The spot was far from perfect, but it would have to do. Ray borrowed a pair of ramps from a friendly stranger, but the ramps wouldn't reach the bed of the truck until we let all the air out of the rear tires. When we finally got the car off the truck, I drove it over to the garage to get it inspected.

I had never been through an inspection process like the one in Daytona. The entry form I signed listed a lot of detailed specifications I hadn't bothered to read very closely, fine print that, it turned out, NASCAR officials were dead serious about enforcing. The inspection crew looked at my car and shook their heads. The head of the competition for the Sportsman division, a guy named Pete Keller, tapped me on the shoulder. "You ain't gonna race this thing here," he said with finality.

"What? Why not?" I was incredulous.

"Well, to begin with, there are no side windows in this car. The rules say all the windows must be in place, and the one on the driver's side must be operable."

"No problem," I said. "Is there a junkyard around here? I'll find windows."

Keller raised his hand. "I'm just getting started," he said. "You've also removed a lot of the sheet metal and bracing. You've cut out the webbing from the underside of the hood and the inside of the trunk, for example. Your car is way too light."

"Are you serious?" I stammered. "Back in Owensboro, everybody does that. The lighter the car, the faster it goes."

"This is NASCAR," Keller said. "And in NASCAR, all the metal stays."

This was not looking good at all. "Anything else?" I asked.

"Yep," Keller said. "You know about Fireball Roberts, right?" Of course I knew about Fireball Roberts. One of NASCAR's most successful drivers, Roberts had died the previous year after a fiery crash at the World 600 in Charlotte. His car had flipped, and fuel from his gas tank had poured into the cockpit and ignited. "New rule," Keller said. "The gas tank must be located inside the trunk and fully secured. Yours is hanging on the bottom of your car."

The next week was a race against time. Ray, Jim, and I arrived at the racetrack before dawn each morning and worked until long after dark. In a junkyard about five miles away, out on Route 92, we found a '58 Ford. We started feverishly cutting pieces out of that car with a torch and taking them back to the track. The cutting part was pretty easy, but the welding part was not. We weren't skilled welders. Jim knew how to repair a tractor, but he didn't have any idea how to work on a race car. Fortunately there were plenty of talented people walking around, and some of them were willing to offer suggestions or lend a hand. Fitting the salvaged window assembly into the driver's side door and getting the thing to roll up and down properly took an entire day. The hood from the wrecked Ford wouldn't fit, so we wound up cutting it apart and then welding the webbing onto the hood of my car, a tedious, time-consuming process. Restoring the trunk and relocating the gas tank proved to be a nightmare, but we kept plugging away. We worked all week, barely stopping to eat and sleep. Finally, as the last hours of practice were slipping away, we finished. I drove the car back to the inspection garage and waited nervously for Keller's verdict. The car passed.

A couple days earlier, on my way back from a quick trip to Steak 'n Shake, I stopped at Kmart to buy a pair of coveralls. NASCAR had made the "fireproof suit" mandatory after Fireball Roberts died wearing only a T-shirt and jeans. The new outerwear was not high-tech. You'd take an ordinary pair of coveralls to the NASCAR guys, and they would dip them in a fire-retardant solution. Then you'd hang them on a fence until they were dry and stiff. Shoes? I preferred Hush Puppies, and NASCAR had no rules covering footwear.

I was shaking in my Hush Puppies when I finally drove onto pit lane and a flagman waved me out onto the track for the first time. I was so nervous, in fact, that when I reached the end of pit road, I turned left onto the flat road course that runs through the infield. To my friends who were watching, it looked like I had just disappeared. With no radio in the car I was completely on my own out there, but I eventually figured out that I was on the wrong track. Flushed with embarrassment, I got the car turned around and headed back toward the front straightaway.

I eased onto the apron at the bottom of the track and gingerly accelerated, eventually drifting into the warm-up lane. When I reached turn 1, I eased off the gas and dropped onto the apron again. I made two laps that way, riding the warm-up lane on the straightaways and clinging to the apron in the corners. After the second lap somebody held up a pit board and motioned me in.

"What's wrong?" asked the first guy to reach me.

I looked at him blankly.

Another guy arrived. "What's the problem?" he asked, concern in his voice. "What's wrong with the car?"

"Nothing's wrong with the car," I said. "I just don't see how this car is going to stay up on those banks. It just doesn't look possible to me."

21

"Did you notice that other cars are staying up on the banks?" they asked.

"Yeah, but I don't know how they're doing it."

The guys looked at each other. "Simple," one of them said to me. "They're holding it wide open."

I was dumbfounded. "You want me to hold this car wide open and go up on those banks?" They nodded. "I'm not your man!" I said. I started unbuckling my seat belt, but they calmed me down and persuaded me to give it another try.

Back on the track I pushed the pedal to the floor and got up some pretty good speed going down the back straightaway. As I was approaching turn 3 everything in me wanted to ease back on the throttle, but I closed my eyes, resisted the urge, and drove right into the turn. When I opened my eyes again I was high on the banked track, flowing through the corner, just as smooth and pretty as you please. Centrifugal force was pulling me toward the right side of the car, but otherwise the experience was not nearly as bad as I had expected it to be. Before long I was riding around the whole track wide open and feeling pretty comfortable.

The car behaved differently, however, during the actual race. We had built the car to compete on quarter-mile tracks, and on those tracks you run big, wide tires—almost like the tires on a dragster—in order to maintain maximum contact with the road in the tight turns. The tires at Daytona, however, are much smaller. My car looked a little funny with those short speedway tires, and I soon learned that the problem was more than cosmetic. All that room around the wheels had aerodynamic implications too.

It was weird. During the race I'd be sailing along just fine, but then my clutch would slip. I couldn't figure it out. Then the pattern became clear: my clutch slipped only when somebody passed me. I was still pondering the problem when two cars passed me simultaneously, one on either side. As the cars blew by I felt my car lift up and heard the engine whine. That's when it hit me. The clutch was fine, but my car was *flying!* When the air pushed aside by the passing cars flowed around my wheels and under the car, it was literally lifting my rear tires off the track.

I suppose it's a miracle I didn't spin out and crash that day. I drove recklessly, aggressively, pushing my car in a way that only an 18-year-old with delusions of immortality can drive. With ten laps to go, I was running in the top ten. Then a couple of cars dropped out, and with five laps to go I was running in the top five. I could taste victory. Suddenly, roaring down the back straightaway with two laps to go, I heard a clattering sound. The engine abruptly quit and the car filled up with smoke. I coasted to the apron in disgust, certain that my motor had blown up.

After the race we pushed the car back to the garage and assessed the damage. Strangely, we couldn't find any oil under the car, and no fluids were leaking from the engine compartment. We lifted the hood and looked at the engine for a minute. Finally, Ray noticed the alternator. One of its mounting bolts had broken, and the alternator had fallen back against the engine, shorting out all the wires in the ignition system. We tilted the alternator back, replaced the bolt, and hot-wired the ignition. The car fired right up and ran like a champ.

Ray, Jim, and I hung around the track for the Cup race, then packed up and headed back to Owensboro. The return trip was bittersweet. We had almost won but had come up empty. Still, I had acquired valuable experience that I was sure would help me in my next trip to the Beach. I didn't know then that that trip was five years away.

CHAPTER THREE

REBEL WITHOUT A CLUE

Some boys grow up under the care of a very involved father or father figure, an older man who is protective and affirming and who coaches them step-by-step through life. Such boys tend to develop an easygoing attitude toward authority, and when they reach adulthood they usually operate pretty well within authority structures. Other boys are compliant by nature and will always turn themselves inside out to please anyone in a position of authority, regardless of how well they are treated in return. I was never either one of those boys. In fact I developed a pattern of independence and protest during adolescence that followed me into adulthood, a pattern that cost me dearly over the years.

My father was a wonderful man and a very hard worker, but he was not what I would call a doting dad. His job as a route deliveryman for the local Pepsi bottler was physically demanding, and it took most of his time. My mother worked full time too. Our family kept growing until there were five kids in our little three-bedroom house. At that point I started staying with my friends rather than going home, and my parents didn't seem to mind. I was still in school, but I started making all my own decisions. I decided what I was going to do and figured out some way to do it.

I didn't play football or baseball in high school. I did play basketball, but never with distinction. My most memorable accomplishment as a basketball player came in my first varsity start, when I got my hands on the ball and promptly scored a basket— at the wrong end of the court! The only sport in which I ever excelled was track, and I wound up walking away from that sport after a conflict with authority.

My track career started early in my freshman year. I was at my desk in homeroom one morning, trading jokes with my friends, when an announcement came over the loudspeaker: tryouts for the track team would be held in the gymnasium that afternoon. A few of my buddies decided to go down and try out, so I said I'd go too.

The tryouts, as it turned out, were nothing more than a brutal endurance test. The coaches lined us up and said, "When we blow this whistle, we want you guys to start running laps around the gym. We'll blow the whistle again when we want you to stop."

The whistle blew, and I took off running. I had no idea at the time, but I had a major advantage over the other guys who were trying out for the team. Physical endurance is mostly determined by physical factors, many of them genetic, and I happen to have been blessed with a body that is designed for endurance. In scientific terms, my body is at the upper end of the scale in its ability to deliver oxygen to the muscles and remove lactates, the chemicals that cause fatigue and cramping. I didn't know that. I just knew I was running, lap after lap, and I was hardly getting tired at all. Other guys started stumbling and stopping and throwing up, and I kept breezing along. Eventually only a couple guys were left. I was starting to get a little tired by now, but I still had plenty of energy in reserve, so I kept on chugging until I was the last man standing. Afterward the coaches gushed their approval. "You're great, kid!" they said. I'd never heard that before in an athletic context, and it was exciting. Finally, I had discovered the thing I could do that nobody else could do. I'd found my claim to fame.

I was a middle-distance runner. I started out competing in the 680-meter event and soon graduated to the 880 (now commonly known as the half-mile). The course was simple—two laps around the oval track—and my strategy was simple too. On the first lap I would hang back and watch, patiently, as the other runners fought for the lead. Then, about halfway down the back of the last lap, I'd take off. I had a great kick, and this was the part of the race I loved most. I would blast through the field, past the leaders, and cross the finish line as they were coming off the fourth turn.

Years later I would apply this same strategy to motor racing. Driving a race car is physically and mentally demanding in the extreme. While other drivers wore themselves out trading the lead in the early going, I would lay back, conserving my strength. Only later in the race, after the leaders were exhausted, would I make my move, lighting the fuse on my reserves and rocketing to the front when the lead really mattered.

As a high school runner I went undefeated in the 880, and by my junior year I had become a bona fide track star, holding the record for my event in the state of Kentucky. My prospects for a college athletic scholarship were bright, but that's when my adversarial attitude toward authority altered the course of my career.

Our track coach was a big, gruff character who had played football at the University of Kentucky. Coach had a mean streak, and his method of coaching involved regular doses of humiliation and intimidation. If you did something he didn't like, he would reach over and knock you on the back of the head with his big, heavy ring—thump!—and yell, "You knucklehead!" I never liked the guy very much, and I was pretty sure he didn't like me.

One afternoon we were practicing at the football stadium, training on the track that runs around the field, and Coach was sitting up in the grandstand, harassing us. He had a Coke in one hand and a moon pie in the other, and he was yelling, "Run, you pansies, run! If you don't pick it up you're going to give me fifty!"

This was just not a good day for Coach to be treating me that way. The more he yelled, the more I fumed. What I wanted to do was go up there and grab him and say, "How about you coming out here and running some laps with us, huh? How about, instead of sitting up there drinking your Coke and yelling at us, you get your big butt out here and run with us?" I guess my displeasure must have shown, because he singled me out for some verbal abuse. When he did that, I stopped, took my shoes off, and starting walking toward the locker room.

"Where in the hell do you think you're going?" he yelled.

"I quit," I said.

"What do you mean, you quit? You can't quit! We're getting ready for a meet against Owensboro High School next Saturday—you can't just walk off."

"Yes I can," I said over my shoulder. "I don't have to run track. I ran because I enjoyed it, and I don't enjoy it anymore."

I never went back. I never ran track again, and that was a shame, because I was very good at it, and I loved to run. I felt like I could run forever.

By the time I quit the track team, I had already acquired other interests: girls, for example, and picking up an illegal six-pack or two to split with my friends. I was also driving on the weekends at the speedway in Whitesville, a paved track that had opened in 1960. I made a name for myself pretty quickly in Whitesville, but my success on the oval brought an unintended consequence: it inflamed my already hostile relationship with the local police.

Several of the Owensboro cops also had race cars, and they would drive on the weekends at Whitesville. They were older than I and had more money than I did, but I consistently came out ahead of them on the track. I was not the most gracious of winners either. As a result some of those cops made a special effort to make my life miserable when they were on the job. They'd pull me over for anything: failure to signal, a missing taillight, an inoperable windshield wiper, anything.

One time I got pulled over for speeding in front of County High School. I hadn't really been going that fast, but the cop who always sat beside the school monitoring traffic ticketed me anyway. The next time I drove past the school, I slowed way down. There was a No Passing zone in front of the school, and pretty soon traffic started piling up behind me, but I refused to go any faster than about 20 miles per hour. I looked over at the cop as I drove by, and smiled. He flipped on his lights and pulled me over again. This time he issued me a ticket for driving too slowly.

Fortunately my grandfather was the deputy sheriff in Owensboro. His name was Lee Phillips, and he was good friends with the judge in town. Whenever I got in trouble I'd call my granddad and say, "Pappy, you gotta call the judge and tell him I'm coming in to see him again today, and see if you can help me out." My grandfather was always making that call and getting me out of trouble, but his influence was limited.

One time I drove over to Murray, Kentucky, to visit some friends at Murray State University, and I got a ticket while I was there. The cop said I had 30 days to pay the ticket, but I thought, *Why worry about a ticket in eastern Kentucky? I live in Owensboro, and I'm never going back to Murray again.* So I just tossed it. Well, lo and behold, they came and got me and took my license because I hadn't paid the ticket. There wasn't anything my grandfather could do to save me that time.

I stayed around Owensboro after high school; college wasn't in the cards for me. I had a bunch of rowdy friends, and we raced on the weekends and hung out all week. Our only purpose in life was to have a good time. One of our favorite forms of entertainment was to get the cops to chase us.

I was sharing a second-floor apartment with a buddy named Steve, who would let me borrow his car occasionally. One Friday night I borrowed Steve's car for a date. I had a little too much to drink that night—okay, a lot too much to drink—and was headed home when a cop tried to pull me over. Naturally I took off. The cop called for backup, and pretty soon I was flying through Owensboro with a couple of cops on my tail.

I ducked into a neighborhood, hoping they'd blow by, but they followed me in. I made another turn and realized, too late, that I was in a cul-de-sac. The cops hadn't followed me into it yet, but it was only a matter of time before they would track me down, so I made a quick decision to cut through a yard to reach the next street.

I was driving around the house, looking in my rearview mirror to see whether they were following me, when suddenly I heard a sharp thump and a clatter, and the car abruptly lurched to a stop. When I pressed the accelerator, the tires only spun. I was stuck in somebody's backyard.

To be honest, I have no memory of what happened next, but the people whose yard I had blundered into gave a detailed account to the police. A car had barreled into their yard and run over their swing set. The driver, a young man, had gotten out and walked around as though he was looking for something, then had shrugged and gotten back in. He had dropped the car into gear and floored it. The car sat there for a minute, screaming, tires smoking, and then it jumped off the mangled swing set and roared away, slinging grass and dirt. They didn't know which way it had gone.

The next morning I stumbled out of my bedroom to find my buddy Steve getting ready for work. I said, "Man, I had the weirdest dream last night. I don't know where I was or what I was doing, but I dreamed I ran over a swing set."

Steve headed out the door for work; I heard his footsteps booming down the steel stairs to the driveway. A second later I heard him charging up the stairs again. He threw open the door and yelled, "That damn dream you had last night tore my car all to pieces!"

The cops came looking for Steve, of course. I made a call to my grandfather, and eventually we got things worked out. I ended up paying for the swing set to make the people happy. That was the least I could do.

Eventually I got a job at Don Moore Chevrolet, selling cars. The job also got me a discount on the Chevy line of automobiles, so as soon as I could afford it I bought a new car, a '69 Chevelle SS with a 396-cubic-inch engine. The car was hot, all souped up at the factory, and I made sure to order it with extra-loud "open chamber" pipes. The week after it arrived, one of my fans on the police force gave me a ticket for loud pipes. I had to go to court, but the judge dismissed the charge when I showed him the paperwork from the dealership proving that the pipes were factory-installed.

On the south side of town, just beyond the South Side Bar, was a two-mile stretch of four-lane highway that was straight as an arrow. That's where we'd go when somebody challenged somebody else to a drag race. The stakes were usually low—we might race for a six-pack or a 20-dollar bill—but the competition could get pretty serious.

Before I got my new car, the fastest street car in Owensboro may have been a '68 Chevelle that belonged to a black guy whose name I don't recall. He and I started harassing each other in a good-natured way after my car arrived, and eventually we agreed to settle the question of who was fastest with a drag race.

As usual, my timing was impeccable. I didn't know it, but the cops had been receiving complaints about hooligan hot-rodders drag racing outside of town, so on this particular night they had set up a stakeout. They sat in the dark with their lights off and watched as we rolled up, stopped, turned around, and sat there side by side, revving our engines. I had my buddy Johnny with me; he was going to be the starter. Johnny was about to get out of the car when two patrol cars suddenly appeared out of nowhere.

The black guy hit the gas and roared away, but I figured my best option was to sit there. After all, I hadn't done anything yet. When the cop shined his flashlight into my eyes, I said, "What seems to be the problem, officer?" just as innocent as you please.

"You know what you were doing," the cop said.

"Doing?" I put on my best puzzled expression. "I was just sitting in my car talking to a guy. What's wrong with that?"

"I'm not going to argue with you about it," the cop said. "Here's your ticket. If you want to argue about it, see me in court." And he gave me a ticket for *attempted* drag racing.

When I got to the courthouse, the judge listened to the charges, then gave me an exasperated look and said, "Okay, tell me what happened."

I had cooked up a pretty good story for the occasion. "Your Honor," I said, "I was just trying to help a guy from out of town. This guy stopped me on the road and asked me how to get to the Dairy Drive-In. I was in the process of explaining to him how to get to the Dairy Drive-In when all of a sudden the cops had me surrounded!"

The judge looked at me for a moment. Then he said, "Can anyone corroborate this story?"

"Oh yes!" I said. "My buddy Johnny was in the car with me. He saw everything."

The judge asked, "Where is this Johnny?"

"He's at work," I said.

"Get him down here at one o'clock, and if he corroborates your story, I'll let you go."

I got on the phone to Johnny right away. "Look," I said, "all you've gotta do is tell the judge that we were just giving this guy directions. That's all you've gotta do. Can you do it?"

"Oh yeah, no problem," Johnny said. "I'll be there in a little while and do it."

At one o'clock the judge called Johnny to the front of the courtroom and had him sworn in. Then he fixed Johnny with a stern stare and said, "Young man, let me explain something to you. Lying under oath is a crime, a crime much more serious than the one with which Mr. Waltrip is charged. Lying under oath is known as perjury, and it will get you fined and thrown into jail. I do not regard perjury lightly. If I find that you have lied to this court, I will make certain that you feel the full weight of the law. Now, I want to ask you a simple question. Were you and Mr. Waltrip drag racing, or were you giving that guy directions?"

Johnny stood stock-still for a second, eyes wide, and then blurted, "We were drag racing, Your Honor!"

I couldn't believe it! Johnny was supposed to be my friend, and he couldn't even tell a little lie when one was necessary! I felt like choking him, especially when the judge found me guilty and took my license.

Afterward Johnny was all apologetic. "Man, I was afraid they were going to put me in jail," he said.

"You dummy," I said. "Couldn't you see that the judge was just trying to scare you?"

I couldn't hold a grudge against Johnny for long, though. The more I thought about it, the more I felt sorry for him. He'd been intimidated, that's all. He'd never been in a courtroom before, and he certainly didn't have the experience of standing before a judge that I did.

CHAPTER FOUR

THE REDHEAD

"Whoa! Who's THAT?"
            "The redhead? That's Stevie Rader."
"Stevie?"
"You know, Stephanie. Carol Rader's little sister."

Carol Rader had been in my class at Daviess County High, and she didn't like me very much. The Raders were not like the Waltrips. We lived on one side of town; they lived on the other. Mr. Rader was the president of Texas Gas, a pipeline company that funneled natural gas from the oil fields of Texas to the Midwest. He was a big man with a Harvard education and the demeanor of a frontier sheriff, and his daughters were the apple of his eye.

Stevie was a good student. She had spent most of her high school years at a private girls' school in Washington, D.C., where she excelled, and her mother had decreed that she would receive her college education at Southern Methodist University in Dallas, the university from which most of her family had graduated. With that understanding, Stevie had persuaded her parents to let her spend her last year of high school in Owensboro. Stevie was two years younger than I. That two-year difference would have rendered her practically invisible when I was cruising the halls of Daviess County High as a student, but now that I was a car salesman with a racing career and she was 18, the cute redhead with the big green eyes and the dazzling smile was anything *but* invisible.

I asked Stevie out on a couple of dates, and she accepted. Our dates were nothing formal or fancy. In Owensboro you picked up your date and took her to the Dairy Drive-In for a cheeseburger and a Coke, and you'd sit in the car and talk and watch your friends go by. Or maybe you'd cruise around for a while and listen to the radio before swinging back into the Dairy Drive-In to see who else had shown up. I was the unofficial king of "the DDI," as we called the drive-in, with my own parking space, and I would often stay there with my friends for hours. My dates with Stevie always ended early, however, because her father enforced a very strict ten o'clock curfew.

My interest in Stevie, and her evident interest in me, set off alarm bells in the Rader house. Stevie had already applied to SMU and had been accepted for the fall semester. Her mother fretted. An ill-conceived romance with a local renegade like me could ruin everything. Her parents tried to distract Stevie by sending her to Hawaii on a three-week vacation, but it didn't work. She came home a week early because she missed me.

One Friday morning I called Stevie to let her know I was planning to take her out that night when, to my shock, she turned me down. "I can't," she said.

"What do you mean, you can't?"

"I mean I can't. I already have a date."

I was momentarily speechless. "Who are you going out with?"

"He's just a friend," she said. "His name is Rob, and he's a family friend from Connecticut. He's coming down for a visit, and I've got to go out with him."

"You're going to go out with Rob and not with me? Really?"

"I'm sorry," she said, "but I have to. He's coming into town and I have to entertain him."

My buddies were surprised that night when I showed up at the Dairy Drive-In alone. One guy asked me, "Hey DW, where's your girl? Didn't you say you had a date with her tonight?"

I shrugged. "Something came up."

An hour or so later I was sitting in my Chevelle, talking with a couple of my buddies, when I saw a familiar car approaching. Stevie's father had just bought her a beautiful ride, a 1966 442

Oldsmobile with a four-speed and three deuces, and here it came, unmistakable. Stevie was behind the wheel, and Rob was riding shotgun. Stevie slowed, stopped, backed up, and pulled into a spot under the lights. Then they ordered Cokes and sat there, talking.

It didn't take long for my buddies to realize what was going on, and when they did they started ragging me mercilessly. "Something came up, DW? Well, we can see what came up. Your girlfriend got a better offer! Looks like you're not as hot as you think you are!" When I explained to them about Stevie's one-night obligation to a family friend, they just winked and chuckled. "Sure," they said. "Right."

Finally I said, "Well, guys, I do feel pretty bad about this, and I think it's time to do something about it. I have a plan. C'mon, follow me."

I walked over to Stevie's car and waved, and she introduced me and the boys to Rob. The guy was plainly out of his element. He was wearing an oxford shirt, khaki shorts, and shoes with no socks, and he had a tan. His fingernails were clean. It was obvious to me that Rob wasn't a mechanic.

"Hey, Stevie," I said, "would you mind popping the hood for a second? I want to show these guys the engine in this beauty—they've never seen anything like it."

"Sure," Stevie said. I pulled the chrome pins that held the hood down, and she triggered the interior release. Then I lifted the hood and gave Rob and the boys a dramatic narrated tour of the engine compartment. As I pointed out the three carburetors, I casually reached over and disconnected the coil wire and slipped it into my pocket. Then I concluded my monologue with a flourish and dropped the hood.

"Thanks, Stevie!" I said. "Nice to meet you, Rob." I shook hands with the guy, and we went back to my car and waited.

I knew Stevie would need to leave for home by 9:50, and sure enough, she started cranking the engine about ten minutes before her curfew. Naturally the car wouldn't start. She pumped the gas a few times and hit the starter, then repeated the same fruitless sequence again. I watched as she spoke to Rob with mounting distress. Finally I jumped out of my car and ran over.

"What's the problem?" I said.

"My car won't start," said Stevie, a note of panic in her voice.

"Well, what's wrong with it?"

"I don't know—it's brand new. I don't know what's wrong with it."

"Pop the hood and let me look at it," I said.

As soon as the hood was up, I slipped the coil wire back into place. Then I tapped on a couple of things and walked around to the driver's door. "Step out for a second and let me try it," I said. Stevie got out of the car and I got in. I cocked my head, waited a couple beats for dramatic effect, then turned the key, and voilà! She fired right up.

Stevie almost collapsed with relief. "You saved my life!" she exclaimed. "I was going to be late, and I would have been in so much trouble if I had to call my dad and tell him my car wouldn't start." She gave me a quick kiss and jumped back in the car and drove away.

From that day on I was a hero in Stevie's eyes. It was a long, long time before I told her what really happened that night at the Dairy Drive-In.

It was the last Friday before Christmas, and the showroom at Don Moore Chevrolet was practically deserted. I picked up my paycheck just before noon, then headed over to Petey's Spotlight Inn for lunch. Several other guys from the dealership were already there, drinking beer and playing shuffleboard. We were all in a pretty festive mood.

Before long we were playing shuffleboard for money. I loved playing shuffleboard, and, since the game was going my way, I directed some of my winnings toward an even bigger prize: an enormous heart-shaped box of chocolates displayed behind the bar. There was a punch-board set up on the bar, and for 50 cents you could punch out one of the holes in it. If you hit the right hole, you'd win the box of chocolates; otherwise you'd win a little jar of hard rock candy. I had a date with Stevie that night, and I was determined to win that box of chocolates for her.

As the afternoon wore on, the boys and I decided that, since it was Christmas, it didn't make much sense to go back to work for a few hours on a dead Friday afternoon. We devoted ourselves instead to some serious competitive shuffleboard, accompanied by equally serious drinking.

Before I knew it the afternoon had slipped away and the after-work crowd was filling up the bar. Since the new arrivals hadn't been drinking as long as I had, my luck at the shuffleboard table started to turn. By now I had accumulated a small mountain of hard rock candy, but the heart-shaped box of chocolates still sat behind the bar. Which reminded me: I had a seven o'clock date! I looked at my watch. Crap! It was already seven o'clock!

"Gotta go, boys!" I shouted, scooping up an armload of hard rock candy and heading for the door. Outside I dumped the candy into the backseat of the Chevelle, on top of a bunch of wrapped Christmas presents I had bought for my family, then jumped in and peeled out of the parking lot in the direction of Stevie's house.

Stevie's family lived on Old Hartford Road, a few miles out of town. I was roaring along that two-lane blacktop at somewhere between 100 and 120 miles per hour, less than a mile from Stevie's house, when I saw a police car easing out of a subdivision just as I went flying by. Sure enough, he flipped on his light and came after me. Of all the rotten luck! The thought that I had been drinking didn't even cross my mind. All I thought was *I can't pick up Stevie with a cop chasing me! I'll have to lose him.*

It was completely dark by now, and there were no streetlights this far out in the country. Still traveling at more than 100 miles an hour, I tried to formulate a plan. Suddenly it struck me. There was a four-way intersection at a low spot in the road about a quarter-mile before Stevie's house. That was it! If I turned my lights off and kept my foot off the brakes when I went through that intersection, the cop wouldn't know which way I'd gone when he got there. I quickly doused my lights and blew straight through the intersection, then looked back to see whether I'd lost him. By golly, it worked! The cop slowed, then turned left. I flipped my headlights back on, and suddenly—I was airborne!

Just past the entrance to the Raders' long, curving driveway, the Old Hartford Road takes a sharp 90-degree turn, and there are high dirt banks on both sides of the road on that curve. I had miscalculated badly, failing to take into account my high rate of speed, and had missed the turn. My car shot up the dirt bank on the far side of the curve and launched toward the heavens, where it seemed to hang forever. I could see the starry sky, and I could hear the rumble of my wheels spinning free. Then, with a jolt, the car landed on the soft earth. I fought for control, trying to keep the Chevelle upright as it tore through the blackness, but it slewed and started to roll. Christmas presents and hard rock candy churned around me. I closed my eyes and hung on for dear life. When the car finally stopped, I was upside down.

I hung there for a minute and checked myself. Nothing seemed to be broken. I unhooked my seat belt and crawled out of the car and looked around. The Chevelle's lights were still on, and the horn was blaring. I could see a house a short distance away. It was Stevie's house. I had crashed in the worst possible location; my car was now upside down in the Raders' front yard!

Suddenly my attention was drawn to a pair of flashing lights coming down Old Hartford Road. Cops! I quickly scrambled up the dirt bank, away from the incapacitated car. Maybe, if the cops didn't find me here, I could convince them that I hadn't been driving the car. Somebody else had stolen my car, run from the cops, and crashed in my girlfriend's front yard! I stopped at the top of the slope and sat in the darkness for a minute, dazed and shivering, and tried to refine my story. While I watched, two cop cars pulled into the yard.

The cops looked inside my car and shined their flashlights around it. They conferred for a minute or two, then went back to their cruisers. Another police car arrived. Suddenly a spotlight ignited and began to sweep in my direction. The light went past me, stopped, and returned. I shielded my eyes. A raspy amplified voice echoed through the cold night air. "You up there! Come on down with your hands up!" The cops cuffed me and pushed me into the backseat of a patrol car.

Up at the house Mr. Rader was at work in his study while Stevie sat near the door, anxiously awaiting my arrival. Her sister Carol was the first to see the flashing lights. "Looks like your date has arrived," she said drily.

Stevie rushed down the driveway toward the commotion. She panicked when she saw the upside-down car, but the officers quickly assured her that no one was hurt. When she asked to see me, they told her I was already gone. They had taken me to the police station in Owensboro for booking.

Stevie ran back to the house and told Carol to get her coat. "Don't say a word to Dad," she ordered. "You and I are going to Owensboro to bail Darrell out of jail."

By the time the girls arrived at the police station, I was locked up in the holding cell in back. I had seen the inside of that cell on several previous occasions, but on this night it was especially crowded. It seemed like the entire criminal element of western Kentucky had been apprehended. There was no place to sit, so I stood at the door of the cell and looked out through the tiny barred window, desperately hoping to see a friendly face. Ages passed. I heard muttering in the cell behind me, and harsh bursts of laughter that made my skin crawl. I had to get out of here!

Finally a door clanged, and I saw a flash of auburn hair at the far end of the corridor. Stevie was here! I looked again. She was accompanied by Carol and a beefy deputy with a jangling ring of keys. Then I saw something that made my heart stop: the hulking silhouette of Mr. Rader lumbering behind them. I ducked away from the window and turned back toward my fellow prisoners. Suddenly jail didn't seem like such a bad place. Maybe I could stay here for a few days, or at least until Mr. Rader was gone.

The deputy unlocked the door, and I meekly followed Mr. Rader and his daughters down the corridor and out to the desk to retrieve my wallet and other personal effects. As we waited there, I noticed a cop leaning against a wall, a cop I knew. He had gained notoriety in Owensboro for shooting a suspect who had been attempting to flee. As we turned to leave, the cop pushed away from the wall and stopped us.

"Is this your daughter, Mr. Rader?" the cop asked, gesturing toward Stevie.

"Yes it is," Mr. Rader answered.

"Well, then, let me offer you a piece of advice. I wouldn't let her ride around with young Mr. Waltrip again if I were you, because the next time I get him in my sights I'm going to shoot him." He cocked a finger in my direction and pursed his lips. He was dead serious.

One night I mentioned to Stevie that I thought we ought to get married. She agreed—on one condition. "You're going to have to talk to Dad and get his permission," she said.

I thought about it for a minute, and then said, "I don't think I can do that."

Stevie was firm. "If you want to marry me, then that's what you'll have to do."

The next day I called Mr. Rader and asked if I could come and talk to him. When I arrived at his office in the Texas Gas building, I found him behind a big desk, a tiny pair of half-glasses perched on his nose, studying a file. He looked up at me and shook his head gravely.

I didn't know Mr. Rader very well, and was therefore unaware that he suffered from a tremor that grew worse when he was tired or under stress. The tremor made him shake his head. All I knew was that Stevie's dad was shaking his head at me before I had even told him what I wanted. I almost gave up then and there, but I forced myself to continue.

Mr. Rader was still shaking his head when I finished. "Stevie is accustomed to a certain standard of living," he said. "How do you intend to support her? What are your career plans?"

"I'm going to be a professional race car driver," I said.

For a long time Mr. Rader didn't say anything. Finally, he said, "If that's what Stevie wants, then that's fine. But I won't support it."

"Thank you, sir," I said, and turned to leave.

"You know," Mr. Rader continued, almost conversationally, "my daughter has been accepted at SMU. It would be a great disappointment to her mother if she did not enroll this fall."

"Uh, we haven't decided about that yet," I said, bolting for the door. I walked unsteadily out of the Texas Gas building and got into my car, my knees shaking.

CHAPTER FIVE

ESCAPE FROM OWENSBORO

Four years after high school I was still living in Owensboro, Kentucky. The Apollo 11 astronauts had just landed on the moon, Woodstock was weeks away, and antiwar activists were planning massive demonstrations in Washington. The nation was in turmoil, and my life was a mess. I'd wrecked my Chevelle, my driver's license had been suspended, and I'd lost my job at Don Moore Chevrolet.

Some things were going my way, however. I was engaged to a great girl, to begin with. I still had plenty of friends, and I was racing on the weekends for an owner named Harry Pedley, and winning regularly.

One night I was drinking with a couple of my buddies, lamenting the loss of my street ride, when a guy named Patrick walked into the bar. Patrick wasn't a member of our group, but he was trying to join. His father had bought him a brand-new '69 GTO, a beautiful car with three deuces and a four-speed. Patrick had been showing off the car all week.

"You still puttering around town in that GTO, Patrick?" one of my friends asked.

Patrick smiled cautiously. "What do you mean?" he said.

"I mean you drive like my granny," my buddy replied. "It oughta be a crime, driving that car the way you do. What have you had it up to? Sixty?"

Patrick opened his mouth, but my buddy cut him off. "You know what you oughta do, Patrick? You oughta let DW show you how to drive that car right. Let him teach you how to powershift it, how to take a corner, stuff like that." He turned to me. "You'd do that, wouldn't you?"

I nodded, warming to the idea immediately.

Patrick hesitated. "Gee, I don't know," he said. "My dad—"

"Your dad didn't buy you that car so you could park it," my buddy said. "He bought it so you could drive it like a man, and there isn't a better guy to teach you how to do that than DW. C'mon! Give him the keys, and let's go."

Patrick looked at me skeptically. "You'll be careful with it?"

"I'll treat it like my own," I said. Patrick grimaced and handed me the keys.

The GTO was spotless, and its interior still had that new-car smell. My buddies climbed into the backseat with a couple of six-packs, and Patrick settled nervously in the front passenger seat. I cranked the engine to life, revved it a couple of times, and grinned at Patrick. "Watch and learn," I said.

On our way out of town we stopped at a traffic light, and a black-and-white patrol car pulled up beside us. I stared straight ahead, praying the cop wouldn't recognize me, and held my breath while I waited for the light to change. As we sat there, one of my buddies reached out the window of the GTO and flipped a beer can over the roof, toward the cop. The can landed on the hood of the patrol car with a clatter, just as the light turned green. I jammed the accelerator to the floor and away we went, tires screaming, with the cop in hot pursuit. The race was on!

A few blocks later another cop joined the chase, and then another, their sirens wailing. I could see their flashing lights in my rearview mirror. It must have been a slow night on the crime front in Owensboro, because before long we had every cop in the county trying to catch us—and this time they were serious.

Eventually about 30 police vehicles were involved in the chase. Since they didn't have a helicopter, the cops weren't able to track our speeding GTO from the air, but they used their radios and worked systematically, relaying our location and direction every time somebody spotted us.

In the past I had always been able to outrun the cops, to get far enough ahead of a pursuer to disappear, but this time they were calculating our trajectory and sending cars ahead of us. At one point I rounded a curve to find a roadblock: two patrol cars parked sideways at a narrow point in the road and officers motioning me to stop. I screeched to a halt, slammed the car into reverse, squealed backward with the tires spinning, and executed a perfect J-turn just like the stunt drivers do in the movies, whipping the GTO around and roaring away as the cops scrambled for their cars. It was fantastic!

Finally we found ourselves in Bon Harbor Hills, a quiet upscale residential section outside of town. Since there were no flashing lights in sight, I pulled into a long driveway and switched my headlights off. I drove all the way up to the house, turned around, then rolled back down the narrow driveway for about 50 yards and stopped. We sat there in the darkness for a few minutes, straining our ears for sounds of pursuit. Patrick was a wreck, rambling incoherently. One of my buddies spoke up from the backseat. "Let me out," he said. "I need to pee."

Moments later the four of us were standing beside the driveway, emptying our bladders, when we heard a car approaching. The car pulled into the driveway and stopped. It was a cop. We stood stock-still in the darkness while the patrol car sat at the bottom of the hill, its motor idling. The cop seemed to be talking on his radio. Finally he put the car in reverse and started to back out of the driveway, but then he suddenly stopped again and flipped on his spotlight. The light darted up the driveway and played across the front of the GTO. He'd found us! We dashed back to the GTO as the patrol car came flying up the hill in our direction.

The cop stopped just a couple feet from our front bumper, blocking us in. I slipped the car into reverse and started backing up, and the cop followed. I kept backing up, and the cop kept coming, crowding us. We were now approaching the top of the hill, where the driveway widened slightly. I stopped. The cop stopped. I punched the gas quickly, jumping backward, then dropped into first gear, feinted right and dodged left, where there was now just enough room for the GTO to squeeze past the patrol car. I gunned the engine and we slid around the cop, our left rear tire spinning crazily in the soft earth beside the driveway. As we did, the cop stepped out of his car, laid his revolver across the roof of the cruiser, and started firing. I could see the muzzle flashes, but the sound of the shots was drowned by the roar of our engine and Patrick's screaming. Finally our tires found traction and we roared down the hill and out into the safety of the night.

Some time later, when my heart had stopped pounding and my breathing had returned to normal, I started laughing at Patrick and my buddies. "I can't believe you guys were scared back there," I said.

"WHAT?" Patrick yelled, his voice still shaky. "Are you saying you weren't afraid? We could have been KILLED! That cop was SHOOTING at us!"

I snorted. "You don't think he was using actual bullets, do you? You think an Owensboro cop is going to shoot guys like us for speeding? Those were blanks! He was just trying to scare us! And it looks like he did a pretty good job on you."

By now we had been running from the cops for so long that we were almost out of gas, so I stopped at a country store for fuel. Patrick pushed his door open and stepped out of the car. Then he cursed.

"DW?" Patrick said.

"Yeah?"

"Would you like to see what those blanks did to my car?"

I got out and walked around to see what he was talking about, and the sight made me weak in the knees. The right side of the car was perforated with dimpled bullet holes.

Patrick was frantic about what his dad would say when he saw the bullet-riddled car, but my concerns were more pragmatic. This car was marked. Any cop who saw the bullet holes would know instantly that we were the ones who got away. If we could somehow make that telltale damage disappear . . .

"I've got it!" I said. "Don't worry boys, I have a plan. We'll drop this car behind Pedley's garage tonight, and by tomorrow night everything will be fine."

Harry Pedley, the guy I raced for, had a garage with a little body shop behind it where Bill, the body man, worked out the dents in my car after a race. I figured that Bill would be able to fill the bullet holes and repaint the GTO in a matter of hours. I'd call him first thing in the morning and tell him to get on the job right away. Tomorrow night, if everything went as planned, we would be able to drive through town in Patrick's unblemished GTO and smile at the cops. That was my plan.

Bill grunted when I called him in the morning. "Okay, I'll do it," he said, tactfully avoiding the subject of how the bullet holes had gotten there. "I think I can get it done by this afternoon."

Later in the morning I decided to swing by Pedley's to see how the work was coming along. I went into the garage and walked into the back, where I expected to find Bill working on the car. The GTO was there, but no one was working on it.

"What's this?" I said to Bill. "I thought you were going to fix the car right away."

Just then, three policemen walked around the corner.

"He's not going to fix that car today," the biggest cop said, reaching for his handcuffs. "He may never fix it. And you're in big trouble, boy."

As it turned out, the previous night had gone worse for the cops than I had realized. Two patrol cars had wrecked during the chase, and a section of private fence had been demolished—not to mention the humiliation the department endured when I got away. I continued to maintain my innocence, however. "This is not my car!" I said. "I wasn't driving it! This is my buddy Patrick's car! I'm just trying to help him get it fixed!"

The cops issued a whole slew of tickets to Patrick since the GTO belonged to him. They charged him with running from the law, destroying public property, speeding, reckless driving, and a raft of other major and minor infractions.

My buddies and I were summoned to appear in court. We got

together beforehand to get our stories straight, and we agreed to testify that Patrick had been driving the car. That seemed like the best solution to me. If I were found guilty of being the driver, I might never be able to drive again.

On the morning of the trial we sat in a hallway outside the courtroom and waited to be called. My buddies went in first, one by one. When my turn came, I took my place on the witness stand, placed my hand on the Bible, looked the clerk straight in the eye, and swore to tell the truth, the whole truth, and nothing but the truth.

The prosecuting attorney asked me whether I'd been driving the car on the night of the chase.

"Before you answer, Mr. Waltrip," the judge interrupted, "I would like to inform you that we have already heard a great deal of incriminating evidence—so much evidence, in fact, that you might want to consider taking the Fifth."

That puzzled me. What had my buddies actually said? Had they been intimidated into telling the truth? I sat there for a couple of minutes, thinking.

"Okay," I said, "I'll take the Fifth."

"No more questions," said the prosecuting attorney.

Patrick was seated at the defense table, his attorney beside him. The attorney stood up. "No questions for this witness, Your Honor."

"The witness is dismissed," said the judge.

In the end Patrick was convicted on all counts. For reasons I never fully understood, the officer who shot at us identified Patrick as the driver of the car. My buddies had indeed folded under pressure, but the prosecuting attorney was able to discredit their testimony and obtain the conviction he wanted. "It's obvious what's going on," the prosecutor told the judge after my buddies and Patrick testified that I had been driving. "It's a setup! These two witnesses have colluded with the defendant to pin the blame on Mr. Waltrip. They think the court will find their false testimony believable because Mr. Waltrip already has a bad driving record and his license has been revoked. Waltrip doesn't have anything to lose, and they'll get away scot-free." The judge bought it. He revoked Patrick's license, imposed a stiff fine, and required Patrick to pay compensation for all the damage.

I left the courthouse that day knowing I had just dodged a bullet, and feeling bad that Patrick had been caught in the crossfire. Next time, I thought, I might not be so lucky. Owensboro was hot. It was time for me to start looking for another place to live.

Stevie and I got married on August 15, 1969. It was a small affair; there was no way the Raders were going to throw a big, fancy society wedding for a daughter who was marrying Darrell Waltrip. My parents and Stevie's parents were there, along with a couple of my buddies and Stevie's sister. That was it. Stevie's mom did her best to smile, but her act wasn't very convincing. Mr. Rader didn't say much at all.

My plan for the honeymoon included a romantic week at the French Lick Resort in Indiana. There was only one hitch: I was broke. My credit card was over the limit, and my total cash reserves amounted to $69. "No problem," I told Stevie. "There's a race in Salem this weekend that pays a thousand dollars, and some friends of mine have a '57 Chevy they want me to drive. My share of the purse will be five hundred bucks. So here's the plan: we'll spend our wedding night at a hotel in Louisville, then drive over to Salem. I'll win the race, and we'll be off to French Lick!"

By the time I'd paid cash for the Louisville hotel, nearly all my money was gone. I couldn't afford a proper meal, so Stevie and I split a cheeseburger for dinner. The following day we drove to Salem and parked on the side of the road near the speedway, watching for my parents' sedan. I knew my folks would be coming to the race, and I needed to borrow enough money to pay the gate fee.

"How much do you need?" my father asked, after we'd flagged them down.

"I don't know," I said, hesitating. I knew my parents lived from payday to payday, just like I did. "Twenty-five dollars?"

"Twenty-five dollars!" Dad opened his wallet. "Sorry, son, but twenty-five is all the money I have, and your mother and Mikey have really been looking forward to seeing this race."

"Ten then? I can pay you back as soon as the race is over."

Dad handed me a ten-dollar bill and wished me luck.

I jumped out to an early lead in the feature race, and I drove like a man possessed as I dreamed of the week ahead in French Lick. I was still leading on the last lap when suddenly Les Snow, one of the veteran drivers on the Automobile Racing Club of America (ARCA) circuit, slipped under me in the third turn and drove me right up the high-banked track and into the fence, wrecking my '57 Chevy and, along with it, my plans for a romantic honeymoon. Stevie and I left the track with $30 and drove back to Owensboro in silence. When we arrived at my apartment, my key wouldn't work, and a note on the door said "Pay Rent or Move Out."

Soon after the wedding, Stevie and I were confronted by the reality that we had come from two entirely different worlds. If we hadn't loved each other as much as we did, our marriage never would have survived, because those worlds collided every day.

Stevie was no longer able to do many of the things that she was accustomed to doing, because we weren't getting support from her family. True to his word, Mr. Rader was not subsidizing our marriage. He did get me a job at Kentucky Electronics, where I worked in the warehouse. Stevie took a low-paying job at the hospital. Between us we managed to pay the rent on a little three-room apartment where the kitchen was equipped with a hot plate and an icebox—no refrigerator—and where we slept on a mattress on the floor. Debutante Stevie Rader, only 18 years old and barely out of high school, had sacrificed her future for this: marriage to a local race car driver who was obsessed with his career. What had she been thinking?

Increasingly my attention was consumed by racing. It had been four years since my trip to Daytona, and I was now driving regularly in the Late Model Sportsman series races on Saturday nights.

One day I received a call from P. B. Crowell, an owner-driver who lived in Franklin, Tennessee. Crowell had raced in Whitesville a few times, and we had become friends. In the spring of 1969, he was testing a new car at the Fairgrounds racetrack in Nashville when something went wrong. The car flipped, and P. B. broke his back. Fortunately he wasn't paralyzed, but the doctors told him that he was looking at a long recovery period.

He asked several different people to drive his car for him while he was recuperating, and now he was calling me for that purpose. Would I be interested in taking a turn in his car on a Saturday night in Nashville? I had raced in Nashville a few times and had always wrecked or finished poorly, and the prospect of driving a better car really appealed to me. "I'd love to!" I said.

The first night I drove P. B.'s car, I won. He had already lined up a couple of local drivers for subsequent weeks, but those guys didn't do so well, so he eventually called me back. The second time I drove his car, I won again. "You know," said P. B. after that race, "if you want to come down here to Nashville on weekends, you can be my full-time driver."

The arrangement worked well. I won consistently in Nashville, where the steeply banked track at the Fairgrounds matched my all-out driving style. Eventually P. B. suggested that I relocate. It would be a whole lot better if I lived in Franklin, close to the shop, he said. That way I could be available throughout the week, and it would be easier for us to race at other tracks.

By this time Stevie and I had been married for three or four months, and our romance was strained. She was enrolled at Kentucky Western College in Owensboro, and when she wasn't studying she was spending a lot of time with her family. When I told her about P. B.'s suggestion, she resisted. She reminded me that she was in the middle of a semester. She liked being close to her mom and dad. She didn't want to move to Tennessee. I said, "I'm sorry, but I'm going to Franklin. If you want to join me, that's where I'll be." And I packed up my things and left.

I liked living in Franklin. My reputation hadn't followed me to this pretty little town, so I was free to start over. The police didn't chase me. I was making pretty decent money, splitting my winnings with P. B., and the regular ride at the Fairgrounds represented a major step in my career. Things were definitely looking up.

About a month after I moved to Franklin, Stevie came to town with her mom for a visit. The two of them strolled down Main Street, checking out the shops and restaurants. The locals they met were friendly, and the town itself seemed inviting and safe. Stevie could see that I was starting to change in this new environment, becoming a little more settled, more purposeful. The romantic spark between us flared again, and she decided to stay.

I won the track championship at the Fairgrounds in 1970. When the season was over Stevie and I bought a house and a car. Franklin was now officially our home. Things were going well for us, and they were about to get a whole lot better.

P. B. Crowell had purchased several of his race cars from Bobby Allison. In fact the car I was driving every week had been built in Allison's shop in Hueytown, Alabama, so whenever we had any questions about it we would have to give Bobby a call. Since Hueytown is not far from Franklin—about a three-and-a-half-hour drive—Stevie and I would sometimes drive down there to pick up spare parts. We'd wind up sharing a meal with the whole Allison clan at the Iceberg restaurant, and I'd hang around the garage for hours, trying to learn everything I could about the racing business.

Bobby was a born teacher. Every teacher likes an attentive student, and I followed him around like a puppy, peppering him with questions and soaking up everything he told me. I was really eager to learn how to set up a car so that it would handle smoothly on the racetrack, and Bobby was one of the smartest guys I ever met when it came to that subject. He understood more about how to make a car work than anybody I knew.

Bobby introduced me to terms I'd never heard before, like "caster" and "camber" and "wedge." To Bobby, setting the front end of a chassis was a science. Camber, he explained, is the way a tire leans in or out at the top, and it can be adjusted by inserting shims in the A-frame. The magic number, he said, is 3½ positive camber on the right front tire and ½ negative on the left front, and he showed me how to make the necessary measurements and adjustments to set the camber perfectly. He then placed the front end on special "front-end plates," placed a caster/camber gauge on each hub, and turned the wheels to measure the caster. He showed me how to check the "toe" by setting up a string along the side of the car, between two jack stands, and measuring the distance from that string to the front and rear tires. The difference between the inside and outside measurements on the front tire was your toe, and there was a magic number there too: 3/16.

Bobby would place a jack under the middle of the rear-end housing, then jack up the car while shaking the left rear tire. When that tire started to slip, he would measure the distance under the right rear tire. If he could place a 7/8 inch socket under the right tire, that was the right amount of "wedge."

I didn't know anything about springs, but Bobby taught me that I'd need a 1,100-pound spring in the right front, a 700 on the left, a 400 here, and a 300 there—and a sway bar. Sway bar? My car didn't even have one, as far as I knew, but Bobby told me that I needed a one-inch sway bar to stabilize the car in turns. He also showed me how to take the temperature of my tires after a test lap, taking readings in the inside, middle, and outside of each tire in order to determine how much surface contact the tire was making with the track.

The more Bobby pontificated about the arcane science of setting up a race car, the more convinced I became that mastering this science would give me a decisive advantage on the track, and I became a devotee of Bobby Allison. Years later, when I was challenging Allison's dominance on the track using the knowledge he had shared with me, our relationship would strain and break, but at the start of my career we were friends. Stevie and Judy, Bobby's wife, became good friends too, and their friendship endured even after Bobby and I became rivals. It was as though our wives made a deal: no matter what the two knuckleheads they'd married might do, they wouldn't let NASCAR affect their friendship. If only Bobby and I had been able to do the same.

CHAPTER SIX

SHAKING THINGS UP

I have been outgoing and verbal ever since I was a kid. Back in elementary school I entered the talent show every year, and I don't remember ever getting nervous onstage. My fellow students elected me "king" of the school a couple of years running—mostly, I think, because I could make people laugh.

I learned the value of humor from my parents. Their main defense against life's disappointments was to take a deep breath and smile, and they taught us kids to do the same. In their view, pain is inevitable in this world, but misery is optional. You can always find something to be grateful for, and you can usually find something to laugh about. That outlook, I've learned, goes a long way toward reducing stress and making you the kind of person other people pay attention to. People will always pay attention to someone who can make them laugh.

And if you want to make people laugh, you have to be willing to say and do surprising things. Most people are too guarded, too careful to be very funny. They think before they speak, and they take the trouble to say the *right* thing. Saying the right thing isn't wrong, of course. Being nice doesn't make you any enemies, but it doesn't really fascinate people either, and it seldom makes them laugh. People laugh at the quick and unexpected reply. They crack up when you say something they have thought about but would never say out loud. And when you make an outrageous claim with a wink and a grin, people pay attention. The more unpredictable you are, the more people are compelled to listen, because they don't want to miss whatever's coming next. That, in a nutshell, is my strategy for self-promotion.

I'm aware that in the opinion of some drivers out there, self-promotion is a bad word. Some guys think that only competence counts. You prove yourself on the track, they say, and drawing attention to yourself before or after a race only cheapens whatever success you might achieve. I always liked drivers who thought that way, because they were easier to beat. Just by making a joke I could mess with their heads. Those drivers would be thinking about me while I was thinking about the race, and their involuntary obsession gave me a competitive edge.

The primary targets of my self-promoting statements, however, were the fans. I learned early on that a little trash-talking before a race stirs up the kind of controversy that fills the stands with paying customers. My outrageous comments might upset some drivers along the way, but the promoters loved me. In my mind, that was how the game—and make no mistake, racing is a game; a serious game, but a game nonetheless—should be played.

Bill Donoho, a promoter in Nashville, was a pistol-packing former assistant chief of police who had served a little time in prison. In 1958 Bill obtained a 30-year lease on a piece of land at the Fairgrounds where he spearheaded the construction of a steeply banked 5/8-mile paved racetrack. The Fairgrounds hosted NASCAR Late Model Sportsman races on Saturday nights, as well as a few Cup races. Donoho was a stern guy who stalked around the racetrack like a drill sergeant. Most people thought he didn't like anybody, but he took a shine to me when he realized that I could help him sell tickets.

Joe Carver, who was the head of public relations for the track at the time, was the first to recognize my willingness to stir things up, and Joe took full advantage of it. He'd drag me all over town for radio interviews, or he'd get me together with Joe Caldwell and Larry Woody, the sportswriters for the Nashville *Banner* and the *Tennessean*. During each interview I'd come up with some wild statement that was sure to raise eyebrows. If a big driver was scheduled for the next race, I'd promise to kick his butt.

Is Bobby Allison coming to town? He'd better bring the entire Alabama Gang, because he's going to have to go through me to get to Victory Circle. Is Richard Petty going to drive this weekend? Really? That old guy should get his prescription windshield changed.

In 1971 Channel 5 in Nashville launched a 30-minute Saturday morning television show called *Pit Stop*. Hosts Joe Carver and Hope Hines would recap the most recent race, talk about the upcoming race, and interview a driver. On the first show Joe and Hope interviewed Coo-Coo Marlin, a local driver whose son Sterling would go on to become very successful on the NASCAR Cup circuit. Coo-Coo's record of four track championships in Nashville would never be broken, but he was not the most talkative guy in town, and his one-syllable responses to the hosts' questions left a lot of dead air. Joe and Hope had to work hard to keep the interview going, and the show ended without the memorable moment they were hoping for.

The following week Joe and Hope interviewed another driver, Flookie Buford, and the outcome was pretty much the same. "Yep," Flookie said. "Nope." When they gave him the opportunity to criticize another driver or second-guess the officials, Flookie ducked and said, "Well, I don't know about that." This was hardly riveting entertainment.

When it was my turn to be on the show, I jumped in with both feet. Whenever Joe and Hope mentioned a driver, I'd make some kind of antagonistic remark. Flookie Buford? He's a backhoe driver, for Pete's sake. (It was true. Flookie owned a construction company.) Coo-Coo Marlin? What kind of a name is Coo-Coo? I was merciless in poking fun at Cale Yarborough. In postrace interviews, Cale had a habit of saying something like "This was the hardest race I ever ran in my life." So I created the Cale Scale. When the hosts asked me to assess the difficulty of the previous race, I said, "Well, on a scale of one to ten, I'd rate that race a four. But on the Cale Scale it was probably a nine." Joe and Hope loved it. From that point on, I was on the show every week.

Like all spectator sports, auto racing is entertainment. And

NASCAR is drama on a grand scale. Drama, of course, depends on conflict: no conflict, no drama. A hero may battle the elements, but the most compelling story is a conflict between good and evil, a hero and a villain. A bunch of buttoned-down nice guys who don't have a bad word to say about each other are, well, boring. These days, when Jeff Gordon gets into a wreck with, say, Jeff Burton, a little shoving match might erupt between the two of them on the track, but when the safety crew arrives they will climb into the same ambulance, and by the time they get to the hospital they'll probably be fine. Apologies will have been exchanged and accepted.

That would never have happened when I was driving. After any of my countless wrecks with Earnhardt, for example, the officials might need a cop to separate us, and there is no way I would have climbed into an ambulance with that guy after a wreck. We were at war. I would have walked to the hospital before sharing an ambulance with Dale, and he felt the same way about me. Our rivalry was real, and the fans knew it. Some fans saw me as the villain, others put Dale in that role, but it didn't matter who wore the black hat on any given Sunday. The point was that every race was a battle of good against evil. It was that drama, more than anything else, that drew fans to the track week after week.

In Nashville I learned how to use the media to antagonize the competition and get the fans talking. My goal was always to be the topic of conversation around town. I wanted the folks down at the diner to say "Did you hear what Waltrip said on the radio? Can you believe that guy? Who does he think he is?" During the driver introductions before each race I usually got more boos than cheers from the crowd during the early years, but that response didn't bother me at all. I just wanted my name to provoke a reaction. The worst response I could imagine was indifference. I wanted my presence to be felt.

Looking back, I must admit that I was pretty obnoxious at times. If I didn't qualify all that well, for example, and a reporter asked me what was wrong with the car, I'd shrug and say something like "It doesn't matter where I start. I'm going to take the lead on the thirtieth lap." Then, when the race got under way, I'd pick my way along and keep an eye on the scoreboard. When it reached 30 laps, I'd jump into the lead, and the media would go crazy. "Waltrip said he was going to take the lead on the thirtieth lap—and he did!"

Not every race turned out the way I predicted, of course, but I always got my name in the paper anyway. Sometimes the headline was "WALTRIP LAPS THE FIELD." Other times it was "MARLIN TAKES THE CHECKERED FLAG, WALTRIP FINISHES LAST." Either way, I got what I wanted most: I got noticed.

Before long other promoters were noticing me too, identifying the Waltrip kid as a gunslinger who could sell tickets. I don't think promoters do this sort of thing much anymore, but back in those days a promoter from Hickory, North Carolina, for example, would call me up and say, "Hey, we hear you've got a pretty fast car. We'll give you five hundred dollars to come over here and beat these boys." Then they'd arrange a remote radio interview, giving me a chance to talk some trash about the local drivers and get their fans all riled up. When race day arrived, the stands would be full. I traveled around a lot during those early days, playing the villain in towns all over the country.

P. B. Crowell and I were competing in NASCAR's second-tier series, which in those days was called the Late Model Sportsman series. (Later these races were renamed the Busch series, and now they're the Nationwide series.) NASCAR awarded driver points only for certain Saturday races, so ambition required travel. You could race at the same track every weekend and try to win the local track championship, but if you wanted to pursue a national ranking you had to travel to different tracks. P. B. and I hauled our car all around the country, following Late Model Sportsman barnstormers like Red Farmer and Bobby Allison to places like Manassas, Virginia, and South Boston.

Ours was a barebones operation in 1970. We had only one car, which we hauled around with a truck and trailer, and our pit crew worked for beer. Not that we needed much of a pit crew; most of the short tracks on the Late Model Sportsman circuit didn't even have a pit road. The race would typically consist of 100 laps, maybe followed by a break for gas and tires and another 100 laps.

I'm not kidding when I say our crew worked for beer. Sterling Beer was our first sponsor. We got that deal through a friend of mine named Charlie, who worked at the Sterling brewery in Evansville, Indiana, right across the river from Owensboro. P. B. Crowell put the Sterling Beer logo on our car, but the brewery didn't actually pay us any money for it. Instead a delivery truck pulled up outside our shop once a week and dropped off 20 cases of beer. That was the deal. When the arrangement with Sterling Beer ended, Pabst Blue Ribbon came aboard as our sponsor under identical terms. No money; beer.

For the kind of help we wanted, however, beer was all the currency we needed. Our guys loved racing and fooling with cars, and they would gladly work their hearts out in exchange for all the beer they could drink. Sometimes we forgot our toolbox when we loaded up and headed off to the track, but we never forgot our cooler. Beer made our world go round.

My relationship with my father-in-law started to thaw in late 1970. In one of her phone calls home, Stevie let her dad know that I would soon be competing in a Saturday race at the Salem Speedway in Indiana, about 100 miles from Owensboro. Mr. Rader let the invitation pass without comment, but as the weekend approached a couple of his buddies mentioned over lunch that they would be driving over to Salem for the race, and they invited him to come along. He agreed to go.

Stevie accompanied me to the track that weekend, and before the race started she pointed out where her father and his friends were sitting. "Right over there," she said. "See him?" Even from a distance there was no mistaking the imposing figure of Mr. Rader. He seemed to be looking at me. I waved. He didn't. I swallowed hard and climbed into my car.

It was a beautiful day for racing. The sky was clear, the air was warm, and the stands were packed. I put Mr. Rader out of my mind as I joined the huge field of cars rumbling toward the starting line. I had qualified near the pole, and when the green flag dropped I quickly charged into the lead. I stayed in front for the entire race, steadily pulling away from the pack. Meanwhile Mr. Rader grew more animated with every lap, rising to his feet and smiling every time my car went by. During the final ten laps he was cheering, and when I took the checkered flag he slapped his buddies with glee and shouted to everyone around him, "That's my son-in-law! That's my son-in-law!"

A few months later Stevie and I attended a dinner party in Louisville honoring my father-in-law. Texas Gas, the company Mr. Rader ran, was affiliated with CSX, a company that operated river barges. CSX had commissioned the building of a new triple-screw towboat for moving barges up and down the Mississippi River, and they had decided to name the boat after Mr. Rader. We attended the official launch and christening of the *Frank Rader* at the boatyard, followed by a grand celebratory dinner at the Brown Hotel.

I was on my best behavior in the elegant dining room. I put my napkin in my lap, sipped carefully from the crystal, and watched Stevie for clues about which fork to use. Suddenly I felt a strong hand on my shoulder, and I turned to see Mr. Elmer, the CEO of Texas Gas.

"Hello, young man," said Mr. Elmer. "Darrell, isn't it?"

"Yes sir," I said, dropping my fork and fumbling for my napkin.

"How's married life?" Mr. Elmer looked at Stevie, who beamed.

"Uh, great!" I said. "It's great!"

"Glad to hear it," said Mr. Elmer. "You're a lucky man. And how's your racing going? Frank tells me you put on quite a show up there in Salem."

I almost choked. Mr. Rader had been bragging about me at work? "Yes, sir," I said. "It's going pretty good right now. I've got a good ride, and I've been winning some races."

"He's been winning a *lot* of races," said Stevie.

Mr. Elmer turned to Mr. Rader, who was seated nearby. "Frank," he said, "how much would it cost to put a car in the Daytona 500?"

Mr. Rader shrugged and looked in my direction. "How much would that cost, Darrell?" he asked.

"I don't know," I said. "A lot, I'm sure. I can find out."

"You do that," Mr. Elmer said. "Find out how much it would cost. We just might put us a car in the Daytona 500."

On the following Monday I called up my buddy Ed Sanders, whose pal Slick Owens worked at Holman-Moody. Sure enough, Ford's factory-backed racing shop had a car for sale, a 1969 Mercury Cyclone. Its price? $12,500—roughly four times the cost of a showroom model. I took a deep breath and telephoned Mr. Rader.

"I've found a car that can run in the Daytona 500," I said. "It costs twelve thousand five hundred dollars."

"I'll go talk to Elmer about it," Mr. Rader said.

About an hour later Mr. Rader called me back with the good news. "Go get the car," he said.

Within a week I had taken possession of my new car and was polishing it inside P. B. Crowell's garage. It was late at night, and everybody else had gone home. The Mercury Cyclone rested under the lights, a contoured behemoth with an angular nose and a flamboyant chrome grille. Beneath the gleaming new body was a used car with a glorious past. Mario Andretti had driven this very car to victory in the 1967 Daytona 500, when it bore the body of a '67 Ford Fairlane, and during the intervening years it had made several other Cup appearances around the country. Now the car was refurbished and ready to roll again, but it was cruelly imprisoned inside a locked garage. Autumn had already arrived. The 1970 racing season was rapidly coming to a close, and the next Daytona 500 was a winter away. As I ran my fingers over its fenders, I could feel the car's impatience. This machine needed to prove itself, and it was pleading for my help.

The next morning I telephoned Mr. Rader. "I've been thinking I should get some superspeedway experience before we show up in Daytona next February," I said. "I mean, I've driven a lot on short tracks, but really I need to find out how this car handles on a two-and-a-half-mile track before the big event. And it occurred to me last night that it's not too late to enter the Late Model Sportsman event that's coming up in Texas."

"That sounds like a good idea," Mr. Rader said.

The event in Texas was a 100-lap race, so I wouldn't need to take a pit crew with me. I quickly assembled a race team of three humans and a dog. With the car loaded onto the trailer, Stevie and I climbed into the cab of P. B.'s truck with a guy named Bo Brady and our dog, Charlie Brown, and headed for the Texas Motor Speedway.

I slapped the dashboard with excitement when we crossed the line into Texas, and when we arrived in College Station I was beside myself. "Two more miles!" I shouted as I maneuvered the truck and trailer through traffic. Suddenly I heard a car horn. A four-door sedan had pulled up beside us, and two guys in Stetsons were waving in our direction.

"Look, honey—cowboy race fans!" I said. "I wonder how they know who we are?"

Stevie looked over at the car. "Uh, Darrell? I think they're motioning for you to pull over. They look like cops to me."

Sure enough, the guys in the car were Texas Rangers, and they were not smiling as they approached the cab. I rolled my window down and fished for my license as Stevie rifled through the glove compartment for the registration. "Do you realize you cut somebody off back there while changing lanes?" one of the Rangers asked. "You almost caused an accident. Some poor female driver was forced to turn into a side street to avoid being run off the road."

"Gosh, officer," I said, "I never saw her. I'm really sorry. I've never been here before, and I'm just so excited about driving in the big race that I guess I wasn't paying attention. In fact I thought you guys were honking at us because you were fans."

The cop squinted at my license, then looked up at Stevie, who gave him a sweet smile.

"Well, Mr. . . . Waltrip," the Ranger finally said, handing back my license, "I'm going to let you go with a warning this time. Welcome to Texas. If you drive on the track like you drove back there, you just might win that race."

At the speedway it soon became apparent that my new Cyclone was faster than any other car in the Late Model Sportsman division. I captured the pole with ease, my average speed nearly five miles per hour faster than Bobby Allison's, who qualified second in a Dodge. When the green flag fell on Saturday afternoon I jumped into the lead, and I led the race until the 52nd lap, when the engine suddenly blew up.

Afterward a reporter pointed out an ironic coincidence. "Your engine failed on lap fifty-two, and that's the number on your car."

I shook my head ruefully. "I guess I should have asked for number one hundred," I said.

Despite the loss, we all felt good about our trip to Texas. The new car had proven itself, and I had proven that I could run with the best on one of NASCAR's long tracks. We had captured the pole. We had held a lead. We were on our way.

It seemed like February 1971 would never arrive. Stevie and I visited family during the Thanksgiving and Christmas holidays, but I spent every other available minute during the winter at the shop, tinkering with the car and circling the Daytona International Speedway in my mind. We planned to enter our Terminal Transport car in the Late Model Sportsman race that would be held on the Saturday afternoon before the Daytona 500. A full contingent of executives from Terminal Transport and Texas Gas would attend the race, and I fully intended to win it.

One day, while I was looking over the paperwork for Speedweeks, I noticed that an ARCA race would be held at the Daytona Speedway a week prior to the 500. ARCA is a race-sanctioning body similar to NASCAR. The organization was founded in 1953 by John Marcum, a former driver who competed against Bill France Sr. in the 1940s. Due largely to the personal friendship between France and Marcum, ARCA was invited to hold races at the Daytona Speedway during Speedweeks beginning in 1964. Since that time ARCA has come to play an important role in the development of NASCAR drivers. Its events are open to hobbyists as well as professional drivers, who often drive older cars that have been retired from the NASCAR Cup circuit. Similar to the farm teams in baseball, ARCA often serves as a stepping-stone to the big leagues for aspiring young drivers. I decided to enter our car in the ARCA race as a warm-up for the main event. It seemed like easy money.

I qualified third for the ARCA race, but on the third lap I was drafting behind the pole-sitter when he blew up and wrecked. Unable to avoid him, I wrecked too. We should have packed up and gone home right then, but the thought of disappointing my father-in-law and the crowd from Terminal Transport and Texas Gas was too unpleasant to bear, so I spent the whole next week in a frantic effort to fix the car. The chassis was bent, but we straightened it the best we could and patched and rigged the rest of the car, pulling it all together in time for the race on Saturday afternoon. Twenty-five laps into that race, however, I wrecked again.

"What are we going to do?" I asked Suitcase Jake Elder, my crew chief, as we surveyed the wrecked car.

"There's one man I know who can fix this car right," Jake said. "His name is Robert Gee."

"What's his last name?" I asked.

"Gee," said Jake. "G—E—E. He worked for Harry Hyde back when I did, building the K & K Dodges, but he recently opened a little business of his own in Charlotte. He can straighten a frame, and he's the best body man I know. Why, you can wad a piece of metal up and give it to Robert and he'll give it back to you smoothed out so perfectly you'd swear it had never been bent. Let's ship the car to Charlotte, and I'll get Robert Gee to fix it."

A week or so later I walked into Robert's shop for the first time, accompanied by Jake. My car was already there, and a big man was leaning against it with his eyes half-closed, the long ash from a cigarette dangling precariously from his lips. The man was pressing a wire welder against the side of the car and pulling the trigger. I had seen a wire welder before; we had always made our metal repairs the old-fashioned way, using a torch and a welding stick that left a ragged, pustular scar, but this guy was making spot-welds. Pfft! Pfft! I grabbed Jake by the arm and whispered, "We've gotta get our car out of here! This guy doesn't even know how to weld!"

In the years that followed, Stevie and I would spend a lot of time at Robert Gee's shop, often sleeping in his house in front of the shop. Like most body men, Robert liked to drink, and his normal routine was to sleep during the day and drink and work at night. Meanwhile a motley succession of drivers and mechanics and relatives would drift through his house and shop.

One evening a bleary-eyed mustachioed young man wearing a dirty T-shirt and Hush Puppies wandered into the shop carrying a half-empty fifth of Jack Daniel's. He regarded me silently for several minutes, taking an occasional pull from the bottle. Finally Robert introduced us.

"This here's Dale," Robert said, in his Virginia twang. "He's married to my daughter Brenda. You may have heard of his dad, Ralph. Dale's a driver and a mechanic."

I walked over to Dale and stuck out my hand. "Darrell Waltrip," I said. "Nice to meet you."

Dale drained the bottle and tossed it into a nearby barrel, where it landed with a clatter, then he wiped his mouth with the back of his arm.

"This your car?" he asked.

CHAPTER SEVEN

THE ROOKIE IS A BRAT

At Robert Gee's shop in Charlotte we reanimated my wrecked 1969 Cyclone, transforming it into a 1971 Cyclone. Our sponsor, Terminal Transport, painted all its trucks brown so they wouldn't show dirt, and since we were required to match our sponsor's colors we dutifully painted the car turd brown. Then, after plastering "95" and "Terminal Transport" on the side of the car, we looked at NASCAR's schedule of upcoming events. As it happened, the next race was in Talladega, at the very superspeedway where our car had competed last. Impulsively we said, "Let's go to Talladega!"

We were going to need a hauler, and one soon arrived. My father-in-law drove up in a retired Maxwell Coffee delivery truck he'd purchased from a used equipment dealer. P. B. agreed to let me borrow his trailer. I owned 16 used "Talladega tires," the wide tires specially made for the Alabama superspeedway, and I loaded them into the truck, along with my only spare part: one gear. Then I went to the local Western Auto store and purchased a small metal toolbox, a few wrenches, a stationary jack, and a pair of light-duty jack stands.

I knew I would need a knowledgeable crew chief at Talladega, so I drove over to Hutchinson-Pagan, where some of the recent repairs had been made, and talked to Dick Hutchinson about hiring one of his mechanics on a temporary basis. "Jake Elder knows the car," Dick said. "He worked on it when Pearson drove it, and he helped with your repairs. If Jake will do it, he can go with you." Jake agreed, and I arranged to rent his services from Hutchinson-Pagan for a week.

Stevie, Robert Gee, and I rode together in the cab of that lumbering, underpowered delivery truck all the way to Talladega. Jake met us there. When we arrived at the garage, Jake went around to the back of the truck, pulled up the overhead door, and swore. "Where's all your stuff?"

"What stuff?"

"Your tools! Your nitrogen bottles and air wrenches! Your pit equipment! Your springs! Where's your *stuff*?"

I shrugged. "This is all the stuff I've got."

Jake pulled the door back down. "Man, you're not ready to race. You don't have anything."

"We'll buy it!" I said. "But listen, the first thing we've got to do is make the race. If we make the race, I'll buy everything we need." Jake stood there for a minute, shaking his head, and finally agreed.

After we had qualified for the race, I went over to see Mr. Hurd, the vendor at one of the tools trucks, and picked out brand-new air wrenches, a new pit jack, and everything else I thought we'd need. The total bill was about $1,000. "You want to pay by check, or do you want me to send you an invoice?" Mr. Hurd asked. I told him to send me an invoice.

Even though we had made the race, there were still some issues with the car. The biggest problem: it was bottoming out on the rough track. A cross-member on the frame was striking the asphalt hard enough to make the car undriveable. Jake grabbed a torch. "We'll just cut that sucker out," he said.

I was appalled. "Whoa! I ain't very smart, but I know you can't do that."

"What do you mean, you can't do that? It doesn't do anything."

"The heck it doesn't! It holds the chassis together!"

"Well, we can't race the car the way it is."

We argued for a while, neither one of us willing to budge. Finally Jake said, "Well, if you're not going to let me do my job my way, I'm going home."

"I guess you'll have to go home, then."

"Fine." And he left.

Not knowing what else to do, I went to see my friend Bobby Allison. Bobby referred my question to his buddy Bill Hamner, who was working on Allison's Chevrolet. Bill came over and looked at the offending cross-member. "Well, that's easy to fix," he said. He called a couple of Bobby's guys, and they modified the steel member, trimming it from its original four-inch thickness to about an inch, giving me plenty of extra clearance under the car.

It had been a long day, and I still needed to hire a new crew chief. When we got back to the Days Inn, however, I found Jake relaxing beside the pool, drinking a beer. I walked up to him and said, "I thought you were going home."

"Nah," Jake said, tossing his empty aside and reaching for another cold one. "I decided to hang around. Did you get that car fixed?"

"Yes, sir, we damn sure did—no thanks to you."

Jake fixed me with an indulgent stare. "I knew you'd figure it out. I thought I'd wait here until you got done, then go back out there in the morning and get on with the program."

Goodyear had introduced a new treaded tire for Talledega in 1972, which the manufacturer promised would improve performance on the superspeedway. Every other race team (with the exception of Jim Hylton's, it turned out) had purchased the new tires, but such an extravagance was beyond the means of our struggling little operation. We arrived at Talladega with our 16 used tires, determined to do our best.

This was my first Winston Cup race, and I had qualified 23rd in a field of 48 cars. When the race got under way, I was astonished to discover that I was driving the fastest car in the field! After just a few laps I was blowing past NASCAR giants Richard Petty, Cale Yarborough, and David Pearson like they were standing still!

What I didn't know was that the new Goodyear tires had proven incapable of withstanding the high temperatures produced by all-out driving on the Talladega asphalt. Some drivers were forced into the pits after just a few laps, and others were slowing way down to prevent their tires from overheating and shredding. I quickly threaded my way through the field and eventually passed James Hylton to take the lead. What a feeling! This Winston Cup racing was easier than I thought! My confidence soared, and I continued driving like a madman until the 99th lap, when my engine blew up.

James Hylton won that race, earning $24,895 in what would be the only first-place finish of his NASCAR career, and Bobby Allison took home $9,465 for his second-place finish. I ended up in 27th place, winning a grand total of $1,465.

The paltry purse didn't cover our expenses at Talladega, but my financial situation quickly improved nonetheless, because my small stock of obsolete tires turned out to be a gold mine. As soon as I was out of the race, other teams started bombarding my crew with offers for my tires. I wound up selling my used tires for $1,500! Ironically, poverty had saved me from going broke. Too poor to buy the newest equipment, I had come to the track with *the wrong tires at the right time.*

I competed in a total of five Cup races in 1972, finishing sixth at Charlotte and turning in two third-place finishes on my hometown track in Nashville. All in all, it was not a bad beginning for a NASCAR Cup career. And since I had competed in only five races in 1972, I was still eligible to compete for Rookie of the Year honors in 1973.

My 1973 season got off to a promising start, with a 12th-place finish in the Daytona 500 and a sixth at Richmond. We were facing a growing mechanical challenge, however; Jake Elder was finding it increasingly difficult to find engine parts for my aging Mercury Cyclone. In March the engine blew up on the 51st lap of the Southeastern 500 at Bristol, a race Cale Yarborough led through all 500 laps in his new Chevrolet Chevelle Laguna. "We need a new car," I told Jake after the race. "I want what Cale's driving." We decided to make the switch to Chevrolet, and our team got to work building a couple of new cars at Robert Gee's shop in Charlotte.

I didn't have any money, of course. I owed everybody and his brother, and if it hadn't been for Wayne King at the Williamson County Bank in Franklin I probably wouldn't have survived the year. Wayne was a buddy and a race fan, but I think he grew to regret doing business with me. I'd write checks for whatever we needed, regardless of the balance in my account, then I'd go down to the bank to see Wayne. The banker would open his desk with a sigh and produce a fistful of checks.

"Here's a check for a hundred dollars," Wayne would say, "and here's one for two hundred, and one for five hundred." He'd read through all the checks, stacking them on his desk, and ask, "Can you make any of these checks good?"

"Not today," I'd say. "But let me tell you, I love the next track we're going to, and the way the car is running now I guarantee I'll be able to make some of them good next week."

Each week, however, brought a problem that only more money could solve. Eventually Wayne would say, "We've got to do something about all these checks, Darrell. We'll make out a ninety-day note to cover them." He'd prepare the note and I'd sign it. Let me tell you, if you want 90 days to go by fast, just make a 90-day note!

In August 1973 a measure of financial relief finally came in the form of a phone call from Bud Moore, asking if I would be interested in driving his car. Bobby Isaac had been driving very successfully for Bud that year, but in the middle of the Talladega 500 Bobby had pulled into the pits, climbed out of the car, and announced his retirement. He had reportedly heard a "strange voice" warning him that he would be killed if he didn't quit immediately.

The thought of driving for an established team appealed to me. I especially liked the thought of somebody else being responsible for the weekly bills. After talking it over with Stevie and conferring with the guys, I accepted Bud Moore's offer. For the final few weeks of the season I drove the #15 car, finishing eighth at Darlington and sixth in Wilkesboro.

It was in April 1973 at the Atlanta Motor Speedway that I secured my reputation as an upstart and a malcontent in NASCAR. After qualifying laps for that race were canceled due to rain, NASCAR announced that starting positions would be determined by the drivers' individual points. Since I was 18th in the point standings at the time, I naturally assumed that I would start 18th, but NASCAR issued a clarification: only the first 17 cars would start according to points. Everybody else had to draw for their starting positions.

I was livid when I heard the news. Within minutes I was stomping around the racetrack complaining to anyone who would listen. Only the first *17* cars will start according to points? This is ridiculous! Why not the first ten, or the first 20? I'm 18th in points and they're going to make me draw for starting position? I ranted and fumed, demanding to know who was responsible for a decision that seemed to be aimed directly at me.

Back in Nashville I had always been able to get redress for my grievances. If I had a problem at the Fairgrounds Speedway, all I had to do was make a fuss, and somebody—Bill Donoho, the officials, *somebody*—would handle it for me. I was ready to give somebody a piece of my mind. I just didn't know who to give it to.

"Oh, Len Kukler is the guy you need to talk to," one guy told me.

"Who's Len Kukler, and where can I find him?"

"He's a NASCAR executive, and he's down at the press box." I headed for the press box at top speed.

Len Kukler was a mild-mannered fellow, a real gentleman, but I didn't know that. When I burst into the media room I found him holding a press conference, explaining to a few dozen reporters the process NASCAR was going to use to determine the starting lineup. The reporters, arrayed in front of him in folding chairs, were languidly taking notes. Len finished his explanation and asked, "Does anybody have any questions?"

"Yeah, I have a question," I said. Chairs scraped and heads swiveled in my direction. I saw a couple of cameras and a few microphones. Len looked a little surprised that there was a driver in the room, but he nodded cordially in my direction.

"I'm eighteenth in the points," I said, "and I'm sure NASCAR knows that. So I want to know why the first *seventeen* guys get to start by points and the rest of us have to draw. I want to know why in the world I have to draw when I'm *eighteenth in the points!*"

Shutters were snapping now, and reporters were grinning. This was too good to be true! A young driver who didn't know any better was challenging a ruling by NASCAR!

Mr. Kukler didn't lose his cool. The reason, he patiently explained, was that only the drivers who had run all the races that year were eligible to start by points. I hadn't competed in all the races. I had skipped Riverside. His explanation made sense, but the reporters, emboldened by my protest, began shouting questions of their own. What had been an orderly press conference suddenly turned tumultuous, and I became the biggest story of the moment. Carried away by the heat of the dispute, I was too naive to understand the folly of what I had done. The media loved me, but I had just stuck a finger in the eye of my sport's sanctioning body. I had marked myself as a contrarian and a troublemaker, and NASCAR would start dealing with me accordingly.

Wouldn't you know, when NASCAR held the drawing for starting positions in the Atlanta race, I drew the last spot. The 18th position was drawn by Charles Barrett, a guy who had never even been to Atlanta before and had only practiced for a few laps. Incensed by the injustice of it all, I continued my campaign. I found Barrett and convinced him that, given his inexperience, he would be a whole lot safer starting at the rear of the field than in the middle of it, and I offered to switch positions with him. He agreed, and we went to NASCAR together. The officials weren't stupid. They could envision what might result from starting a greenhorn in the middle of the field, so they reluctantly conceded and allowed us to make the swap. In the end, however, it was all for naught.

I was running strong in the race, holding my own with David Pearson, Cale Yarborough, Buddy Baker, Richard Petty, and the rest, when something broke on the car during the 160th lap and I had to drop out. I wound up taking 33rd place and winning a purse of $935—just $35 more than the last-place finisher. Barrett finished 18th and won $1,200.

I fully expected to drive again for Bud Moore in 1974, but in December 1973 Bud called me with bad news. He told me that George Follmer, a driver who also competed on the Grand Prix and U.S. Automobile Club circuits, had approached him with a deal. If Bud would let George drive his car that year, RC Cola would sponsor it. It was a package too sweet to resist. Bud regretfully told me that he had taken the deal, leaving me without a ride.

I quickly made phone calls of my own, scrambling to reassemble my team. Terminal Transport agreed to sponsor me, pledging $25,000 for the season. Jake Elder reenlisted as my crew chief, and Robert Gee signed on again as the body man. Ray Fox Jr. rejoined the team, along with Larry Reagan. We may not have had much money, but we were loaded with talent, and we were determined to compete.

I didn't have a specialized pit crew in those days; nobody did. Whoever worked on the car in the shop during the week also pitted on Sunday. Five men went over the wall during a pit stop, not six like today, and tire changers had to carry their own tires. Anybody, including the truck driver, was liable to be pressed into service. You might be sitting in a Waffle House on Saturday, run into somebody who raced at the local dirt track, and say, "Hey, do you want to help on our pit crew tomorrow?" And they'd come to the track on Sunday and pit your car for you.

Roles on the pit crew were fluid; anybody could do anything. Robert Gee was an experienced gas man—that's what he'd done for Harry Hyde—so he usually gassed the car. Jake Elder didn't need to be going over the wall, but he would usually change the right front tire, and Ray Fox would change the right rear tire, and whoever could jack the car would be the jack man.

A good pit stop in those days took about 20 seconds. Nowadays, of course, a 20-second pit stop would put you half a lap behind. It was Ray Evernham who revolutionized the pit stop when he became Jeff Gordon's crew chief in 1992. Ray started focusing on little things that other people were ignoring. He was the first to have a specific group of guys whose sole job was to pit the car. Today everybody has a designated pit crew, along with a coach and a training program. Like special teams in football, the pit crew has become a project in and of itself.

I managed to start a total of 16 Cup races in 1974. By midseason I was ranked 19th in the points and was winning just enough purse money to keep us going. Here and there I'd find ways to bring in a little more money, driving in a Late Model Sportsman race, for example, or approaching a local Chevrolet dealer and offering to paint his name on my hood that week for a thousand bucks. We were operating hand-to-mouth, barely surviving from week to week.

Meanwhile a handful of NASCAR drivers were prospering. NASCAR had a bonus program they called the Winner's Circle, which was limited to ten drivers. If you were in the Winner's Circle, you received an extra $10,000 per week, just for showing up. To me, the whole arrangement seemed unfair. The rich were getting richer, while guys like me were getting poorer. Finally, in frustration, I placed a telephone call to Bill France Jr. at the NASCAR office in Daytona.

"I can't keep going," I told Mr. France. "I'm broke. I know you have this Winner's Circle program, but guys like me who aren't there yet can't make it on what we're being paid."

"What do you want?" Bill France asked tersely.

"I need some help," I said. "Maybe the racetracks could help. I spend my own money to go to these tracks week after week, and they don't help me at all."

"So how much do you need?"

"Well, I'd like to have ten grand," I said. "I know I can't get that much, but five thousand or even twenty-five hundred from a track would make a big difference to a little operation like mine."

The line went silent for a few seconds. "Okay, let me work on it," Mr. France said.

True to his word, Bill France Jr. made phone calls on my behalf. John Riddle, the former Air Force general who ran the racetrack in Dover, Delaware, was the first promoter to help me. He gave me $2,500 to race at Dover Downs. L. G. DeWitt at Rockingham, Paul Sawyer at Richmond, and a number of other promoters who appreciated the ambition of a struggling young driver also lent a hand. I was grateful for their assistance, and I tried to show my gratitude by competing hard in every race. Even though I did not win a single race in 1974, I did almost win Darlington in September, and in all the other races I drove like a demon until my engine blew up or my tires were gone or I wrecked. I didn't just show up to take the money and run.

In those days most of the fans were rooting against me, often because of something I'd said in an interview. Other drivers were wary of the media and avoided reporters whenever they could, mostly because they didn't want to be quoted saying something that might upset NASCAR. I, by contrast, used the media to relay messages to NASCAR. As I saw it, the officials weren't going to pay much attention to the private complaints of a young driver like me, but those same officials did read the newspapers, and they hated negative publicity. NASCAR would pay attention to my complaints if they were in the newspapers.

My suggestions for improving procedures at NASCAR, which I was not shy about sharing with the media, did not endear me to the NASCAR establishment or my fellow drivers. I was still largely oblivious to the political intricacies of the motor racing world. My brash attitude, when interpreted in light of my connection to Stevie's dad, fed the popular misconception that Darrell Waltrip was a spoiled rich kid who had been bankrolled into NASCAR by indulgent relatives. Most people had no idea that I was just a poor boy from Kentucky who was scratching to survive from week to week.

When the 1974 season came to a close, I took the money Terminal Transport was giving me for the upcoming season and invested it in improving the car. I bought an engine and a lot of parts from Junior Johnson. We got off to a rocky start in 1975—a broken axle at Daytona, a blown engine at Richmond, a wreck at Rockingham—but then we found our groove. In the next seven weeks I finished sixth at Bristol, fifth at Atlanta, seventh at Wilkesboro, second at Darlington, second at Martinsville, and fourth at Talladega. Then, on May 10, 1975, I won my very first Winston Cup race before a hometown crowd at the Nashville Speedway. It was Mother's Day, and Mom was there to see me win. One of my prized possessions is a photograph taken that day in Victory Circle. The photo shows me standing triumphantly beside the car with my parents, my grandparents, Stevie, and my 12-year-old brother, Michael.

Nashville was home to Marty Robbins, the country music star who was also NASCAR's most beloved nonprofessional driver. I raced against Marty often at the Nashville Speedway, where it was not unusual for him to exit the feature early so that he could get to the Opry in time for his performance. Marty was a legitimate driver. Over the course of his career he competed in 35 Winston Cup races, finishing six times in the top ten.

Maybe it was the popular singer's crossover to driving that gave Jim Donoho his big idea in 1975. Jim, the son of speedway owner Bill Donoho, had plenty of friends in the music business. His idea? An album of country standards sung by NASCAR drivers. He titled the project *NASCAR Goes Country,* and recruited Cale Yarborough, Buddy Baker, Bobby Allison, Richard Petty, David Pearson, and me to sing on it.

On our first night together, we all went to dinner and then

went out on Jerry Bradley's dad's boat to have a few drinks and socialize. The next day we went to Bradley's barn in Mt. Juliet to record. The Jordanaires were there to sing backup for us, and Jim had brought in some of Nashville's top session musicians to play, guys like Charlie McCoy on harmonica and Bobby Thompson on rhythm guitar and banjo. Everything was great—until it came time for the drivers to sing. We were awful, truly awful. When Richard Petty sang "King of the Road," you could hardly understand what he was saying. What's more, the very fact that Richard had been chosen to sing that song made Cale Yarborough mad. "Why Richard?" Cale complained. "He's not the King of the Road—I am!"

Marty Robbins was in the studio with us that morning, trying to offer guidance and encouragement. After one particularly off-key rendition of "99 Bottles of Beer on the Wall," he stepped out from behind the control board in mock horror. "Y'all are about to set country music back twenty years! I'll make a deal with ya. If y'all will stop singing, I'll stop driving!"

Eventually we started drinking, and the alcohol seemed to improve our performance. We got a little braver, a little more vocal. Pretty soon we were having altogether too much fun. I had never laughed so hard in my life. Here we were, five of the most competitive guys on the planet, doing something none of us knew how to do. Each man had to take a turn inside the soundproof recording booth, and while he was in there the rest of us would cut him to pieces. Buddy Baker butchered "Just a Bowl of Butterbeans." Cale belted out "Six Days on the Road," David Pearson warbled "Maybelline," and Bobby Allison recited "Watch Out for the Matador." I was pretty sure my performance of "I Can Help" was the best of the group, but that's no compliment. Marty Robbins was right.

By the time the music people finished producing the record, however, it sounded pretty good. After he'd heard it, Bill Donoho offered me $10,000 for my share of the profits. I turned him down flat. "How crazy do you think I am? This record is going to sell *millions*!"

In the end, Bill's offer was approximately $9,999 more than I earned from sales of *NASCAR Goes Country*. The entire marketing plan for the record consisted of Jim selling the thing out of the trunk of his car at races. Most of the 25,000 copies wound up in Jim's basement, which, I guess, was a pretty good place for them.

On July 4, 1975, I finished fourth in the Firecracker 400 at the Daytona Speedway, passing Donnie Allison on the last lap. Donnie had taken the pole for that race, averaging 186.737 miles per hour in the #88 car owned by DiGard Motorsports. I had known Donnie for years, ever since my days with P. B. Crowell, and Donnie had been driving for DiGard since the team launched in 1973. The new team had made a number of impressive showings, but Donnie had not yet made it to Victory Circle. It wasn't his fault.

DiGard's biggest problem was that their engines kept giving out. Mario Rossi was the engine builder, and they were experimenting with nitrous oxide during qualifying. (DiGard wasn't the only team to use that banned fuel additive. Rumors of nitrous use circulated through the garages, but nobody complained to NASCAR about DiGard because the new team wasn't winning races. And besides, other teams had secrets of their own.) The DiGard car would typically set a blistering pace during qualifying, but their engines simply could not sustain that level of performance for an entire race.

Bill Gardner, who shared ownership of the DiGard team with his brother-in-law, Mike DiProspero, was growing impatient. After I edged out Donnie in the final lap of the July Daytona race, Bill Gardner exploded. He was reported to have said something to this effect: "I'm sick and tired of getting outrun by that ragtag Waltrip operation. I'm spending thousands of dollars every week and they don't have two nickels to rub together, so why can't we beat 'em? I don't know who that kid is, but I want him in my car!"

After the race, Stevie and I drove down to Vero Beach to spend a couple days relaxing at her family's vacation home on John's Island. On the way back to Charlotte, I stopped by the Daytona Speedway to pick up my purse money, the $6,210 I had earned for my fourth-place finish on the Fourth of July. As I was leaving the office, somebody stopped me in the hall and asked, "Hey Darrell, have you seen Jim Gardner?"

"No." I was mystified by the question. Jim was Bill Gardner's brother, and I had no idea why he would want to see me.

"Well, he's looking for you."

"For me? Why?"

"DiGard wants to hire you."

"Well, that's ridiculous," I said. "Why would I want to drive for them?"

A few hours later Stevie and I pulled off the interstate for gas and a couple of Pepsis. As I was walking from our car to the soda machine, I was surprised to see Jim Gardner sitting in his car at another pump. He saw me too, and his face registered disbelief. Jim quickly climbed out of his car and strode in my direction. "Darrell?" he said. "Where have you been? We've been looking all over for you!"

"I've been at the beach with Stevie," I said. "Why?"

"My brother wants you to drive the DiGard car."

"Now? In the middle of the season?"

"Yes," Jim said. "He wants to make the change right away. Whaddaya say?"

I shook my head. "Sorry, Jim, I can't do that. It doesn't make sense. I have my own cars, my own people, and we're doing real well. I'm just not going to abandon everybody and everything halfway through a great season."

"Well, think about it," Jim said.

When we pulled back onto the highway, I told Stevie about my strange conversation with Jim Gardner.

Stevie was incredulous. "You told him no?" she said, her voice rising. "Darrell, have you lost your mind? Do you have any idea how broke we are? This sounds like a real chance. I think you should consider it."

"Well, what would I do with Jake and all the guys?" I asked.

"Just take them with you," Stevie said.

I thought about it for a minute. "That's a possibility, I guess."

Stevie and I continued debating the DiGard proposal all the way through Georgia and South Carolina, and by the time we reached Charlotte I had conceded that driving for Bill Gardner was the right thing to do. When we got to the shop, I gave Bill a call.

"Look," I said, "I'll drive your car for you, under one condition. You have to hire Jake, my crew chief, and you'll need to give a couple of my other boys a job too."

"Done," Bill Gardner said, and we made a deal.

The DiGard shop was located in Daytona, right across the street from the Daytona International Speedway. I think Bill Gardner believed that there was some advantage to planting his flag within sight of NASCAR headquarters, some magic to be wrought by proximity, but the remoteness of the shop in relation to all of the other tracks on the circuit meant a lot of extra travel for our team. It also meant that the boys and I were forced to live far from home. Jake and Robert Gee and I took rooms at the 8 Day Inn across the street from the track and hunkered down for the duration.

I drove my first race for DiGard at Talladega on August 17, and was in the lead on the 39th lap when the engine blew up. Two weeks later I was forced to drop out of the Darlington race on the 61st lap when the engine overheated. The following week in Dover, I made it to the 82nd lap before the engine failed. That catastrophe was followed by a broken timing chain in Martinsville and a dead battery in Charlotte. By then I'd had enough. Back at Robert Gee's shop in Charlotte, we took one of my cars and painted it up as the #88 DiGard car. The engine in that car had been built by Robert Yates, who was working for Junior Johnson at the time. We took our car with the DiGard paint scheme to Richmond and won the race.

*   *   *

One Friday night while we were in Charlotte, Stevie and I drove over to the Charlotte Fairgrounds Speedway, a local dirt track, to watch Dale Earnhardt race. I'd grown to like Robert Gee's son-in-law, and in repayment for his help in getting my car ready for Richmond, I had come up with some money to sponsor his dirt-track car that night. This was the first time I would actually see Dale race.

Dale's dad was Ralph Earnhardt, a former cotton mill worker and one of NASCAR's early drivers. A gifted mechanic who built his own cars, Ralph had dominated the dirt tracks around Charlotte. Tragically, Ralph died suddenly of a heart attack in 1972, at the age of 45. Robert Gee told me that Dale drove like his dad, maybe better.

I had done just enough racing on dirt to know I wasn't cut out for it. There were two tracks near Owensboro when I was a kid: a paved track in Whitesville and a dirt track at Ellis Park. I raced go-karts at both of them. On the paved track I'd lap the field, but I would always struggle at the Ellis Speedway. Eventually they paved that track too, and then I won everything.

My skills were perfect for driving on pavement. I was adept at holding a tight line through a turn, making a smooth transition, altering my trajectory in a split second without sacrificing speed. My finesse depended on solid traction, what the racing folks call "grip." Dirt-track racing, by contrast, requires an entirely different set of skills. On dirt, you sling your car around the track. Cars slide through the corners and churn down the straightaways, sending billows of dust rolling through the stands.

As I sat in the bleachers on that sticky summer night, eating gritty popcorn and drinking lukewarm beer, I watched Dale Earnhardt with growing admiration. Dale's car was not the fastest on the track, but it was clear to me that this kid had already mastered the art of racing on dirt. And he had fire in his belly.

In just a few years, of course, Dale would bring his aggressive attitude and distinctive style of driving to the paved tracks of NASCAR. The skills he acquired on dirt, including the uncanny ability to control a car that seemed to be out of control, would leave less experienced drivers shaking their heads with wonder. Team members and rivals alike would marvel at his ability to guide a wreck around a racetrack. The worse the car, it seemed, the better he could drive it. That night in North Carolina, Dale's raw ability and steely determination were on full display.

On the last lap of the feature race Dale spun out the local favorite and took the checkered flag. Stevie and I clambered down from the stands and trotted out onto the track to congratulate him, but as we approached Dale's car I heard a commotion and felt Stevie squeeze my hand. An angry mob was advancing toward us from the opposite direction, hurling threats at Dale as they came. I quickly swung Stevie around and pulled her toward the parking lot. "Nice race, buddy!" I shouted over my shoulder. "See you back at the shop!" Then we ran.

CHAPTER EIGHT

PLAYING HARDBALL
IN THE BIG LEAGUES

In my first full season with DiGard Motorsports I won three poles and just one race, Martinsville. I did manage to finish eighth in overall points, but mechanical problems with our #88 Gatorade car prevented me from finishing in 14 of the 30 races on the schedule that year. Almost every week it was something different: a cracked cylinder head at Riverside, a broken rocker arm in Daytona, a transmission failure in Wilkesboro, a broken valve in Talladega, a bad rear end in Nashville, followed by blown engines in Dover and Michigan. On the Fourth of July at Daytona, after being forced from the race on the 43rd lap due to yet another blown engine, I vowed that things would change.

Mario Rossi was still the motor man for DiGard in 1976, and the team was still located in faraway Daytona Beach. I had been hounding Robert Yates, who was the best motor man I knew, to come to work for DiGard, but Robert wouldn't hear of it. "I've got everything I need in Wilkesboro," he would say every time I called him. "And that drive up and down the highway from Daytona to wherever the race is that week? That's ridiculous. I ain't moving to Daytona."

I kept after Robert, week after week, and finally he offered a conditional surrender. He agreed to come to work for DiGard if I could convince Bill Gardner to move the team to Charlotte. I had been pressing Gardner for just such a move for some time. The team owner was reluctant to give up his prized location on Fentress Boulevard in Daytona, but I eventually persuaded him that any benefits we might gain from holding that location were far outweighed by the talent pool we could draw from in Charlotte, where most of the other NASCAR teams were located.

At the end of the 1976 season we moved the whole team to Charlotte. Robert Yates was now the motor man, and other great guys, including Buddy Parrot, Harold "Frog" Fagan, Ducky Newman, Bobby Jones, and David Iff, joined the team. When the new season opened in 1977, the results of our focus on quality improvement were immediately apparent. DiGard's Gatorade car completed more than 94 percent of the laps on the circuit that year, and engine problems forced us to retire early from only three races.

My first superspeedway win, which came at Darlington on April 3, 1977, marked an important turning point in my evolution as a driver. Critics had dismissed me as a "short-track guy," a driver who would never be a serious threat on a superspeedway. By winning on NASCAR's toughest track, I finally proved that I was a force to be reckoned with. In the process I also made an enemy of my old friend Bobby Allison.

With six laps to go in the Rebel 500, I was running behind Bobby, David Pearson, and Richard Petty, who were battling for the lead, when J. D. McDuffie and Dick Brooks suddenly tangled in turn 4 on the opposite side of the track, strewing wreckage across the asphalt. Under the rules at that time, drivers raced back to the caution flag when the yellow lights came on. Since this race would probably end under caution, I knew that whoever got to the line first would win the race. I saw my chance, and I went for it.

By the time I reached turn 3, David and Richard had collided and were out of contention, and Bobby was limping toward the flag with a flat tire and a badly torn-up car. I didn't know whether to go around him on the inside or the outside because he was weaving so badly. As we came off turn 4, Bobby got into some water from Brooks's radiator and went a little sideways. I managed to get by him—barely—and beat him to the line by about a foot. The race ended under caution, and I was declared the winner.

Bobby was furious that I had passed him the way I did, and he complained loudly that it was a dangerous move. Chris Econo-maki, who was working for ABC, interviewed me in Victory Circle. "Wellll, Darrellll," Chris said in his inimitable way, "Bobby Allison is a little upset with you today." I shrugged. What did it matter if Bobby was upset? I'd won the race, and I'd won it fair and square.

Four weeks after Darlington I won my second superspeedway race, at Talladega, taking the checkered flag with a very controversial last-lap maneuver. In those days every race strategist in the pits and in the stands understood that you should not be leading a race on the last lap. The lead car was a sitting duck. Cale Yarborough had perfected the "slingshot" move that would propel him past the leader at the very last minute, and he had timed that move perfectly to win race after race. Everybody respected the slingshot. If you were going to win a race, you wanted to be in *second* place, not first, going into the final lap.

With five laps to go at Talladega I was in the lead, and my crew chiefs, Buddy Parrot and David Iff, were screaming at me on the radio, "Slow down!"

"Shut up, you guys!" I hollered back. "I know what I'm doing!"

When the white flag came out to signal the last lap, I was still in the lead, followed closely by Cale Yarborough, Donnie Allison, and Benny Parsons. We were running single-file at the top of the track, following the groove beside the wall that was the fastest way around the long oval. As we went into turn 1 I checked my mirror—and then did something completely unexpected. I cut my car hard left and dove to the bottom of the track! The change in direction caused my car to lose momentum, but I was compensating for the reduction in speed by taking a shortcut across the end of the track. Cale, Donnie, and Benny were taking the longer way around.

When we came off of turn 2 I could see that I had increased my lead by about 100 yards. The other three cars had not sacrificed speed, however, and they came barreling into the back-stretch with a head of steam. I stayed on the bottom of the track and watched as they caught up with me. Then, as we went into the third turn, I drove right back up the track and cut in front of them, barely clipping Cale's front left fender in the process. The contact caused Cale to get loose; his car started to wiggle, and Donnie and Benny were forced to check up to avoid hitting him. With that, the race was mine.

I had made a risky move and it had paid off. My reputation was growing. In just a few short weeks I had gone from being a short-track punk to a superspeedway hero.

Later in the year I won again at Talladega, this time driving in relief of Donnie Allison after my engine failed on the 106th lap. That race, the Talladega 500, was the last time in NASCAR history that a Cup race was won by a relief driver.

Our momentum continued to build in 1978, when we once again won six races. I led a total of 2,173 laps that year and finished third in total points.

I had been building a little Busch series car in the shop in Charlotte, intending to race it on Saturday nights to make a little extra money. Time was scarce in 1978, however, and we had made very little progress on the car.

One Friday night Dale Earnhardt stopped by the shop while we were working. His face was streaked with dirt. Dale was carrying yet another bottle of Jack Daniels in one hand and a trophy in the other.

"Man, I've gotta get off these dirt tracks," he said. It was a familiar refrain. Anybody who hung around Dale for very long knew how tired he was of kicking around on dirt. He was desperate to get into NASCAR.

"Hey, Darrell," Dale said, "when are you going to finish that little Nova and let me drive it for you? I swear nuthin's been done on that car in a month." He was right. Work on the Busch car had definitely stalled. Suddenly I had an idea.

"I'll tell what I'll do," I told Dale. "If you'll finish the car for me, I'll let you drive it in the big race that's coming up in Nashville. You finish the car, and you can race it."

Dale slammed the trophy on the workbench and grabbed my hand. "Deal!" he said.

He lost no time in getting to work. Dale was a versatile mechanic, capable of doing almost anything, and his enthusiasm for this project was infectious. A couple of friends, including a big guy named Darrell Cruz, soon pitched in, and before long they had finished up that little car. Dale then tinkered with it endlessly until the weekend of the Nashville race arrived.

On the Monday after Dale's debut in Nashville, I received an avalanche of telephone calls from my friends at the Fairgrounds Speedway. "Why did you let that Earnhardt guy drive your car?" they demanded angrily. "That guy's crazy! He wrecked everybody over here! If you ever let that guy come to Nashville and drive your car again, we'll get you barred from the track!"

I still liked Dale, but that was the last time I ever let him drive my car.

Ken Squier, the standard-bearer for NASCAR announcers, had become a good friend of mine. We had first met in 1973, during my rookie year, when Ken decided to shoot a segment about the new kid from Kentucky for a television special he was putting together. After a Sunday race at Talladega, Ken and I climbed into an airplane and flew to Owensboro, and the following morning we shot a little a standup piece at the Whitesville racetrack. Ken and I clicked immediately, and over the course of the next few years he would occasionally invite me to join him in the broadcast booth to provide color commentary during a race.

Even as late as 1978 no major NASCAR race had been covered flag-to-flag by any of the big three television networks. Networks sometimes aired highlights of major races or taped the races for later broadcast, but nobody in network television had yet recognized the mass appeal of stock car racing as a live event.

The prevailing wisdom limited NASCAR's potential audience to illiterate Southern rednecks, a minority demographic that did not excite the interest of station owners in most parts of the country.

Ken Squier, to his great credit, believed passionately that a national audience would respond favorably to live coverage of NASCAR. In the fall of 1978, after CBS had finally agreed to experiment with live flag-to-flag coverage of the upcoming Daytona 500, Ken took me with him to New York to attend the annual CBS affiliates meeting. Our mission was to sell the station owners on carrying what Ken was now calling "the Great American Race."

Dessert was being served in the vast New York ballroom when Ken and I were introduced. We stepped up to the microphones and delivered an enthusiastic dog-and-pony presentation, hyping the Daytona 500 as the "Super Bowl of Stock Car Racing," but you could barely hear us above the din of scraping silverware, the clink of crystal, and the roar of station owners still engaged in table conversation. Nobody paid us any attention. It was clear to me that this crowd had no interest at all in NASCAR.

When we were finished, I went back to our table and dropped into my chair with a sigh. Beside me sat a burly guy I had just met, a retiring football coach that CBS had hired to provide color commentary for its coverage of NFL football. His name was John Madden. Madden slapped the back of my seat. "Tough room," he said, sympathetically. "But for what it's worth, I think your thing sounds exciting. I'll be watchin'."

Suitcase Jake Elder had earned his nickname by never staying too long with any team. Even though his formal schooling had ended at the third grade, Jake was so knowledgeable about the mechanics of racing that fresh job offers were constantly coming his way. At the end of 1978 he broke the news to me: he was leaving DiGard.

"Gonna go work for Osterlund," Jake told me. "He's hired

Dale to drive his Cup car next year, and I'm gonna be Dale's crew chief."

Rod Osterlund was a real estate mogul from California, a wealthy race fan whose latest ambition was to add a Winston Cup Championship to his list of accomplishments. For the 1979 campaign, which would be Osterlund's third season as an owner, the wily investor had opened his wallet, hiring the best talent available and authorizing them to purchase any equipment they would need to get the job done. Dave Marcis, a stubbornly independent driver famous for wearing wing-tip shoes when he drove, had been Osterlund's driver in 1978, but Osterlund was on the look-out for fresh talent, and he found the driver he was looking for in Dale Earnhardt. Dale had stepped in as a last-minute replacement for Osterlund's regular driver in a Late Model Sportsman race in Charlotte in late 1978 and had almost won the race. After watching Dale's impressive performance in another Saturday-night race in Atlanta a couple weeks later, Osterlund offered him the wheel of his unsponsored Chevy Monte Carlo for the 1979 Winston Cup season. This was Dale's big break, and he would make the most of it.

Our DiGard team opened the 1979 season with a bang, running away with a win at the Winston Western 500 in Riverside, California. A month later we were at the Daytona International Speedway, where the track had just been repaved for the first time since the speedway opened in 1959. The grip of the new asphalt surface brought fresh speed to Speedweeks. Buddy Baker blazed a track record during qualifying, capturing the pole with an average speed of 196.049 miles per hour, and I won one of the two 125-mile qualifying races on Thursday afternoon to secure the fourth starting position for the Daytona 500.

It rained all through the night before the Daytona 500, and on the morning of the big race rain continued to sweep across the track. The green flag was scheduled to drop at one o'clock. As the fateful hour approached, drivers and crews stood beside their idle cars and the broadcasters fretted. NASCAR's contract with CBS guaranteed that the race would start on time. If the race were postponed, CBS would switch to alternate programming and NASCAR would not get paid.

In reviewing its contract with NASCAR, however, the lawyers for CBS had failed to spot a loophole—a loophole of which NAS-CAR was well aware. Just as time was about to expire, NASCAR ordered the race to be started under a yellow flag. After all, the television contract did not specify how *fast* the cars had to be traveling when the race started.

Meanwhile the same storm that had lashed Daytona with rain had traveled up the East Coast and was now dropping fat flakes of snow on the mid-Atlantic seaboard. The storm, which would become known as the Presidents' Day Blizzard of 1979, would dump more than 18 inches of the white stuff on Washington, D.C., by Tuesday morning and paralyze the city for a week.

That afternoon more than 21 million Americans, many of them trapped in their homes by the snow, wound up tuning their televisions to CBS's live coverage of the Daytona 500. The network had introduced in-car video and low-level trackside cameras for the event, innovations that would give viewers an unprecedented experience of the action on the track, but for the first 30 minutes of the race all the audience saw was a parade of colorful cars sedately circling the speedway while Ken Squier and the other members of the CBS broadcasting team bravely manufactured suspense out of absolutely nothing.

Finally, after 15 laps, the green flag came out and we were off. On lap 32 Bobby Allison and Cale Yarborough swerved to avoid hitting a careening Donnie Allison, and all three cars went spinning through the muddy infield. By the time Yarborough had repaired his car and rejoined the race he was two laps behind the leader.

Tension built as the race wound on. Buddy Baker retired with a blown engine on the 38th lap, and on lap 52 a three-car wreck sent David Pearson, Gary Balough, and Ronnie Thomas to the garage. Meanwhile, through a total of seven caution flags, Yarborough steadily worked his way through the field until he was once again challenging Donnie Allison for the lead.

All the fans were on their feet for the final lap as Yarborough made a bid to pass Allison on the "superstretch," the long back straightaway between turns 2 and 3. Accounts of what happened next vary widely, depending on the perspective of the observer. Yarborough famously described it this way: "I was going to pass him and win the race, but he turned left and crashed me. So, hell, I crashed him back." Donnie Allison's account was entirely different. "The track was mine until he hit me in the back," he said. "He got me loose and sideways, so I came back to get what was mine. He wrecked me, I didn't wreck him." Both cars collided with the outside wall on turn 3 and wound up sliding into the soggy infield.

After the two leaders wrecked, I suddenly found myself in position to win the Daytona 500! Richard Petty flew past the stricken Allison and Yarborough, who were climbing out of their cars, and I was right behind him. I drew up to Petty's bumper, and as we came out of turn 4 I made a last-ditch attempt to slingshot past him on the inside, but I couldn't do it. Richard Petty won the race.

As soon as the television cameras had captured the finish, they turned their attention to the infield, as Ken Squier said those now-famous words: "There's a fight!" Yarborough and Allison had climbed out of their cars and engaged in a heated argument. Bobby Allison, who was a lap down anyway, pulled off the track and came to the aid of his embattled brother. Within seconds a punch was thrown. Then, as a national television audience looked on in astonishment, the helmeted combatants rolled in the muddy infield, flailing furiously.

The next morning NASCAR was the talk of the entire country. The story even made the front page of the sports section of the *New York Times*. THE *NEW YORK TIMES*! What had been dismissed as the strange obsession of a small Southern minority had suddenly gained national attention. NASCAR was about to go mainstream.

* * *

The race for the championship in 1979 came right down to the wire. I won seven races that year, more than any other driver, but I made two crucial mistakes late in the season that ultimately cost me the championship.

I made my first serious mistake in September, during the Southern 500 in Darlington. I was a lap ahead of the rest the field, dominating the race and driving like a maniac. Buddy Parrot and David Iff kept begging me to slow down, warning me that I was taking too many chances. I wouldn't listen. Darlington, the "Track Too Tough to Tame," is notoriously unforgiving; it demands total concentration from a driver. On that day, however, my focus was elsewhere. I was fixated on defeating the Silver Fox, David Pearson.

Pearson, who drove with surgical precision, had won more races at the Darlington Raceway than anyone else. If I could beat David Pearson at Darlington, I thought, I could prove that I deserved to be considered in the same breath as one of the legends in the sport. I was a lap ahead of him, but that wasn't good enough for me. As my crew waved frantically from the pits and Buddy screamed on the radio to take it easy, all I could think about was *lapping him again.*

Hubris finally caught up with me with less than 50 laps to go, when I attempted to pass a lap car on the outside in the first turn. It was a bonehead move, entirely unnecessary, and it defied a simple rule that every sensible NASCAR driver respects: Don't pass on the outside in turn 1 at Darlington. If you do and you're crowded at all, you will wind up in the wall. And that's what happened. Buddy Arrington went into the turn a little low, and I went in on the outside. Buddy pushed up a little bit, I got into the loose stuff, and WHAM! I hit the wall and spun out. David Pearson went on to win the race. I finished 11th.

Although it wasn't evident at the time, I essentially lost the championship that day at Darlington. My mistake dealt a serious blow to our pursuit of the season trophy, but the damage was far greater than the loss of a few points. I was demoralized by the loss, haunted by the knowledge that my own stupidity had caused it. Worse, I had lost credibility with my team. The crew was so angry with me that they didn't want me to drive the car the next week.

I was still holding on to a 53-point lead in mid-October when my campaign for the championship was sideswiped again, in Wilkesboro. The other Chevy teams were running Monte Carlos in that race, but at the request of the manufacturer we had built a little two-door Caprice designed specifically for North Wilkesboro's tight .625-mile oval. The Caprice was a sweet race car, the class of the field, and I could have won the race if I hadn't miscalculated again.

Late in the race I made the decision to pass Bobby Allison for the lead. It was a rash decision, made in the wrong spot and at precisely the wrong time. As we came off turn 4, I passed Allison on the outside—an insult to any good driver—and in the process made myself vulnerable. Bobby came up and nudged me as I went by, clipping my left rear quarter-panel, and sent my car spinning down the track. I fought the wheel for the length of the front straightaway and almost regained control, but I ran out of room in turn 1 and wound up against the wall, wrecked. The yellow flag came out, and NASCAR personnel went to work clearing the track of debris from my car.

My crew was furious with Allison, convinced (as I was) that he had wrecked me on purpose. They worked quickly to patch the car, and soon I was back on the track, laps behind the leaders but capable of keeping pace with anybody. Benny Parsons was in the lead by this time, but his lead was far from secure. Bobby Allison was close behind him, and Bobby's car was faster than Benny's. Passing is difficult in Wilkesboro, but it seemed inevitable that Allison would slip past Benny eventually. Allison was going to win the race unless he ran into trouble. I decided to be Trouble.

When the two lead cars caught up with me, I let Benny by. Then I started running interference for him, blocking Bobby. Soon NASCAR sent my crew chief a stern warning. "Tell DW to give Bobby room to race," they ordered, "or we'll black-flag him." I disregarded the message and continued blocking Bobby until, true to their word, NASCAR waved me into the pits with a black flag and held me there for two laps. I fumed as I watched Bobby close the gap with Benny Parsons. When NASCAR finally allowed me back on the track, I immediately caught up with Bobby and switched tactics. This time I went to the top of the racetrack, along the wall, and stayed there. I ran right beside Bobby Allison for the rest of the race.

Bobby knew exactly what I was doing, of course, but I couldn't be charged with blocking him because I wasn't in front of him. I gave him the whole bottom of the racetrack, which was the fast groove, but I gave him no room to pass. When we came up on a lap car, that car would move to the middle and Bobby would be forced to back off while I went around it. When Bobby caught up with me again, I'd stick right beside him, bird-dogging his every move, until we reached the next obstruction. Bobby never did get back to Benny, and Benny won the race.

NASCAR's current points system, which was then less than five years old, assured a tight race for the championship. In the old days, NASCAR had used an arcane and ever-evolving calculus to determine the winner of the season championship. In 1974, for example, points were based on total money winnings, multiplied by starts, divided by 1,000. But in 1975, Bill France Jr. had asked a public relations official, Bob Latford, to devise a simple and equitable points system. In the Boot Hill Saloon in Daytona Beach, Latford and two friends, Phil Holmer and Joe Witlock, had worked out the new system on a napkin. Under this system NASCAR would assign equal value to all races, regardless of length or purse, awarding points on a sliding scale based on finishing order, and bonus points for winning a race, leading a lap, and for most laps led. This was a system that the fans and drivers could understand, and it produced real drama late in the season. When the sun went down on North Wilkesboro that evening in 1979, my lead in the race for the season championship had dwindled to just 17 points, and Bobby Allison and I had become bitter rivals.

By Ontario, the final event of the 1979 season, my once-imposing lead in the championship race had dwindled to a mere 2 points. Richard Petty, who had already won the championship six times, was poised to strike. If I could finish the race ahead of Richard, the championship was mine. But it was not to be. Richard finished fifth at Ontario. I finished eighth. Petty captured his seventh Winston Cup Grand National Championship by a margin of 11 points.

In the weeks and months that followed, I replayed that season endlessly in my mind. If things had only gone differently in either Darlington or Wilkesboro, I told myself, I would have won the championship hands down. I tended to focus on Bobby Allison and the rotten thing he did to me in Wilkesboro, but in my heart I knew that only one person was responsible for the way things had turned out: I had beaten myself. And I had let my team down. In my determination to prove myself by winning every skirmish, I had lost the war, and I had nobody to blame but me.

The Rookie of the Year trophy in 1979 went to Dale Earnhardt. Dale had driven brilliantly that year, finishing 11 times in the top five, and he'd ended the season ranked seventh in overall points, despite missing four races due to a fractured collarbone he sustained in a wreck at Pocono. Dale had earned his first win in Bristol on April Fool's Day. Bobby Allison and I had battled for the lead for most of that race, but Dale slipped around me with 27 laps to go and outran both of us to the checkered flag.

My adversarial relationships in 1979 were not limited to Bobby Allison and the NASCAR establishment. I was also increasingly at odds with my owner.

At the end of the 1979 season Bill Gardner called a meeting of the entire team and vented his unhappiness with our second-place finish in the championship race. "I have one thing to tell you guys," Gardner said. "I'm never going to compete for a championship again. I spent a fortune this year on new engines, new parts, and equipment because you guys promised me a championship. I opened my checkbook and you didn't deliver. So don't be asking me for any more money next year. You already have your inventory for the 1980 season."

The 1980 season got off to a promising start with a first-place finish at Riverside, but things quickly went haywire after that. The mechanical curse returned, and we were hamstrung by Gardner's refusal to spend money on parts. We somehow managed to win five races that year, but I was forced to retire early from 12 of the 30 races due to mechanical problems.

In May or June 1980 Cale Yarborough pulled me aside one Sunday morning after a drivers' meeting. Cale had been driving the #11 car for Junior Johnson since 1973 and had compiled a phenomenal record, stacking up 55 victories in just eight years and winning an astonishing 26.73 percent of the races he started. He had won the Winston Cup Championship three consecutive times. After his victory in the 1977 Daytona 500, he became the first NASCAR driver to appear on the cover of *Sports Illustrated*. He was a genuine superstar, and he was driving for the best owner in the business.

Cale Yarborough and I were not even casual friends. He disapproved of my brashness, and he ridiculed my eagerness to speak my mind. He had dubbed me "Jaws," a nickname the media had seized upon with delight. I had learned to keep my distance from him, and I could not imagine why he would want to talk to me now.

Cale made small talk while the room cleared. When he was finally certain that nobody else was within earshot, he leaned in my direction. "I'm going to give you some of the best advice you'll ever get," he said.

"Okay . . . ," I said, warily.

"Go see Junior Johnson," he said.

"Why?" I asked, mystified.

Cale sighed. "I haven't told Junior yet," he said, "but I'm going to be leaving his team at the end of this season. I've agreed to drive next year for M. C. Anderson. As soon as I let Junior know, he'll be looking for a driver. I know he's been watching you, and he likes the way you drive. You should let him know you're ready to take the job when the time comes."

Doing my best to conceal my astonishment, I thanked Cale and walked back to the garage in a daze. This was epic news. Driving for Junior Johnson would be like playing football for Vince Lombardi or baseball for Casey Stengel. Junior was universally respected as the smartest and most resourceful owner in NASCAR. Like any great coach, he was capable of taking any player to the next level. He could make me a better driver than I would ever become on my own. The prospect of my driving for him was almost inconceivable.

I didn't know it at the time, but when Junior learned that Cale was leaving there were two hot young drivers to whom he seriously considered offering the job: me and Dale Earnhardt. Fresh off his Rookie-of-the-Year season, Dale was tearing up the tracks in 1980, and he would wind up winning the season championship in only his second year on the circuit. On his way to the trophy, however, Dale was wrecking a lot of cars—his and other people's. He drove so aggressively that the average weekly repair bill for his team was astronomical, and he was always antagonizing somebody. Since I couldn't afford to mistreat the DiGard cars after Bill Gardner made it clear that he would not be buying new parts for us, I was forced to drive more carefully than I'd driven in the past. All things considered, Junior concluded that my expense-to-revenue ratio would be better than Dale's. I would take better care of Junior's equipment, and I wouldn't be causing as many headaches on the track as Dale would.

Junior sent Henry Benfield to tell me that he would like me to drive for him next year if I could get out of my current deal. That, I knew, was the sticky part: there were still three years left on my contract with DiGard, and Bill Gardner was a master negotiator.

Despite his dissatisfaction with the team, Bill Gardner had been pressing me to sign a lifetime contract. When I told him that I would like to buy my way out of the current contract instead, he shook his head emphatically. Impossible, he said. He wouldn't even discuss the terms of a potential buyout. If I would read the contract carefully, he told me, I would understand why.

The DiGard attorneys had written a contract that, for all practical purposes, was unbreakable. The language of the agreement defined Darrell Waltrip as "priceless and irreplaceable," and because of that definition the contract could be said to have no monetary value whatsoever. There was therefore no basis on which we could negotiate a price. Under the terms of the contract, no dollar figure could be assigned to my services as a driver. Because I had naively signed the contract, I could not buy my way out of it. I was obligated to drive the DiGard car for the next three years whether I wanted to or not.

I called my father-in-law to discuss my dilemma, and he advised me to hire a good lawyer. The best lawyer I knew was Dave Alexander, so I went to see the famous attorney at his office in Franklin, Tennessee.

At the time of my visit, Dave was immersed in a huge lawsuit against multiple railroad and chemical companies. He was representing the families of people killed by a toxic spill in Waverly, Tennessee, and the case was going to trial. "I'm too busy to help you right now," Dave said, "but my son-in-law, who just graduated from Boston College, has just moved to town. His name is Ed Silva. If you trust my recommendation, I'll get Ed to look this contract over."

"That's fine," I said, and I went to see Ed.

The fresh-faced young man who welcomed me into his office did not fit my image of a high-powered attorney, and he certainly wasn't Southern. This guy was from Boston, and his accent made him sound like the Yankee owners whose "unbreakable" contract I was trying to escape. Ed spent several minutes looking through the document, flipping the pages and furrowing his brow while I fidgeted in my chair. Finally he laid the contract on his desk and looked up. "I'll get you out of this contract," Ed said. "But first, you're going to have to teach me a little bit about NASCAR."

By the time I finished educating Ed Silva about racing, we had become friends. We traveled together to Connecticut a couple of times to meet with the owners and try to initiate negotiations, but those forays ended in failure. Bill Gardner wouldn't even discuss possible ways of terminating the contract. "You cannot buy your way out of this deal," he repeated whenever we raised the subject. "The contract has no value. There is no way to put a price on it."

DiGard's attorney was always present during these meetings, and over time Ed developed a professional relationship with the guy. The two attorneys became quasi-friends, treating each other with the kind of professional courtesy that one shark extends to another. One day, Ed placed another telephone call to the DiGard attorney to talk about the Waltrip contract.

"Let's just say, hypothetically, that we offered you a hundred thousand dollars for the contract," Ed suggested.

"No, no, no," the DiGard attorney interjected. "Absolutely not. That's unacceptable."

"*Per year,*" Ed continued. "A hundred thousand dollars for each year left on the contract. That would be a total of three hundred thousand dollars."

"Well, that would be a good offer," the attorney replied. "But you can't put a price on the contract."

"Oh yes you can, and you just did!" Ed said triumphantly.

"What are you talking about?"

Ed called Bill Gardner and notified him that the DiGard attorney had acknowledged a price of $300,000 on the Darrell Waltrip contract. Negotiations were no longer stalled. The attorneys eventually worked out an agreement. I would be released from my contract upon payment of $300,000. The payment would be made and the release would be signed at a time and place to be specified by DiGard.

DiGard's demand for payment finally came late on a Friday afternoon in early January. We were ordered to meet at a bank in Charlotte at nine o'clock the following Monday morning with $300,000 in cash. The banks had already closed by the time the demand arrived, and they would not reopen again until after the deadline had passed. If the money were not paid on time, DiGard warned, the release would not be signed. Furthermore, I would be served with an injunction barring me from driving in NAS-CAR, and any team or sponsor who dared sign me to a contract would be barred from competing as well.

By this time the marketing people at Pepsi had agreed to have Mountain Dew sponsor Junior Johnson's #11 car in 1981 if I would drive it. Junior had agreed to advance me $100,000 against future earnings, and Pepsi had offered a $100,000 advance as well. As soon as the DiGard demand arrived, I called Junior. He said that he and Pepsi would find a way to get their money over the weekend. The last $100,000, Junior said, I would have to come up with on my own.

I certainly didn't have $100,000, but I knew somebody who did. Although she was reluctant to ask her father for the money, Stevie picked up the phone and explained the situation to her dad. Mr. Rader immediately called the president of the Owensboro National Bank.

Stevie and I had been planning to drive to Louisville that Saturday to see the road version of *Fiddler on the Roof,* but we jumped into our Corvette and drove to Owensboro instead. On Saturday morning Mr. Rader met his friend at the bank, withdrew $100,000, and gave it to Stevie and me. We then drove to Louisville, carrying more money than I'd ever seen at one time in my life, and went to see *Fiddler on the Roof.*

Stevie and I returned to Franklin on Sunday night, and at six o'clock Monday morning Ed and I caught a flight from Nashville. At nine o'clock on Monday morning we were sitting in the bank in Charlotte when the DiGard gang arrived.

We all went into a conference room and sat around a table while the attorneys went through the paperwork. But just as Bill Gardner was about to sign the release form, he stopped and put his pen down. "Wait a minute," he said. He got up and left the room, along with his attorney and his brother and a few other guys, while the rest of us just sat there looking at each other.

When the DiGard group returned, Bill said, "We need twenty-five thousand dollars more."

"WHAT?" I was aghast.

"We forgot about the Busch Clash," Bill said. The Clash (now known as the Budweiser Shootout) was the first competitive event of Speedweeks in Daytona, a 20-lap "all-out sprint" between the pole winners from the previous season. The Clash did not pay points, but it did pay cash: $50,000, to be exact. "You'll be competing in the Clash because you won poles in our car," Bill said. "So we want half the money."

"Okay, I'll pay you half the money if I win," I said reluctantly.

"No," Bill said firmly. "We want half the purse, and we want it today. Twenty-five thousand dollars or the deal's off."

That extra demand wiped out every nickel Stevie and I had in the bank, but it was worth it. When we walked out of the bank that day I was $325,000 poorer, but I felt great. I had paid a staggering amount of money for my freedom—nearly a million bucks in today's dollars—but I was free. I had made an investment in my own future, and I was determined to make that investment pay off.

CHAPTER NINE

DRIVING FOR JUNIOR

Cale Yarborough's supporting cast was still intact when I arrived at Junior Johnson's garage as the new driver. Crew chief Tim Brewer (who now works for ESPN) and premier engine builder Harold Elliot headed Junior's all-star team. I was thrilled to be joining such an elite group, but Junior warned me that the guys were not nearly as excited about his hiring decision as I was. My reputation as a hothead and complainer had preceded me. I was known to cuss my crew when things went wrong, or find fault with the car, or blame another driver, or criticize somebody else. At that point in my life, I wasn't in the habit of taking responsibility for failure.

Junior warned me that I would need to win over the crew. "Bill Allman is probably the key guy in the garage," Junior said. Bill was an old fellow who worked in the engine room. He had been with Junior for years. "If Bill decides he likes you, everybody else will like you too," Junior said. "But you're going to have to sell yourself. Bill's not real high on you right now."

When I walked into the engine room, Bill looked me up one side and down the other as the room grew quiet. "So you're the hotshot that's going to take Cale's place, huh?" Bill said.

"Yeah, I am," I replied evenly. "I'm the guy."

"Well, I've gotta tell you, you don't look like much."

I heard shuffling and chuckles behind me.

"You've got big shoes to fill," Bill continued. "I guess you know that."

"Yes, I know that. But I think I can do it."

The old man reached into the bottom drawer of his toolbox and pulled out a Mason jar filled with clear liquid. He poured a generous amount of the stuff into a battered cup that was resting on his workbench, then waved the jar in my direction. I was carrying a cup of coffee at the time. "Dump that coffee out," he ordered. I complied, and Bill poured moonshine into my styrofoam cup.

I lifted the drink to my nose and took a whiff. The fumes made my eyes water. This was pure white lightning—it smelled like rubbing alcohol—but I thought, *I've got to drink it or this old guy will think I'm a wimp.*

I stood there for a second while Bill took a big swig and set his cup on the workbench. I could feel the other guys watching me. I gamely raised my cup in a salute, took a deep breath and braced myself. But just as the moonshine reached my lips, the bottom fell out of the cup! The hooch had eaten through the styrofoam.

As the laughter died away, I crumpled what was left of the ruined cup and tossed it aside. "If it's all the same to you," I said to Bill, "I'll pass on the drink. Let's talk about the car."

NASCAR had shortened the cars for the 1981 season, reducing the wheelbase from 115 inches to 110 inches. That may not sound like much, but the change in length and body style completely altered the cars' aerodynamics. The new cars were difficult to drive, and none of the teams had yet worked out all of the mechanical complications created by the change.

Our team had taken a big Monte Carlo, a car with a 115-inch wheelbase, cut it down to the required 110 inches, and turned it into an '81 Buick Regal. I hated that car. I hated everything about it. Inside the shortened cockpit I kept banging my knees on the dashboard because my seat wouldn't go back far enough. The steering wheel was in the wrong spot. The car handled all wrong. Tim Brewer listened to my complaints after every test lap and made all the adjustments he could. When we went to Daytona for Speedweeks, I won the Busch Clash. I also won my qualifying race to earn the outside pole in the 500, but on the 117th lap of the big race the engine blew up.

The next week, in Richmond, I was in a foul mood. I complained to Tim Brewer about the butchered, cobbled-up monstrosity he expected me to drive. Every test lap confirmed my conviction that ours was probably the worst car in the history of NASCAR. Imagine my astonishment, then, when we won the race! I could hardly believe it. And the following week in Rockingham, the first race ever broadcast on ESPN, we won again!

We won two more times in the next month, at Bristol and Darlington, but those victories were followed by six straight losses. The drought drove me crazy. With each unsuccessful finish I grew more agitated, and I tried to manage my mounting anxiety by badgering Tim Brewer to make adjustments to the car. Tim and I started to argue. He wanted the car one way; I wanted it another. I thought he didn't know what he was talking about; he thought I didn't know what I was talking about. We were bickering and bellyaching and fighting all the time. Meanwhile the losses continued.

One Saturday in early June, after an argument in the garage at the Texas Motor Speedway, Junior Johnson called Tim and me into the trailer and told us to close the door. I could tell he was angry.

Junior didn't waste any time. "Boys, I want to tell y'all something," he said. "I'm sick of you both. And I'm just about to fire you both. I mean it! If you two dumbasses don't get out there and start working together to get this car running like it's supposed to, you're both going to be looking for a job."

This was a new experience for me. My previous owner had told me I *couldn't* leave; this owner was saying that I might *have to* leave! The prospect sobered me. As we walked back to the garage, I looked over at Tim and said, "You know, Junior Johnson don't say stuff like that just to annoy you or scare you. He's serious. And I don't want to lose my job."

Tim nodded. "I don't want to lose my job either."

"Well, we'd better get our heads together, then."

Our team had a lot of ground to make up in our pursuit of the championship. Bobby Allison was well in the lead with 2,256 points, and we were in third place, 341 points behind. By the end of August we had reduced Allison's lead to 50 points. After Richmond on September 13, Allison was only 3 points ahead. In Dover on September 22 I finished 15 seconds behind Neil Bonnett to take second place. Bobby finished third. I had caught him! With six races left in the season, I had overtaken my archrival in the race for the championship, and I was leading by 2 *points*.

Bobby drove great for those last six races, but I won four in a row. He won the final race, the Winston Western 500 at Riverside, but my sixth-place finish was good enough to preserve our lead in the points and secure my first Grand National Championship. I had won by a 53-point margin.

My championship campaign didn't endear me to the Sunday crowd. There were plenty of die-hard Allison fans, Yarborough fans, Petty fans, and others who were more than a little displeased to see their heroes eclipsed by the upstart from Owensboro. I was starting to build a loyal following of my own, but on any given weekend my fans were vastly outnumbered. One hot-selling T-shirt at the time said "Anyone but Waltrip." When my name went out over the loudspeakers during driver introductions, the cheers were drowned out by the boos. Once again, in the epic serial drama known as NASCAR, I had become the villain.

The 1982 season brought big changes to the Junior Johnson team. The boys still missed Cale Yarborough, who was driving part time for a wealthy guy in Savannah named M. C. Anderson. During the off-season Cale let his old buddies know that his new employer would give them a substantial raise if they would relocate. Tim Brewer and Harold Elliot found the offer irresistible. They tendered their resignations to Junior and rejoined Cale, taking about half the team with them.

There's no doubt that Cale was an easier driver to work for

than I was, and not just because I was a hothead and Cale was a cool customer. The differences between us stemmed in large part from our approach to racing. Cale was an incredibly versatile driver, able to adapt his driving style to whatever car he was given. He worked hard in the cockpit, sometimes wrestling the car around the track and forcing it to do things it didn't want to do. In cowboy terms, Cale was a bronco buster. I had no interest in busting broncos. I didn't want to fight with my car; I wanted a well-trained, obedient car that was tuned to my specific driving style, a style that depended on finesse rather than force. During the years we were close, Bobby Allison had taught me a ton about setting up a car, how to make the hundreds of tiny adjustments that affect handling and braking and acceleration. I knew exactly what I wanted from a car and had definite opinions about how to get it, and I was never satisfied until I got what I wanted. That intensity made me a difficult driver to work for.

The sudden loss of his crew chief exasperated Junior Johnson, and it also opened an old wound. Back in the 1970s another crew chief, Herb Nab, had abandoned Junior's team to accept a better-paying job with Junior's former driver Bobby Allison. Junior was determined not to let it happen again. "I'm not hiring any more crew chiefs," he declared. "I'm not going to make any more crew chiefs rich. *I'll* be the crew chief."

Nobody could argue with Junior's decision, of course. He filled the other vacancies, hiring Mike Hill and Doug Richert, who had been Dale's crew chief when he drove for Osterlund in 1979 and 1980, along with a few other guys, but he made it clear to everybody that he was both the owner and the crew chief on this team.

The 1982 season started poorly for us, with a 20th-place finish at Daytona and 27th-place finish at Richmond. I was consumed with getting the car right, but it seemed that whenever I dropped by the shop to discuss preparations for the next race, Junior would be gone coon hunting or off doing something else. One day I got my boss on the phone. "Junior," I said, "I need a go-to guy. You know I love you to death and I'll do anything you tell me to do. I understand that you're the crew chief, but when I call the shop and you're not there, or when I come up there and you're gone, I've gotta have somebody to tell what I need done to the car."

"Well," said Junior, "who do you want? Who would make a good go-to guy?"

I had already given this question considerable thought. Jeff Hammond, the jack man, was one of the youngest members of the team. He had never been a crew chief, but he was very intelligent and hard-working—and he was somebody I could talk to. I knew Jeff hadn't liked me much at first, but we had developed a bit of a rapport. "How about Hammond?" I suggested. "When I need something done, I'll just call Hammond and talk to him, and he can relay the message to you."

"Fine," Junior said. "Jeff can be your go-to guy."

The season improved temporarily after that. We won five of the next eight races to pull within 60 points of Terry Labonte in the race for the season championship, but then a series of mechanical problems—engine failures at Dover and Charlotte, a blown piston at Riverside, a busted connecting rod in the July 4 race at Daytona—left us, at midseason, 186 points behind the new leader, Bobby Allison.

Meanwhile the routine at the garage was degenerating into a rodeo. We were trying to race a car by committee, and it wasn't working very well. I'd tell Jeff what I wanted, and he would relay the message to the shop and notify Junior. Sometimes, however, Junior would veto my instructions and issue different directions to Mike Hill. The guys in the shop were getting conflicting messages, Junior and I were both getting frustrated, and poor Jeff Hammond was caught in the middle.

Finally Junior threw up his hands and capitulated. "Fine," he said, after enduring yet another tirade from me about the chaos at the shop, "I'll appoint a crew chief. You seem to get along okay with Hammond, so starting today, Hammond is the crew chief." Junior gave the rest of the boys the news, and from that point on we began pulling together as a team. With 14 races remaining in the season, we had a common goal: to catch Bobby Allison—again.

If anything, my rivalry with Allison had intensified in 1982. Bobby was now driving for DiGard, the team I had publicly divorced in 1980. The DiGard people wanted vindication, and Bobby, I was certain, wanted revenge. He had a score to settle with me.

With Jeff Hammond as the official crew chief, our team won five of the next nine races. By the time we arrived in Charlotte for the running of the National 500 on October 10, we had drawn to within 15 points of Allison. He dominated the Charlotte race, leading the field for 281 laps, but he ran into engine trouble late in the race and wound up finishing ninth. I finished 14th. Bobby had increased his lead to 37 points. There were four more races to go.

The following week, in Martinsville, I battled Ricky Rudd and Richard Petty and came away with the win. Bobby finished 19th. Now the chase for the championship had flipped: we led Bobby by 37 points with only three races to go.

Bobby and I thundered down the homestretch of the 1982 season neck-and-neck. He led the field for 127 laps in North Carolina on October 31, but I slipped past him to take the checkered flag. I tried to do the same thing the following week in Atlanta, but Bobby held on to that lead and came away with the victory. Now there was only one race left, the Western 500 at Riverside, and I held a razor-thin 20-point lead in the chase for the season championship.

On the final day of the season the DiGard team finally faltered. Bobby never led that race, and he completed only 111 laps due to an engine failure. I led the race for eight laps and finished third. That's all it took. Once again the chase for the Grand National Championship was decided by the final race of the season, and once again I had overtaken Bobby Allison for the win.

The second championship tasted even sweeter than the first. Winning one championship is a great distinction, but one such win can be dismissed as a fluke. To win two of them, and to win them back-to-back, gives you a higher level of legitimacy. At least that's what I was thinking on the Monday before Thanksgiving, as Stevie and I drove home from the airport with the trophy in the trunk of our car.

From time to time Stevie had voiced concern about my safety on the track. What would happen if I got into a wreck? I always told her not to worry, because the only people who get hurt in race cars are the ones who don't pay attention. It's the guys who don't really know how to drive, I explained, the guys who put themselves in precarious situations and don't know how to get out of them, the guys who drive over their head—it's *those guys* who get hurt. I was different. I knew how to handle every situation I got into. I eventually convinced Stevie to put those thoughts out of her mind, just as I did. She was married to Superman, after all, and you can't hurt Superman.

After two spectacular seasons in the Buick Regal, Junior decided to switch cars. Herb Fishel, the GM rep who had over-seen Buick's racing division, was moving to Chevrolet. Herb wanted us to move too, so we switched to the Monte Carlo. And what a switch it was! Our team had mastered the Buick; we knew almost everything about that car that there was to know, but with the move to the Monte Carlo all that knowledge was instantly obsolete. Everything about the new car, from setup to the way it drove, was radically different. We *really* struggled with that car as we prepared for the upcoming season.

The 1983 season opened at Daytona on a picture-perfect Sunday. The stands were packed. Cale Yarborough had become the first driver to post an average speed of more than 200 miles per hour during qualifying, but on his second qualifying lap he had lost control and flipped, totaling his car. Now, as the Daytona 500 got under way, track records were being broken. I was still struggling in the Monte Carlo. I had fallen a lap behind the lead-ers, including Joe Ruttman (another driver from Franklin, Ten-nessee), Dale Earnhardt, Dick Brooks, and Cale Yarborough in his backup car, when suddenly, on the 64th lap, smoke started billowing from Earnhardt's car. Dale coasted to the apron with a blown engine. The yellow flag came out.

In those days you were allowed to race back to the start/finish line before proceeding under caution, and I saw this flag as an opportunity to get back on the lead lap. I was making my move, coming out of turn 4 at breakneck speed, when suddenly Dick Brooks was right in front of me—and he had slowed way down. I hit the brakes and ducked left, managing to avoid rear-ending him, but my brakes locked and my car started to lift and slide. It slid sideways down the track for several hundred feet, hardly slowing at all, and slammed into an earthen embankment near the entrance to pit road. The impact was tremendous, the biggest thud I'd ever felt in my life, and it shot my car back up the track, where it crashed into the concrete retaining wall. Then the mangled car slipped into the path of oncoming traffic.

I was too dazed and disoriented to know what was happening, and the car was so badly damaged that I couldn't have controlled it anyway. Cale Yarborough missed me by inches. Joe Ruttman, who was right behind Cale, had no time to take evasive action, but my car miraculously kept moving and he missed me too.

I was conscious when the paramedics pulled me from the car and laid me on a stretcher on the track. They waited for the track to clear so that the ambulance could come and get me. Jeff Hammond was kneeling beside the stretcher, and I was asking him what had happened as cars kept going past us on the high side of the track. The Sta-Dri that the crews had spread on the track to absorb the oil from Dale's engine was being blown in our direction by the passing cars; I could feel the grainy material pelting my face and hands. Suddenly I raised up off the stretcher, grabbed Jeff, and said, "It's raining, Jeff, it's raining! That's why I crashed—it's raining!"

Jeff turned to the paramedics. "You'd better get him to the hospital right away," he said. "He's delirious."

The ambulance delivered me to Halifax Hospital, where the doctors checked me over and released me. Somehow the medical staff missed the signs that I had sustained a serious concussion. The doctor gave me some Tylenol with codeine and told me to be careful driving home.

The next morning Stevie and I packed our bags in the car, put our dog, Charlie Brown, in the backseat, and headed for home. After a few miles on the interstate, Stevie asked me to pull over. "Let me drive," she said. "Your driving isn't too good right now."

"I don't know what's wrong with my driving," I said. "I feel fine."

The following Thursday we went to Virginia for the Richmond 400. Bobby Allison edged out Dale Earnhardt to win that race. I qualified fourth, but I burned up a gear on the 149th lap and didn't finish.

The following Thursday we went to Rockingham for the Carolina 500, where Dale Earnhardt wound up in the wall just as the race was suspended due to rain. NASCAR scheduled the completion of the race for the following weekend, so Stevie and I drove back to Franklin to rest. On the way home Stevie told me I should stop taking the Tylenol. She said it was making me act weird.

About midday on the following Wednesday, sitting at home, I suddenly had the feeling that I had just woken up, and I had no idea how I'd gotten there. I was completely bewildered. I didn't remember crashing at Daytona, or racing at Richmond, or driving to Rockingham. The preceding two and a half weeks were a total blank.

On the next Sunday, after a third-place finish in the Rockingham race, the enormity of what had happened at Daytona suddenly hit me. I had nearly been killed! I was not invincible after all! My sense of superiority had been a delusion. Darrell Waltrip was as prone to mistakes and as vulnerable to tragedy as any other man on the track. This sudden recognition of the fragility of life and my own human frailty affected me profoundly. In the weeks that followed, I couldn't shake the feeling that something about the way I was living needed to change.

CHAPTER TEN

LEAP OF FAITH

Ann and Leonard Isaacs, who were good friends of ours, had invited Stevie and me to visit a new church they were attending in Nashville. The church, which was led by Dr. Cortez Cooper, met in the cafeteria at Hillsboro High School. I had never gone to church on a regular basis, and I had always maintained that I couldn't. After all, I raced on Sundays, and I couldn't go to church on my off weekends because I needed to rest. This church, however, met on Wednesday nights. Our friends knew that Stevie and I were home on Wednesdays, so there really wasn't a polite way to decline their invitation.

Dr. Cooper had grown up in Bristol, Tennessee, not far from the racetrack, so he knew about racing and he recognized me when we showed up at church for the first time. It turned out that he was a sports fan, a real man's man. Dr. Cooper could talk about baseball, football, or just about anything a guy would want to talk about, and he was a good listener too. More than that, he had an ability to explain the Bible in ways that a regular guy like me could follow. When he taught on Wednesday nights I found myself listening intently, and when I went home I could actually remember what he had said. Much to my surprise, I found that I liked going to this church.

April 1983 was a pretty good month for our team—we finished second at Darlington and first at Wilkesboro and Martinsville—and the fans were booing me heartily again. It was after the Wilkesboro race that a member of Junior's team approached me with a suggestion. The guy's name was Roger, and he was a very strong Christian. "You know," Roger said, "when you get out of the car after a race, all you ever talk about is your pit crew and yourself. Did you ever think about giving the Lord any credit for some of the success you've had?"

"I don't know, what do you mean?"

"I mean maybe you could thank the Lord when you're standing in Victory Circle, maybe acknowledge that he protected you, took care of you, and got you there."

Roger's suggestion didn't resonate very strongly with me at the time, but when I faced the reporters on the following Sunday after winning at Martinsville, I thought, what the hell, I'd give it a try. I looked at the cameras and said, "I want to thank God for a safe race and for the success we had today."

I was astonished by the number of fans who responded to that one little statement, and their response made me feel a little guilty. People kept coming up to me and saying, "I didn't know you were a Christian!" I wanted to say, "I'm not," but I knew that wasn't the feedback they were looking for. Instead I just said, "Yeah, I kind of keep my faith to myself."

My inner crisis deepened unexpectedly on May 1, 1983, during the Winston 500 at Talladega. I was roaring down the front straightaway on the inside of Phil Parsons, fighting to control the Monte Carlo, when all at once my car hopped over into the side of Phil's car and sent him barreling into the concrete retaining wall. That created one of the biggest wrecks I had ever seen, sending cars spinning everywhere. I watched helplessly as Phil's car flipped and tumbled down the banking from around the start/finish line all the way to the first turn, finally toppling onto Ricky Rudd's car. Nine cars, including mine, were swept up in that crash. As I surveyed the carnage, I was pretty sure I had killed Phil Parsons. Even later, after they told me Phil was going to be okay, the awful sense of dread lingered.

Two months later I finished 20th in the Firecracker 400 at Daytona on the Fourth of July, eight laps behind the leaders, and came home from that race depressed. My early lead in the chase for the season championship had disappeared. I was now

212 points behind Bobby Allison, and it seemed like things were getting worse instead of better. I knew that Junior was getting annoyed, and I could sense the frustration in the crew too. Everybody was working as hard as they could to salvage the season, but things just weren't coming together for us at all.

It was hot as Hades inside the cafeteria at Hillsboro High School on that Wednesday night in July 1983. Stevie and I were sitting side by side in the sweltering heat, and Dr. Cooper was talking about our relationship with the Lord. There were plenty of other people in the stifling little room that night, but it felt like Dr. Cooper was talking directly to me. He was saying that the Christian faith was meant to be a personal thing, a daily thing, a regular friendship between you and God, and that if you don't know the Lord in that kind of personal way, then, well, you have to ask yourself whether you really are a Christian.

When he described the Christian life that way, I had to admit that I didn't have anything resembling a relationship with God. My knowledge of God was theoretical, not personal. God was a hazy authority figure who lived far away, a judge who kept a record of my sins and would one day punish me for them. The idea that God had already dealt with my sins, that he wanted a relationship with me in the same way that any parent wants to be reunited with a runaway child, and that he was ready to walk with me through the messiness of my life—that idea had never struck me like it did that night. "You can begin a relationship with God tonight," Dr. Cooper said, "and you can settle forever the question of your eternal destiny."

When the sermon was over Stevie and I went out into the hallway with Dr. Cooper. We got down on our knees right there in the hallway of that little high school, and I asked God to come into my life and take it over.

I'm not sure what I was expecting from that simple prayer. I know that religious conversion is a cataclysmic event for some people, one that falls on them from out of the sky and transforms them instantly into somebody completely different, but it didn't happen that way for me. For me, that prayer launched a gradual process that, in many respects, is still under way. I had to feel out my new faith in the beginning, take stock of what I was losing and what I was gaining with each new step. In the back of my mind, I'm pretty sure I was hoping to reform my life and make God happy so that he would let me win more races. I thought maybe God would look down from heaven and say, "Darrell's a really good guy, he should win this week." That's an immature way to think about a God who, in the words of Jesus, is so gracious and generous that "he causes the rain to fall upon the just and the unjust alike," but that's at least part of what I was hoping for in the beginning.

As it turned out, my performance on the track did improve in the second half of the season. I finished in the top three in ten of the next 11 races, winning two of them, and by the first weekend in November we had almost caught Bobby Allison and DiGard. With two races remaining in the season I was in second place in the chase for the season championship, only 27 points behind the leader.

The Atlanta race was crucial. If we finished that race and Bobby didn't, the championship would almost certainly be ours, but Junior was not content to let our hopes rest on the chance that our rivals would stumble. Junior was convinced we had to win the race outright. At Atlanta we needed to outrun Bobby Allison, not outlast him.

We had one special engine in our arsenal that was more powerful than the others. Its reliability was questionable, but this engine was capable of generating enough horsepower to outrun the rest of the field. After debating the merits of each engine, Junior made the decision: we would run our most powerful engine at Atlanta.

For a while it looked like Junior's decision would pay off. I qualified better than Bobby, but it was not long before the engine started to fade, and I finished in ninth place. Bobby finished third, increasing his lead to 64 points. That would be enough to give Bobby Allison the Grand National Championship for 1983.

* * *

One day in the early 1980s, Stevie received a phone call from Grover Adkins, who worked on the 21 team. Grover was a friend of Jack Billmyer, a sales executive at Honda, and he was calling to ask whether Stevie would like to have a Honda to drive. Our financial situation was improving—my share of winnings had gone from $41,085 in 1975 to $341,045 in 1982—but Stevie naturally said yes to the offer of a free car, and soon there was a Honda Accord parked in our driveway.

Honda dealerships were appearing here and there at the time, usually in converted gas stations. The dealerships were small, and the cars were tiny little things. I hadn't paid much attention to them.

Stevie loved her little Honda. She raved and raved about the way it drove, but I never even bothered to get inside it. Why should I, when I had a big, comfortable American car to drive? Finally, after a year or so, she convinced me to take her little sedan for a spin, and I was amazed to discover what a sweet car it was. Sure the Honda was small, but it drove well, handled tight, and ran good. I was really impressed.

At that time the Honda people were trying to change their company image in America. They had opened their first American auto assembly plant in Marysville, Ohio, in 1982, and they wanted Americans to start thinking of the Honda as a domestic product, a car an American would drive. Jack Billmyer, a former Ford dealer from Danville, Virginia, was a huge race fan, and he came up with an idea for gaining credibility with the red-blooded American car-buying public: get respected NASCAR drivers to open dealerships. As the story was relayed to me, Jack was offering dealerships to Cale Yarborough, Neil Bonnett, Dick Brooks, and me. Would I be interested? I had always loved cars, and I'd grown up around the car business, so I said yes, I'd be interested.

A few days later one of Honda's regional sales executives from Atlanta came to see me. I drove him around Franklin and pointed out a couple of old gas stations I thought we might be able to convert to a Honda dealership. Within days I received a call from Jim Cardiges, the head of sales for Honda, asking me to come to Los Angeles. I flew to California and sat down with Jim, and he gave me a letter of intent. I was going to be in the car business!

Before I knew it, though, the project started to snowball. The next time the Honda executive from Atlanta came to see me, he was carrying plans for a gigantic building they were expecting me to build. The cost of my "free" dealership had escalated to $2 or $3 million, and the enterprise was growing more complex by the day. I didn't know what to do. One of my friends advised me that I could sell the letter of intent for $1 million, and I seriously considered doing it.

Finally I called up Rick Hendrick and told him about my opportunity and dilemma. In addition to his racing team, Rick was in the car business in a big way. He owned multiple dealerships, so I knew he had the experience I lacked. I told him, "If you help me, I'll help you."

"I'll do whatever you want," Rick replied. "We're in the Honda business. We build Honda stores every day. I'll send my people over and we'll help you get going."

Three of Rick's guys arrived in Franklin a few days later, bringing their plans and the general contractor they had been working with, and we went looking for a suitable building site. By the time I had chosen and purchased the property where my new dealership would be located, I knew I couldn't handle the business on my own. This project was too big for a greenhorn like me. I called Rick again and said, "Let's partner up." Rick agreed, and we made a deal: I would own the store, and he would manage it. Rick sent his people in, and before I knew it the dealership was staffed and stocked and up and running. That was in 1985, and we've been in the car business ever since.

Junior Johnson and his close friends Ralph Seagraves and T. Wayne Robinson, marketing executives for R. J. Reynolds, had come up with the idea for a new event, an all-star race. As they first conceived it, this race would be the centerpiece of a fan festival hosted by a different track each year, not unlike Major League Baseball's annual All-Star Game. Only those drivers who had won a race the previous year would be invited to compete in the 70-lap spectacle, and the purse would be huge: $200,000 for first place. The first running of "the Winston" would be held at the Charlotte Motor Speedway on Saturday, May 25, 1985, the day before the Coca-Cola World 600.

Junior was so obsessed with winning the first running of the Winston that he hired a special team to build a car specifically for that race. The team spent about three months on the project, taking the new car to the wind tunnel and doing more telemetric testing on it than Junior had done with any other car he'd ever built.

In the meantime Junior personally oversaw the building of a special engine. It was not an illegal engine; after all, the NASCAR officials tore our engines down and inspected them after nearly every race, and anything illegal would result in our disqualification. But this motor was as lightweight as Junior could possibly make it. He ground down the rods until they were as slender as toothpicks and did everything else he could think of to save weight without sacrificing horsepower. The result was practically a drag-racing motor. It would turn more RPMs than any of our normal motors, Junior warned me, but this motor would not last forever. It was a time bomb. We would light the fuse on it when the flag fell on the Winston, and we'd hope it would last to the end of the race.

The race was scheduled for Saturday afternoon, after the Nationwide race. Since the Indianapolis 500 was scheduled for the same weekend, R. J. Reynolds chartered a Boeing 737 to ferry any interested media from Indianapolis to Charlotte and back again for the new NASCAR race.

The rules for this race included a mandatory green-flag pit stop, which we were required to make within a ten-lap window. Junior decided that we would make our stop at the end of that window, at the last permissible moment. That way, he reasoned, we would have fresher tires at the end of the race than if we'd pitted ten laps sooner.

Harry Gant pitted at the first opportunity and took four new tires, then used that fresh rubber to build a substantial lead. When I came out of my pit stop, Harry was a straightaway ahead of us; he was going into turn 3 as I came off turn 2.

The laps were ticking down, and I was not getting any closer to Harry Gant. Suddenly I heard Junior's voice on the radio. "Durrel," Junior drawled, "do you want to win two hundred thousand dollars, or do you want to win seventy-five?"

"Two hundred, Junior, two hundred!"

"Well, boy, you better get up on that wheel, 'cause you're runnin' outta time."

I drove that car as hard as it would go. I drove it like I'd stolen it, and pretty soon the interval between Gant's car and mine started to diminish. I drew closer and closer, and by the time the white flag came out, I was there. Harry was hugging the bottom of the track and I was at the top as we went into turn 1, and I sailed around him on the outside. We come off turn 2 side by side, and then I began to pull away. I beat Harry to the third turn, and by the time we came off turn 4 it was obvious that I had the race won. I was jumping up and down in my seat as I came across the start/finish line, my hand out the window waving to the crowd, when suddenly—KA-BLOOEY!—the motor blew up. I could hear parts clanging and grinding as the engine ground to a stop, and I nearly broke my arm trying to get both hands on the wheel so I wouldn't wreck the thing. We had to push the car into Victory Circle.

Almost immediately rumors began to circulate that I had blown up the engine on purpose. I couldn't believe it. People were saying that our engine was illegal, and that I'd blown it up to prevent the NASCAR officials from inspecting it. Some people even thought that Junior had installed a demolition device in the motor, which he had detonated by remote control after I crossed the start/finish line. The entire premise of these allegations was ridiculous. An engine that blows up does not *disappear*. There may be a hole knocked in the side of the block, or a piston might be mangled, but the motor isn't *pulverized*. The NASCAR officials can still tear the engine down and tell whether or not it was legal. Our engine had been powerful but fragile, and the timing of its demise had been fortuitous, nothing more. But to this day I still encounter people who give me a wink and a nod when I deny that I blew up my engine on purpose after winning the Winston in 1985.

I was ecstatic with my win, and very pleased with the car that had won it. It was a shame the engine had blown up. "I sure wish I could drive that car in the race tomorrow," I told Junior, as we stood in the garage with Jeff Hammond after the race.

"Well, you can," Junior replied. "NASCAR told us that if we ran a car in the Winston, we could run the same car in the 600 if we wanted to."

I looked over at the car we had prepared for the next day's race. It was a fast car—I'd qualified fourth in it—but I couldn't help but think that the car I'd just driven was faster. "Are you okay with switching engines?" I asked.

Junior nodded, then looked at Jeff Hammond for his opinion. "We can do it," Hammond said. He called the guys, and they set to work.

On Sunday morning a NASCAR official looked at our car and shook his head. "You can't run that car," he said.

"Yes, we can," said Junior.

The official planted his feet and crossed his arms. "No, sir, you cannot. Unless you've had a wreck, you cannot enter a car in this race other than the one you qualified in. You'll have to put the engine back in the original car."

Junior was livid. "There ain't enough time for that, and you know it!" he protested, but the official was unmoved.

After the official left, Junior told the crew to start packing up; he was going to withdraw from the race. I turned to Jeff Hammond. He was my only hope. "I think we can get it done," Jeff said. "It'll be awful tight, but I think we can put that motor back in the other car in time for the race." Junior reluctantly agreed to let him try.

Two minutes before the race was scheduled to begin, I was standing out on the start/finish line in my uniform, without a car, looking anxiously toward the garage. Suddenly I caught sight of commotion at the gate, and my car hove into view, pushed by a panting Jeff Hammond and the rest of the crew. I ran to help, and jumped into the seat just as the command came over the public address system. "Gentlemen, start your engines!" I pressed the ignition, and the engine roared to life.

I led that race for 91 laps and crossed the start/finish line 14.64 seconds ahead of Harry Gant to win it. In just two days I had won $290,733, more money than I'd ever won in a single weekend. It was a very good weekend indeed.

The 1985 season was a lesson in the value of consistency. From the very first race at Daytona, it was clear that Bill Elliot's new Ford Thunderbird was the fastest car in NASCAR. Elliot set a new track record during qualifying at Daytona with an average speed of 205.114 miles per hour, and he crossed the finish line in his qualifying race an astonishing 37 seconds ahead of the second-place finisher. The rest of us couldn't keep up with him on the straightaways, and "Awesome Bill from Dawsonville" won the Daytona 500. At Talladega, Elliot lost two laps of track time due to a broken oil fitting but still came back to *lap the field twice under the green flag* and win the race! He won at Darlington too, to become the first driver to win three of NASCAR's four major races in a single season and claim the Winston Million, the million-dollar prize offered by R. J. Reynolds. Bill Elliot was so dominant that year that everyone assumed he was a cinch to win the championship.

Our Chevy was not as fast as Elliot's Ford, but we were more consistent. Elliot won 11 races in 1985, while we won only three, but we finished 18 times in the top five and 21 times in the top ten. Elliot finished 16 times in the top five and 18 times in the top ten. His win at Darlington on September 1, 1985, gave him a 206-point lead in the chase for the season championship, but by the end of the month we had cut his lead to 23 points. Then Elliot was forced from the Wilkesboro race by transmission trouble, and I finished 14th to pull ahead by 30 points. My lead shrunk by ten points the following week at Charlotte, then widened to 15 points at Rockingham. Once again the chase for the season championship came down to the final race at Riverside, where Bill encountered mechanical problems on the road course and finished a disappointing 30th. I finished the race in seventh place to claim my third national championship in four years.

Junior Johnson was not satisfied with winning the season championship in 1985. We had won only three races all year, and he hated losing races. It's my opinion that Junior would rather win a race than win a championship. He was irked by the evident superiority of the new Fords and was further annoyed by the fact that Chevrolet was starting to help other owners. We had once been Chevy's number-one team, but now Rick Hendrick and Richard Childress were getting plenty of attention and assistance from Chevy too.

Junior was also starting to grow disenchanted with me. He had never been a fan of older drivers—he always said that he wanted "a driver in his late twenty-nines"—and I was now 37 years old. As Junior saw it, success was making me soft. He thought I had lost my desire, my aggressive edge, and he pointed to one particular race early in the 1986 season as proof that things had changed.

Five long years had passed since Dale Earnhardt had won his first Winston Cup championship, and Dale was hungry for another trophy. More than the trophy, Dale craved the recognition and respect that multiple championships would bring. I was living in the spotlight in 1986, and it was obvious to everybody that I was comfortable there. My new faith had calmed me down a lot. I was NASCAR's top money-winner and a three-time champion; the fans were warming up to me, and the media loved the sound bites I tossed their way. Dale Earnhardt, in contrast, was still self-conscious and awkward around the media. Although he lacked the refinement and poise that some of the other drivers had when television cameras were around, he knew he could drive with the best of us, and he was determined to prove it to the world. To reach that goal, he would need to defeat the man who was currently at the top of the pile: me. The friendly relationship we had enjoyed during our early years would change. Dale was gunning hard for the top spot, and the fact that I was holding the trophy meant that he was gunning for me.

My unfolding rivalry with Dale Earnhardt was a replay of history. Only five years earlier I had been in Dale's position, battling an old friend for the championship. Bobby Allison had been my mentor during the 1970s, helping me in countless ways. Stevie and I had spent lots of time with Bobby and his wife, Judy, often staying overnight with them at their place in Hueytown during the years when Bobby was challenging Richard Petty and Cale Yarborough for the championship. Bobby's rivalry with the dominant Petty had flared into open warfare at Wilkesboro in 1972, when Allison drove Petty into the wall with three laps to go. After that race Petty told reporters that the feud had gone too far. "It must stop," Petty said. "He's playing with my life out there, and I don't like that."

My friendship with Bobby Allison had ended when I became a serious contender for the NASCAR championship. The goodwill between us vanished when I was the guy in Bobby's rearview mirror—or worse, when he was the guy in mine. I hadn't wanted our rivalry to become a personal thing, but Bobby had taken it personally. My friendship with Dale Earnhardt was about to follow a similar trajectory, but this time I would be in Bobby's place and Dale would be in mine.

The battle lines were drawn in the second race of the 1986 season. Dale had almost won the Daytona 500 the week before, but he had run out of fuel near the end of the race and had finished 14th. This week, in the Miller High Life 400 at Richmond, Dale got to the front early, and he led the race for 299 laps. I stalked him, waiting for an opening. With about 15 laps to go I made a move on the inside, but Dale cut me off. I gave him a shot and got him loose, but he somehow recovered and chopped me off again. This time he looked over from his customary position low in the seat and twirled a finger in my direction. The message was clear: "Hit me again," he was saying, "and I'll spin you out."

Earnhardt and I continued to battle as the race wound down. Finally, with only three laps to go, an exasperated Junior Johnson came on the radio. "Durrell," he said, "pass that s.o.b. *NOW!*" What was I going to do? My owner was ordering me to make a move, but Earnhardt had promised to spin me out if I tried. "All right, boss," I replied. I went into turn 1 deep on the inside, my left tires in the dirt, and slipped beside Dale, then pushed him up the racetrack. When we came out of turn 2 I had nosed ahead to take the lead. The race was mine!

At that moment Dale did exactly what he'd promised to do. He turned left, hooking my right rear quarter-panel and sending me spinning into the wall. The contact wrecked Dale too, but his car was still drivable after it hit the wall. Young Kyle Petty cruised past both of us to capture the first Winston Cup victory of his career. Dale limped across the finish line in third place, leaving me to survey the smoking remains of my demolished car and contemplate what had happened. Like Richard Petty at Wilkesboro in 1972, I was well aware that I had encountered the unbridled competitiveness of another driver, with consequences that easily could have been fatal.

Dale sat sheepishly in his car after the race and tried to downplay the incident. "I just got hung up with ole Darrell and we got in the wall," he said when a reporter pushed a microphone through the window of his Chevy Wrangler. "That's just racin'. There ain't nothing to it."

Stevie was furious after the race. She and Dale had always enjoyed a warm relationship, but when she walked past the Childress garage after the race she fixed Dale with an accusing glare that made him look away.

When Dale saw Stevie the following week at Rockingham, he tried to defend himself. "You know I didn't mean to wreck Darrell back there in Richmond," he said.

Stevie whirled, fire in her eyes. "Don't you tell me that, Dale Earnhardt," she said. "We both know what you did. And you could have killed my husband!"

Dale ducked in tacit admission. "Sorry," he said.

NASCAR fined Dale $5,000 for reckless driving after Richmond. They also required him to post a $10,000 bond and placed him on probation for the rest of the season. He appealed the fine, however, and within a week NASCAR had reduced the penalty to $3,000, returned his $10,000 bond, and lifted his probation. My fans were incensed by that decision. The Waltrip-Earnhardt feud was on, and for once I was wearing the white hat.

CHAPTER ELEVEN

CHASING DALE

Junior Johnson had earned a reputation as the best engine builder in NASCAR, but by 1986 his dominance as a motorman was being challenged. Waddell Wilson's engines were making a lot of power for Harry Ranier. Bill Elliot, his driver, was breaking speed records on the superspeedways, and Richard Childress had made Earnhardt's car faster than ever. People were starting to say that Junior's engines were not as good as they used to be. Our motors were turning out 585 horsepower, while others were now producing up to 650. On the short tracks and road courses, where the car and driver were more important than the engine, we could still be competitive—we won at Bristol and Wilkesboro and Riverside in 1986—but on the tracks with long straightaways, the other guys were running away from us.

Early in the season, after back-to-back engine failures at Martinsville and Talladega, Junior and I got into a big argument about horsepower and the quality of the engines. I knew the subject was dangerous ground. Junior always said you could criticize his coon dogs, his mules, or anything else he had, but you'd better not say anything bad about his engines. I was convinced that the engines were our biggest problem, and I kept bringing it up.

During testing for one race, the crew installed seven different motors in my car, and I didn't like any of them. Junior was exasperated. "That's the best engine we've got," he said, when I pronounced the last one unsatisfactory. "We don't have any others."

"I can't talk about this now," I said. "I have to go do an interview."

When I returned to the garage about an hour later, I found the crew taking the motor out of the car. Confused, I asked Jeff Hammond what was going on. Junior had gone into the hauler and pulled out an old slug of an engine, a spare we'd been dragging around for four years. "If Darrell doesn't like that last engine," Junior had told the crew, "just wait till he tries this one!"

It wasn't just the engines either. Junior had sold 50 percent of his operation in 1982 to a wealthy California industrialist named Warner W. Hodgson, who happened to be a huge fan of Neil Bonnett. Hodgson had tried to persuade Junior to put Neil in the #11 car instead of me, but Junior wouldn't do it. Junior had expanded instead, adding a second car to the team and hiring Neil to drive it. I didn't like the arrangement. I liked Neil Bonnett, but I thought the second car was a distraction. I told Junior that we had taken one dominant team and turned it into two mediocre teams. In my view, we didn't have enough parts and pieces to do one team right, let alone two.

In the middle of this frustrating year I was talking on the phone with Rick Hendrick, my partner in the Honda dealership, when Rick brought up the subject of my contract with Junior, which was set to expire at the end of the season.

"Are you going to drive for Junior again next year?" Rick asked.

"As far as I know," I said. "I haven't heard any different."

"Well, if anything comes up, I've got a deal for you," Rick said. "By the way, how much is Junior paying you?"

"I'm making $150,000 a year, plus expenses and half of what I win."

"I'm talking to a sponsor who really likes you," Rick said. "I could sign a deal with them, but only if Darrell Waltrip is the driver. With that deal I could pay you $500,000, plus your expenses and half of what you win."

I was floored. "Are you serious?"

"Yes, I am. No pressure, though. I just wanted you to know that in case anything comes up."

I thought about my conversation with Rick for a couple of days, and then decided it wouldn't hurt to go talk to Junior about it. I found him in his office. He was reading a magazine, a pair of half-glasses perched on the end of his nose.

"What do you want, boy?" Junior said without looking up.

"I need to talk."

"What do you want to talk about?"

"Well, I got a phone call from Rick Hendrick."

Junior tossed the magazine aside and leaned back, and I knew I'd made a mistake. In the three years since Hendrick had started his team, Junior had watched Chevrolet divert an increasing percentage of its support from our operation to Hendrick Motorsports. He complained that Rick was getting the best Chevy stuff now, better stuff than we were getting.

"Oh yeah?" Junior's expression tightened. "What did he want?"

"He told me he had an opportunity for a sponsor, that this sponsor would like me to be the driver, and that he would pay me $500,000 a year to drive his car." Junior raised his eyebrows as I continued. "I just wanted you to know that. I'm not looking to leave or anything. I like driving for you, but I have been making $150,000 ever since I got here, and I'm thinking that when it comes time to renegotiate, maybe I could get a bump in my salary."

Junior grunted. I knew his philosophy. He had always taken the position that winnings, not salary, are the key to a driver's prosperity. Junior might not offer you a salary as high as the one you'd get from another owner, but if you drove for Junior Johnson you would win more races and therefore earn more money. He made you responsible for your own success. Looking back at my own earnings since 1982, it was hard to argue with his philosophy. When I could see that our conversation wasn't going anywhere, I excused myself and left the office.

A week or so later I walked into the shop and immediately

sensed a strangeness in the air. All the guys stopped working and gathered around me. "What's going on, boys?" I asked.

"Why didn't you tell us you were leaving?" one of them asked.

"What? I'm not leaving. Who said I was leaving?"

"Junior came out the other day and said you wouldn't be our driver next year because you were going to go drive for Rick Hendrick."

"Hey, wait a minute!" I said. "That's a bad misunderstanding! I didn't tell him I was leaving—I just told him about a conversation. I thought I made it clear that I wasn't looking to leave. I just wanted to let Junior know what was going on."

"Well, you'd better go talk to him and straighten it out, because he told us you wouldn't be back next year."

"Boy," Junior said, when I finally tracked him down, "if anybody will pay you that kind of money, you'd be a damn fool not to take it. Now just go on and take it."

I was crushed. Sure we argued at times, but I really liked working with Junior and the guys. We were a family, and we had accomplished great things together. I had enormous respect for Junior, but I also knew he had a habit of severing any relationship that went sideways. He even had a humorous way of announcing it. If you'd inquire about somebody who wasn't around anymore, Junior would say, "Oh, he died."

"Really? Wow, I didn't even know he was sick."

"Yeah, he died. He won't be around here no more."

We were halfway through the season, and I was already dead.

The finality of Junior's decision panicked me, because two weeks had gone by since Rick had mentioned the deal, and I had never called him back. What if the potential sponsor had gone away, or fallen in love with another driver? I hurried to a phone and called Rick. "We need to talk," I said. I drove down to Charlotte, sat down with Rick, and worked out a deal. The sponsor, it turned out, was Procter & Gamble, and the brand they wanted to promote would mark a key change in the evolution of my image. I'd spent most of my career driving high-speed billboards for drinks: Sterling Beer, Pabst Blue Ribbon, Mountain Dew, Budweiser. When 1987 rolled around I'd be carrying the squeaky-clean colors of Tide detergent.

On November 2, 1986, Dale Earnhardt won the Atlanta Journal 500 by a full lap to clinch his second Winston Cup championship. I finished the season second in the standings. Alan Kulwicki was named Rookie of the Year. The runner-up for that honor was my little brother, Michael, who ran a full schedule with Bahari Racing in 1986 and wound up ranked a respectable 19th.

After the 1986 season Stevie and I sat down to pray about a huge decision we were facing. Would we follow through on adopting a child?

Stevie had miscarried twice since we'd started trying to have kids a few years earlier. The miscarriages were awful, wrenching losses. We had consulted a top doctor in Nashville, a fertility specialist who was well known for his work with celebrities, and he determined that Stevie's body had been affected by a drug her mother had taken during pregnancy. He told us that the likelihood that she would ever have a successful pregnancy was low. At that point we had applied to an adoption agency in East Tennessee. We had been approved and were scheduled to sign the papers for a baby in just a couple of weeks.

It was now December, and suddenly Stevie was pregnant again. The adoption agency would not allow us to postpone signing the papers, because they had a policy against allowing anyone over 40 to adopt, and I would be turning 40 in February. What should we do? If we chose not to adopt and Stevie suffered another miscarriage, then we'd be left without a family. After praying about it together, we arrived at a decision. We would allow the baby in East Tennessee to go to another family, and we would place the future of this biological child in God's hands.

*   *   *

Rick Hendrick is a great believer in recruiting top talent, and his commitment to excellence was on full display when he announced that Hendrick Motorsports would field a third team, the Tide team, in 1987. Waddell Wilson would be the engine builder for the new team, I'd be the driver, and every other team member, from the fabricators to the pit crew, was an all-star. Almost immediately people started referring to us as Hendrick's Dream Team. Our expectations for ourselves were sky-high. We were going to win a ton of races that year and waltz away with the championship.

The 1987 season was a good lesson for me. It turns out that the best team is not necessarily the one with the most talent. The best team is the one that plays as a team. We were a collection of superstars with strong egos. We were all leaders, and every one of us had his own ideas about how the team should be run. Since we had all won races before, we were certain that our opinions were right. The whole thing was a disaster. I quarreled nonstop with Waddell Wilson. Alliances started to form within the team. In the meantime we couldn't even come close to winning a race. We finished eighth at Daytona, 20th at Richmond, 21st at Wilkesboro. In all of May and June we didn't lead a single lap.

As the situation on the Tide team deteriorated, I found that I really missed Jeff Hammond—not just his expertise, but his flexibility. Hammond was a guy who would listen to me. If I felt strongly about a course of action, he wouldn't argue. He would make certain I'd considered all sides of the issue, but then he'd accept my decision and go make it happen. Even if my decision turned out to be flawed—and many of them were—at least we were both committed to a strategy and were moving quickly to execute it. We weren't paralyzed by indecision or hamstrung by competition. Hammond and I got things done, and I think that's the main reason we had good success together.

I had built a 10,000-square-foot shop over on Hudspeth Road in Charlotte, across the street from Robert Gee's old place, where I'd first met Dale Earnhardt years earlier. This was where I kept the Busch car I raced on Saturdays, and it gave me an idea.

I placed a phone call to Rick Hendrick.

"Rick," I said, "something's gotta give. This team ain't working."

"That's obvious," Rick said. "What do you suggest?"

I had given the matter considerable thought, and I had checked with Jeff Hammond about the feasibility of my idea. Jeff was still at Junior Johnson's, where Terry Labonte was driving the Budweiser car I had left behind, but he wasn't the crew chief anymore. Tim Brewer was the chief, and Tim and Jeff weren't getting along very well. He thought my idea was a good one.

"Here's an option I've been thinking about," I said to Rick. "How about I hire Hammond, and he and I get a group of guys together, and we move the Tide number seventeen car into my shop over on Hudspeth Road? You wouldn't have to pay me any rent or anything, and it would give us a chance to refocus the team."

"I don't know," Rick said.

"C'mon, Rick. We've gotta make a change—we're going nowhere."

We talked it over for a while, and finally Rick agreed to let me move the team to my shop. It was less than two miles from Rick's building to mine, but that was far enough to give me the independence I was looking for. Hammond signed up right away, and the two of us set out to salvage the season.

It wasn't easy for me to concentrate on racing that summer, because Stevie's pregnancy was always in the back of my mind. By May we knew she was carrying a girl. I tried not to let Stevie see my anxiety, but I worried constantly about that little baby. Would she ever see the nursery we had prepared for her?

Jessica arrived on September 17, 1987, the very picture of health. As congratulations poured in from friends and fans, Stevie and I basked in the afterglow of our daughter's birth. At the age when many couples are sending their first child off to college, we were bringing ours home for the first time. And "home" now meant more than it had meant before. After all those years of waiting, God had blessed us with a child.

Ten days after Jessica was born, I found a vase with a single rose resting on the seat of my race car at the Martinsville Speedway. Attached to the vase was a note. It read, "Win this one for me, Daddy."

I led the Martinsville race for 130 laps before surrendering the lead to Dale Earnhardt. For the next 200 laps Earnhardt battled with Terry Labonte. I pitted early, which put me a lap behind the leaders, but with about 20 laps to go, Earnhardt finally pitted too, making it possible for me to get back on the lead lap with him and Labonte. A caution flag with ten laps to go allowed all three of us to get new tires. When the green flag came out again there were three laps left in the race, and Earnhardt, Labonte, and I were bumper-to-bumper-to-bumper on our way around the short oval. Earnhardt, of course, refused to give Labonte an opening, and I couldn't get around Labonte. On the last lap Labonte tried to pass Dale on the outside, and Earnhardt squeezed him into the wall. As they went into the third turn, Labonte went low. It looked to me like Terry was about to give Dale a tap in retaliation for trying to put him in the wall. I hit Terry, and he hit Dale. Both of them spun out, and I slipped past them to win the race.

Martinsville was my only win in the 1987 season. Still, our reconfigured team had managed a remarkable turnaround, and I finished the season fourth in the points. The season champion, for the second consecutive year, was Dale Earnhardt. Dale had been a commanding presence all year. He had led 35 percent of the laps he'd run. He had won 11 races and finished 21 times in the top five, and he had won more than $1 million.

The most memorable moment of the 1987 season came in the Winston All-Star Race at Charlotte on Mother's Day. That race is run in three segments, and is capped with a thrilling ten-lap sprint to the finish line. It was during this sprint that Dale Earnhardt made the save that has gone down in NASCAR legend as "the pass in the grass."

Indisputably Bill Elliot had the quickest car on the track that day. He led the entire race, followed doggedly by a determined

Earnhardt. In the first lap of the ten-lap sprint, Earnhardt bumped Elliot going into the first turn, pushing him into Geoffrey Bodine. The contact caused both Elliot and Bodine to spin out, allowing Earnhardt to take the lead. The field was restarted, and the battle between Elliot and Earnhardt heated up. Earnhardt used every blocking maneuver he knew, cutting off the faster Elliot time after time to maintain the lead. As they came out of the dogleg on the third lap, Earnhardt swung in front of Elliot and the two collided. The contact sent Earnhardt careening off the track into the infield—but he never took his foot off the gas! His car chewed across the grass like a bass boat skimming over a lake, never losing forward momentum, while Dale fought for control. Incredibly, he straightened out the car and drove back onto the track still in the lead!

A couple laps later Earnhardt pushed Elliot into the wall, and Elliot was soon forced to the pits for a tire change. Earnhardt went on to win the race, crossing the finish line less than a second ahead of Bodine. Elliot was furious. On the cool-down lap he bumped Earnhardt from the rear, and he veered toward Earnhardt's car again as they approached pit road. NASCAR fined Earnhardt and Elliot each $2,500 for the fracas and required Dale to post a $7,500 bond, which would be returned to him after seven races if no further incidents occurred.

"If I coulda got back on that racetrack, I'd a wrecked him," the normally mild-mannered Bill Elliot said later. "I've never been so mad in my life." Elliot told reporters that Earnhardt's dirty driving was cheapening the sport and making it more dangerous. "We're not kids," he protested. "We're not Saturday-night wrestlers. We're racers. The thing is, he liked to wreck me and several others on the track." Elliot was disgusted by Dale's take-no-prisoners style of racing. "If a man has to run over you to beat you, it's time to stop. I'm sick of it. Time and time again. If that's what it takes to be a Winston Cup champion, I don't want it."

* * *

The Riverside International Raceway in California had hosted NASCAR races since 1972 and had been the setting for the end-of-the-season championship race since 1981. But it was being sold. Its prospective new owner had announced plans to build a shopping mall on the property. Bobby Allison, who still regarded me as his nemesis, had won six Cup races at Riverside during his career, more than any other driver. I had won five. The final race on the winding road course in June 1988 was my last opportunity to match Bobby's record as the winningest driver at Riverside. I wanted that win, and so did Bobby.

Bobby and I raced each other hard through the 2.62-mile course. After a pit stop we were working our way through the field, swinging around the sweeping right-hand turn into the short front straightaway, past the start/finish line, then through a left-hand turn and down a little straightway and into a very sharp right-hander that leads up into the S curves. As we approached turn 9, a dogleg left, I got under Bobby and he cut me off. I almost wrecked to keep from hitting him. I gathered myself and ran him down again. I caught him near the start/finish line, and we raced side by side down the short straightaway into a right-hand turn. On this turn, the guy on the inside has the advantage; the guy on the outside has to lift or he's going to go off in the dirt. That was my perspective, anyway. Bobby saw it differently. Rather than ease off the accelerator and let me by, Bobby turned hard into the corner. I drove into him, and the collision sent both of our cars sailing off the racetrack. I slid backward into a barrier that protected the safety workers, damaging it, and Bobby's car came to rest in a billowing cloud of dust. Both cars sustained radiator damage, but they were still drivable, so we cranked them up again and made our way back out onto the racetrack. Soon the red flag came out; the officials stopped the race for more than 25 minutes while repairs were made to the barrier I had struck. We were stopped on the front straightaway, and I saw Bobby climb out of his car and head in my direction. He had to be restrained. He was going to whip my ass, he said, because I had tried to wreck him.

Neither one of us won the final race at Riverside. That honor went to Rusty Wallace. Dale Earnhardt, who had never won a race on a road course, led the race for seven laps, but he was penalized three places after he passed the pace car under a yellow flag, and he finished fourth. Bobby Allison finished 22nd, and I exited the race on the 85th lap when my engine overheated.

The following week we were at Pocono. Bobby had a bad qualifying run and wound up having to qualify on the second day. He would start the race in the 28th position; I would start in ninth.

The night before the race Bobby Hillin and his wife, Kim, came over to our motor home for a visit. Hillin was Allison's driving mate on the Miller Beer team, and he and Kim were among our closest friends. On this night, however, they lingered much longer than usual. As the evening passed my normal bedtime, I started looking at my watch, but our guests didn't seem to take the hint.

Finally, Bobby Hillin sighed and said, "I can't believe I'm doing this, but I've got to tell you something. Bobby Allison is going to try to wreck you tomorrow."

"What?" I said, startled.

Hill looked at his wife, then at me. "Bobby is still so angry about Riverside that he said when he gets to you tomorrow he's going to put you in the wall, and he hopes it hurts you."

"You've got to be kidding," I said.

Hill shook his head grimly. "You know how Bobby can get when he's mad. He just won't let go of it. It doesn't help that he's having a bad weekend. His car is not running good. He's qualified poorly. He's mad at the team, but most of all he's mad at you." Hill stood up to leave. "So watch yourself out there tomorrow," he said.

"Thanks," I said. "I will."

The next morning I was sitting next to my brother in the drivers' meeting. After the litany of announcements, Dick Beatty, the NASCAR official, looked out at the assembled drivers and asked, "Do you have any questions?"

Bobby Allison leaped to his feet. "Yeah, I have a question," he said. "What do you do about some asshole that wrecks you during a race for no apparent reason other than he just doesn't want you to win the race? What do you do about that?"

Bobby looked over to where Michael and I were sitting. Michael jumped to his feet. "I'm not the asshole!" Michael said, and everyone laughed.

"Bobby, you just need to settle down," Dick Beatty said. "That was last week. You just need to put that behind you and find a way to handle it."

As I climbed into the car, I told Jeff Hammond to keep me updated on Allison's location throughout the race. "Let me know when he gets close to me," I said, "because I'm just going to let him go. I don't want to tangle with Bobby today."

On the second lap of the race, the caution flag suddenly came out. I came down the long back straightaway to see Bobby's car sitting there with another car stuck right in the driver's door. A soft tire had sent Bobby into the wall and spinning across the track so quickly that the car behind him had no time to react. Jocko Maggiacomo had driven straight into Bobby running wide open. The accident looked horrendous, and I found myself praying that Bobby had survived. The race was stopped while the unconscious Bobby was extricated from his demolished car and airlifted to a hospital in Allentown, where he was listed in critical condition. Bobby would never race again. His broken bones would mend, but the head trauma he suffered in the collision would leave him with equilibrium problems that ended his career.

In the years that followed, Bobby would suffer more tragedy. His youngest son, Clifford, was killed in an accident during practice at the Michigan Speedway in 1992, and the following year his son Davey died in a helicopter accident at Talladega. Still, Bobby soldiered on. When he was inducted into the NASCAR Hall of Fame in 2011 I was genuinely pleased. Bobby Allison is a force of nature, the founder of a racing dynasty and a true hero in the sport of motor racing. Our professional relationship was a stormy one, but I feel fortunate to have been his friend.

*   *   *

Dale Earnhardt broke my single-season record for total winnings in 1988, racking up more than $2 million in purse money. His bid for a third consecutive championship, however, came up short. Bill Elliot won the championship that year. Dale finished third in the standings, and I finished seventh.

At the annual awards banquet in the Grand Ballroom of the Waldorf-Astoria Hotel in December, I found myself standing next to Earnhardt in a reception line. Dale leaned sideways and took an exaggerated look at the side of my head. "You know, there's a new product called 'Just for Men' that will probably take care of that," he said.

"Take care of what?"

Dale pointed. "All that gray there."

"Really?" I touched my hair self-consciously. The introduction of a new hair-coloring product for men was news to me. "Do you use it?"

Dale snorted. "Hell no, I don't need it," he said, and walked away.

A few weeks before the start of the 1989 season, I slipped into a drugstore and bought a package of Just for Men. I didn't tell anybody about it, and since I wasn't sure how quickly the stuff might wear off, I decided to put it away until my next public appearance.

When I arrived in Daytona for Speedweeks in February, I unpacked my suitcase in the hotel and read the hair-coloring instructions carefully. They looked simple enough. I laid out the tubes and applicator and towels on the bathroom counter and went to work, and in no time at all—voilà!—I saw a 20-year-old looking back at me from the mirror. The transformation was remarkable.

The next morning, after admiring my new look in the mirror, I went out to the track. It was a sunny day, unusually warm. I strolled through the garage area, shaking hands and shooting the breeze with friends, signing autographs and posing for pictures with fans, chatting with reporters. People were staring at me, and I smiled inwardly at my little secret.

Early in the afternoon one of the marketing guys from Procter & Gamble caught my eye and cocked his head. He walked to a corner of the garage and I followed him.

"What did you do, Darrell?" he said. "Wash your hair in Tide?"

"What do you mean?"

"I mean your hair is . . . red."

"My hair is not red."

"Oh yeah," he said, nodding emphatically, "your hair is red."

I went into the bathroom and checked the mirror. My hair looked a little different, but it certainly wasn't red. Back outside, though, people continued to stare, and for the next few days the guys on the crew ribbed me mercilessly about my hair. When Stevie arrived in Daytona, she confirmed it. The new shade wasn't obvious indoors under artificial light, but outdoors in natural sunlight my brown hair now shimmered with a distinct red tint. I decided to make the best of it. "Maybe having hair the color of yours will bring me luck," I told Stevie.

During a practice lap on the Wednesday before the Daytona 500, Dale Earnhardt was blasting down the tri-oval at more than 190 miles an hour when he suddenly lost control. His black #3 Chevy lifted, twisted, tumbled end-over-end, slammed into the fence, and disintegrated. Miraculously Dale walked away from the wreckage, wincing in pain but refusing medical attention. An hour later he was back on the track in another car. Nothing was going to keep Dale from the biggest race of the year.

I started the 1989 Daytona 500 on the outside pole, beside my teammate Kenny Schrader. Geoff Bodine, in the other car fielded by Hendrick Motorsports, started in the tenth position, behind Earnhardt. The field thinned on the 73rd lap, when Jody Ridley, driving in relief of the injured Bill Elliot, touched the wall, triggering a ten-car pileup. I saw a car ricochet off the wall in front of me, but I somehow made it through the chaos of spinning cars unscathed.

Schrader led the race for 114 of its 200 laps, with Earnhardt close on his heels. I stayed within range of the leaders as the race wore on, aware that sooner or later they would have to stop for fuel. We had all pitted at the same time, on lap 147. NASCAR rules do not allow a fuel gauge in the car, but we all knew that a race car will travel 50 laps on a full load of fuel. If a caution flag didn't give us the opportunity to refuel without losing track position, we would all run out of gas three laps from the finish line. As Schrader and Earnhardt broke away from the pack, Jeff Hammond came on the radio to say that we were shifting to our backup strategy. I was going to draft off anybody and everybody in order to conserve fuel.

With 11 laps to go, Kenny and Dale ducked into the pits for a splash of gas. I had been driving conservatively, feathering the accelerator and drifting inside the air currents produced by other cars. "Stay out!" Jeff ordered. Could I wring three extra laps from a single tank? It was a huge gamble, but it was our only realistic chance to win the race.

Alan Kulwicki, who had also decided to gamble on gas, took the lead on lap 191. I drafted behind him, keeping a nervous watch on my fuel pressure gauge. On lap 197 Alan was forced to the apron by a flat tire, leaving me in the lead. If I could make it to the finish line without running out of fuel, the race was mine!

With two laps to go, I felt the car hiccup, and the fuel pressure gauge dropped. "I'm out!" I shouted into the radio.

"Shake it up! Shake it up!" the crew screamed. I swerved back and forth on the track and the engine picked up again.

I was cruising down the backstretch on the final lap, holding my breath, when the car suddenly faltered and the fuel pressure gauge dropped to zero. I swung desperately across the track, my heart sinking. Stevie closed her eyes. The crew stood on tiptoe. "That's it! I'm out!" I said in dismay. An eternity passed—and suddenly the fuel pressure gauge jumped and the engine stuttered back to life! I coasted across the finish line under the checkered flag and ran out of gas on Victory Circle.

When I clambered out of my car, I was so elated by the win that I broke into an impromptu dance. Right there before a national television audience, I celebrated with my own version of the "Icky Shuffle," capping it off by spiking my helmet in a touchdown flourish. "I've won the Daytona 500! I've won the Daytona 500!" I was scarcely able to believe it. I turned to the nearest reporter. "This is Daytona, isn't it? Don't lie to me! I'm not dreaming, am I?"

Earnhardt's reaction was more subdued. When an interviewer asked him to comment on my decision to stay out on the track rather than pit for fuel, Dale said, "I didn't think he would make it. I'd like to see that gas tank."

A month after the Daytona 500 I was in Atlanta for the Motorcraft 500. In my room at the Airport Hilton, I noticed that a bit of gray was starting to reappear at my temples. Maybe a second application of the manly hair coloring would remove the gray and also eliminate the reddish tinge the guys had been kidding me about. I pulled the supplies from my suitcase, repeated the procedure, and surveyed the results. My appearance had not improved. Yes, the gray was gone, but now my hair was redder than ever. I could see the ochre tone myself in the bathroom mirror. If I let the guys see me like this, I would never live it down.

I remembered that there was a beauty parlor downstairs in the hotel, so I called down there and got one of the beauticians on the phone. Without identifying myself, I said casually, "Hey, I put some color in my hair and I want to get it out. What do I need to do?"

"You could come down here and we could take care of it for you," the girl said.

That wasn't going to happen. I was not going to risk becoming a public spectacle. "Uh, I'd rather just take care of it myself. What do I need to do?"

"Well, to get that color out you'll have to get some stripper."

"Stripper? What does that do?"

"It'll get all the color out."

"Okay, so if I go get some stripper and put it on my hair, it'll get that stuff out that I put in it?"

"Exactly."

I donned a hat and sunglasses, slipped down the emergency stairs, then drove to the drugstore and bought myself some stripper. Back in the hotel I put the chemical on my hair. The bottle said to leave it on for five minutes, so I checked my watch and looked in the mirror. My hair was starting to turn bright yellow. *Man, this is some weird stuff,* I thought. *I guess that's what it does before you wash it out.* After five minutes I stepped into the shower and washed the stripper out. I washed and washed and washed. When my hair was squeaky clean, I toweled it dry, looked in the mirror, and gasped. My hair was as yellow as a caution light!

In a panic I called down to the beauty shop again and got the girl back on the phone. "Hey, you told me if I put this stuff in my hair it would take the color out!" I said, accusingly.

"That's what it does," she replied. "It takes the color out of your hair. Now you have to dye it back the color you want."

I was stunned. "I have to dye it? I don't want to dye my hair anymore—that's why I called you in the first place. I wanted to take out the color I put in."

"Well, you're going to have to dye it," she said. "Unless you just want to leave it the color it is now."

I checked the mirror, hoping for some improvement. I looked like Dobie Gillis. "Can you come up here and do it for me?" I asked.

"Sure," she said. "What's your room number?"

I told her.

"And what's your natural hair color?"

"Dark brown."

"Okay, I'll be up in a little while. And don't worry. When I'm done, you'll look normal again."

A few minutes later I heard a knock on my door. When I looked through the peephole, I saw Stevie standing there. My parents were with her. I quickly opened the door, grabbed Stevie by the arm, pulled her inside, and slammed the door again, leaving my parents outside.

Stevie gave me a confused look. "Why are you wearing that hat?" she asked. I pulled the hat off, and Stevie collapsed in helpless laughter. "What have you done?" she asked, when she had caught her breath. I was in the middle of telling her the story when she stopped me. "Your mom and dad are still standing out there in the hall."

"I don't want them to see me this way. Go back out and tell them I'm not feeling good. Tell them I've got a headache. Get them into their room and then come back, okay?" Stevie nodded, stifling a giggle, and left.

Stevie returned just as the girl from the beauty shop showed up. We went into the bathroom and the girl applied the dye. We waited a few minutes, then washed it out. As soon as my hair was dry I looked at Stevie for a verdict. She grimaced. "It's red again," she said. I checked the mirror. She was right.

"We probably need to leave the dye on longer," said the girl.

Stevie looked at her watch. "There's supposed to be a Bible study here in our room tonight," she said. "People will be showing up any minute."

"Don't let anybody in!" I said. "Move the meeting to Mom and Dad's room. Tell folks—I don't care what you tell them. Just don't tell them I'm getting my hair fixed."

Stevie left, and the girl went through the whole process again. This time my hair came out a very dark chocolate brown, with a red tint. The girl threw up her hands. "That's all I can do," she said apologetically.

The next morning I wore a hat to the track. I wore that hat all weekend. Whenever it was time for me to get into the car, I'd pull the hat off and slam my helmet on immediately, before anybody could get a good look at my hair.

Earnhardt led for most of the race on Sunday afternoon, but

I was on the lead lap 15 laps from the end when the caution flag came out for the last time. Dale and I both pitted quickly, and I barely beat him out of the pits. The green flag came out with nine laps to go, and Dale was never able to pass me after that. I held him off to gain my 75th career Cup victory.

I pulled to a stop in Victory Circle and was just about to get out of the car when I suddenly remembered my hair. My dad was running toward the car, his expression jubilant. He was wearing a Tide hat. Dad stuck his head in the car to give me a hug, and I snatched the hat off his head. "Thanks for the hat, Dad," I said, and climbed out of the car. Then I hugged him.

In the months that followed I continued to dye my own hair, and I became pretty proficient at it. In fact I eventually starting cutting my hair too, something I continue to do to this day. That fine $50 haircut you see every week when the Fox Sports camera pans the broadcast booth? That's all me, baby. I get exactly the haircut I want every time, and I get to keep the 50 bucks.

Me with baby brother, Mikey.

My first ride. I raced this go-kart at Ellis Park Speedway and elsewhere.

Carrying the checkered flag in the car owned by Harry Pedley's Garage.

Me and the Redhead. Check out those sideburns!

In Victory Circle with Junior Johnson and Stevie after my first win
at Talladega, 1977.

With Dad, Mom, and Stevie during my rookie year, 1973.

In New York with Junior Johnson after
my first championship season.

With Jeff Hammond after a
grueling race at Martinsville.

My first Cup win, Mother's Day Weekend 1975 in Nashville.
Brother Mikey is at lower left, beside my grandfather. Jake Elder
has his arm around my grandmother.

Hanging out with Junior Johnson.

Hugging Mikey on pit road.
I'm not sure when this was taken.

My barrel roll at Daytona, 1991.

Neil Bonnett at far left, Dale Earnhardt at far right.

Stevie with Dale.

Presentations after a horse race at Dover Downs. *Left to right:* Dave Buckson, me, Cale Yarborough, Dale Earnhardt, Bobby Allison, Dennis McGlynn, Mike Joy.

Taking a break
with Mikey
and Dad.

Mike Joy interviews
me and baby Jessica.

With Dale,
James Garner, and
Cale at the "50
Greatest Drivers"
banquet in Los
Angeles. During
NASCAR's 50th
Anniversary
celebration, I was
named Driver of
the 1980s.

With Sarah, Stevie and Jessica—and our dogs, Olivia and Trusty Boy.
Am I a blessed man, or what?

CHAPTER TWELVE

NO PAIN, NO NAPROXEN

My victory in the 1989 Daytona 500 marked the beginning of a good year for the Tide team. We were hitting our stride. I won in Atlanta in March and in Martinsville in April, and at the end of May I was running strong in the Winston when Rusty Wallace wrecked me.

By now the all-star race was being run in three segments: a 75-lap segment with a mandatory green-flag pit stop, a 50-lap segment, and a final ten-lap segment. Rusty won the first segment and I won the second, setting us up for a duel in the ten-lap sprint for the $200,000 purse.

I took off strong in the third segment and was driving away from everybody, but my car had developed a little push; it tended to drift up the track in the corners. To keep the car from moving up the hill, I eased off on the accelerator as I went into the turns, almost coasting, then floored it as I came out onto the straight-aways. I was still holding the lead, but by the time there were two laps left, the redhead from St. Louis was hard on my tail. I could pull ten car lengths ahead of Rusty on the straightaways, but he would draw up to my rear bumper in the corners.

I knew that Rusty's car wasn't fast enough to pass me. I figured he knew that he was going to finish second, and I figured he would be content with that. I figured wrong.

As we reached the third turn on our way to the white flag, I decided to go easy through the corner. My car was really pushing by now, and I didn't want to give Rusty a chance to get under me. I went low into the corner, rolling just a little too easy, and

Rusty came in hard. Just as I was about ready to accelerate, he clipped my left rear fender and sent me spinning off down the front straightaway and into the grass, tires smoking and grass flying, as the yellow flag came out and boos cascaded from the stands.

Since the rules for the final segment required all ten laps to be run under a green flag, the officials set the field for a restart. I expected to be returned to the head of the field, where I'd been when Wallace clipped me, but NASCAR officials sent me to the rear instead. I was aghast at the ruling, angry with both Wallace and the officials, and the fans were in an uproar. I managed to work my way up to sixth or seventh place during those final two laps, but there was simply not enough time to catch Rusty again. When he took the checkered flag, irate fans started booing and throwing garbage onto the track.

Jeff Hammond and the rest of my crew were furious. They charged toward the entrance to Victory Circle, converging there with the members of Wallace's pit crew, and suddenly fists began to fly. As the melee spread, a security officer grabbed Stevie and hustled her away from the pandemonium, toward the safety of the garage area.

Back in the garage a reporter asked me what I thought about Rusty Wallace. "I hope he chokes on that two hundred thousand dollars," I said.

Meanwhile, as the outrage grew, telephone operators at the track received threats against Rusty and the NASCAR officials. The police were summoned, and Rusty was transported out of the racetrack on the floor of a patrol car. A contingent of FBI agents accompanied him to his home, where they placed him and his family in protective custody for the night.

The reaction of this crowd was new, at least for me. I was accustomed to angry fans, but this was different: the fans were on *my side* this time, and they were angry with the *other* guy! The role reversal almost gave me whiplash.

The next day I went back to the Charlotte Motor Speedway and won the Coca-Cola World 600. The fans went wild.

By the end of the season I had won six races, including both races at Martinsville, and I had won more money than any other driver that year. The most satisfying recognition I received, however, came at the awards banquet in New York, when the results of the Most Popular Driver voting were announced. Like the all-star selections in baseball, the Most Popular Driver award is determined by ballots cast by the fans. If the fans had been asked to name their Most Hated Driver, I would have won that award hands-down several times during my career, but this year they had selected me as NASCAR's Most Popular Driver. I could scarcely believe it.

I was not playing the bad guy anymore, but every drama needs a villain. Somebody must wear the black hat on Sunday. I'd worn that hat for years, and now it was someone else's turn. In what seemed to signal his acceptance of the role, Dale Earnhardt had changed colors and sponsors in 1988. The cheerful blue-and-yellow Wrangler Jeans car that he had piloted since 1981 was retired, and he rumbled onto the track in the GM Goodwrench car, with its sinister black paint scheme. Earnhardt now looked more menacing than ever. The new look earned him a nickname, "the Man in Black," and his ominous presence on the track prompted some pundits to refer to him as "Darth Vader." If the hisses of the fans bothered him, he never let it show. He wanted to win races, not popularity contests, and he was not going to play nice for the sake of appearances. Dale knew he had his own cadre of passionate supporters in the stands, but I never heard him obsess about the size of his fan base. He had more important things to think about. Above all, he wanted another championship.

Earnhardt was leading the points race late in the 1989 season, but a broken cam shaft at Charlotte on October 8 and a late spinout at Wilkesboro on the following Sunday cost him dearly. Rusty Wallace wound up winning the championship, a mere 12 points ahead of Dale.

* * *

The rising popularity of NASCAR had caught the attention of Hollywood. The 1990 blockbuster movie *Days of Thunder,* produced by Jerry Bruckheimer and Don Simpson, brought the excitement of stock car racing to a global audience. Most of the racing footage for the movie, which starred Tom Cruise and Robert Duvall, was shot at the Daytona International Speedway. Rick Hendrick was heavily involved behind the scenes, and like several of the other drivers I got pretty involved too.

We were testing for the Daytona 500 while the movie was being shot. I was trying to be helpful to the movie people, acting as a technical adviser, but my main concern was preparing my team for the upcoming race. It was a challenge. The garage area was cluttered with special show cars that would be wrecked for the film, and my crew was being called upon to work on them. It seemed like every time I wanted something done, the guy I needed was gone on movie-related business. I was starting to get annoyed.

Late one frustrating afternoon I opened the door to my hauler to find a mob of strangers inside it. "All right, you people," I said loudly, "I don't know who you all are, but I want you out of here. Now!"

The crowd parted, and I saw Tom Cruise and Paul Newman staring at me.

"Except for you two," I said lamely. "You two can stay."

Paul Newman wasn't in the movie. He'd come to the track to test a car. Unlike Tom Cruise, who, when it came to driving, was an excellent actor, Newman was a legitimate talent behind the wheel. He was part owner of an open-wheel racing team, and he competed in all kinds of races around the world. Newman is the only guy I ever asked for an autograph. He gave me one.

I had a few good lines in *Days of Thunder,* but none of my scenes made it to the final version of the film. The huge budget for the film depended, in large part, on revenue from product placement. Corporations paid the movie studio big money to feature their products and logos on screen. Plenty of corporations anted up, but Procter & Gamble refused to participate. As a result the

Tide car never appeared in the film and all my work ended up on the cutting-room floor. It would be another 15 years before I would finally get my big break in the movie business, as the voice of announcer Darrell Cartrip in the Pixar animated film *Cars*.

We went to Daytona in 1990 with the same car we'd won with in 1989 and found that everything had changed. Suddenly I couldn't get out of my own way. I finished 14th in the Daytona 500, a lap behind the leaders. Earnhardt finished fifth, and my brother finished eighth. We continued to struggle in the weeks that followed, with a 12th-place finish at Richmond and a sixth at Rockingham. At Atlanta, a race we'd won the year before, we weren't even close. Earnhardt won, his first victory in a season that would see him win nine races and capture his fourth championship. I finished 26th at Atlanta, in a car that was running so poorly that at one point we parked it in the garage to work on it.

Rick Hendrick had launched his own in-house engine program that year with a young man named Randy Dorton, and I blamed the engines for most of our problems. As the weeks passed and our troubles continued, the frustration of losing started to get to me.

One day in April I got a call from Rick Hendrick's office telling me to be at a studio in Charlotte at 8 a.m. the following Monday for a photo shoot, part of a promotional program for a sunglasses company.

"How much does it pay?" I asked. I wasn't eager to spend my Monday morning away from home, but an unexpected paycheck would help take the sting out of it.

"It doesn't pay anything," came the reply. "It's part of your contract."

I was in a dark mood when I arrived at the studio on Monday morning. Some of the Tide people were there too, and they weren't very bubbly either. Procter & Gamble had become accustomed to seeing their Tide logo on national television on Sunday afternoons, basking in Victory Circle, and it hadn't happened yet this season. They weren't getting what they had paid for, and they wanted to know what was wrong.

"I'm not sure," I said. "I think we're just not getting the engines we need."

"Well, what are you going to do about it?" they asked.

"I don't know," I said. Then I added casually, "I feel like I could do this a lot better if I was doing it by myself."

The Tide people looked around to make sure nobody else was listening. "Would you ever think about starting your own team?" they asked.

"I've considered it," I said.

"Well, if you decide to do that, let us know."

On my way home that afternoon I kept replaying those words in my mind. *If you decide to do that, let us know.* What were they saying? Were they saying that if I were to start my own team, Tide would want to be involved? Or were they asking to be notified if I planned to start my own team so that they could make other plans? I didn't know.

Rick Hendrick called a few days later to ask what the problem was and why I was being so hard to work with. "It's a bad year, that's all," I said. "We're just having a bad year."

We were still winless in May, when the Charlotte race rolled around, and I decided I'd had enough. "I think it's time to go out on my own," I told Stevie late one night. "I started out with my own team, and I'm happiest when I can run the show the way I want to. I'm going to start my own team."

Looking back on it now, I can see what a dumb decision that was. I had nothing, really. The only thing I owned was the shop, which Rick was renting from me. Everything in that shop belonged to Rick, not me. I owned the four walls, but he owned all the inventory.

I called Rick up and said I wanted to have lunch. We went to the Mayflower, a little seafood house in Concord, just the two of us, and I told him what I was planning. I would finish out the year driving for Hendrick Motorsports, and the next year I was going to start my own team.

Rick was shocked and hurt by my decision. We were long-time friends, as well as business partners, and he had not expected me to quit.

"Well, who's your sponsor?" Rick asked.

"I don't know."

"What about Tide?"

"I don't know," I said. Rick gave me a sideways look that let me know I shouldn't be trying to take Tide away from him. He didn't say it directly, but I got the message loud and clear: *Find your own sponsor.*

On the first weekend in July, still winless, we were back at Daytona for the Pepsi 400. The television show *Entertainment Tonight* had come to Daytona that weekend to follow me around, and they were in the garage filming everything we were doing to the car. I went out for the last few practice laps on Friday afternoon, and the car was not to my liking. Specifically, I didn't like the seat. I had come up with the idea of turning the seat a little to the left, since I'm always looking to the left when I'm driving, and the crew had gone to a lot of trouble to tweak the seat for me. After testing it, I had to tell them that the seat made the car feel funny. I instructed them to put it back the way it was and get the car ready to race. They were not pleased.

Some of the other teams were still out on the track practicing, so I took the reporter from *Entertainment Tonight* over to the coach lot for a better view of the track. We climbed up on top of my motor coach with a cameraman, and I started explaining what the teams were trying to accomplish in practice. Suddenly we were interrupted by a member of my crew, who had run over from the garage.

"We need you to come back to the car for one more run," he said.

"I don't want to make any more runs," I replied. "I'm done for the day. Just fix the seat back the way it was and it will be okay."

"It's not the seat. We think we may have found something in the engine that will really help it, and we'd like to verify the new settings. We need to make a run to be sure we've got it jetted right." I jumped down, threw my uniform on, and ran back to the car, the reporter following me.

There were no leg braces in the car when I got there. The braces, which had only recently been introduced, were designed to confine a driver's legs in the event of a crash, keeping them out of the pedals and preventing them from being mangled. My crew had removed the leg braces while working on the seat, and they hadn't reinstalled them yet. I scarcely noticed and didn't care, since I was just going to go out and make a couple of laps for a plug check.

I hopped in the car and tore down pit road just as practice was coming to an end. A big pack of cars was going by, led by A. J. Foyt's car. A. J. wasn't driving, though. He had gone to an Indy car race somewhere that day, and Dale Earnhardt had agreed to shake down the car for him as a favor.

I caught up with the pack on the back straightaway and followed them into the third turn. Suddenly the rear-end line blew off A. J.'s car and started spraying grease everywhere. Almost immediately, the cars between Dale and me started spinning and colliding. There was smoke everywhere and I couldn't see, but I managed to make it all the way through the wreck without hitting anything. As I came off turn 4, however, I spun out too. My car wound up sitting in the middle of the racetrack, stalled.

Jeff Hammond started hollering on the radio. "Get out of there! Get out of there!" I tried desperately to restart the car, but the engine wouldn't crank. "Cars are coming!" Jeff screamed. I looked back at turn 4, where a huge cloud of smoke hovered over the track. Suddenly a car emerged from the smoke, headed straight for me. There was no time to react. Dave Marcis drove straight into my driver's door doing about 160 miles per hour.

I woke up on Saturday morning in Halifax Hospital with no memory of what had happened. I found myself lying in a hospital bed with my leg in a contraption that was making it go up and down. I had broken my femur, busted it twice and split it. I had a broken arm, broken ribs, and a concussion.

Stevie was sitting by my bedside, watching the race on the television. My first thought was that somebody had beaten me up and tied me to this bed to keep me out of the race. Stevie had to calm me down. After a while friends started stopping by—Junior and Flossie Johnson, Kenny Schrader, and others—and then the surgeon, Dr. Albert Gillespie, came in to check on me.

Stevie had wanted them to airlift me to Indianapolis, where I could be operated on by Dr. Trammel, the orthopedic surgeon who was renowned for his ability to repair the injured legs of Indy drivers, but the doctors at Halifax Hospital told her that my injuries were too serious; I could not be moved. David Stringfield, the president of Nashville's Baptist Hospital, was at the race that weekend, and he helped Stevie research alternatives. Dr. Gillespie came highly recommended. Stringfield got Trammel and Gillespie on the phone. Gillespie described my injuries and what he was planning to do about them. Trammel agreed that that's what he would do, so they went ahead with the operation to fix my shattered leg. It took them 15 hours to do it.

Three days later I was getting restless. Even though our team was having a bad year, I was still eighth in the points, and the point race was all I could think about. It still might be possible to salvage the season, *but only if I were starting races.* I knew NASCAR took a Sunday off between Daytona and Pocono, and I figured I could heal up enough during the two-week break to at least run one lap at Pocono. To get points for the race I needed to drive only one lap before turning the car over to a relief driver, and to enter the race I would need to make only one lap during practice.

The next time Dr. Gillespie came around, Stevie conferred with him in the hallway. "Darrell keeps talking about getting back in the race car," she said. "He thinks he'll be able to drive in less than two weeks. Tell me, how long will it be before my husband can drive again?"

"Considering the severity of his injuries," he said, "I'd say it will be six months to a year before Darrell will be able to get back in a race car."

Stevie grabbed the doctor. "Look at me," she said. "Go ahead and tell Darrell all you want to about his injuries, but please—*please*—don't tell him he won't be able to drive for six months to a year. He will die if you do. He will have a heart attack." Dr. Gillespie gave her a noncommittal smile and came into the room. He described my injuries and the surgical procedures I had undergone, and then, glancing apologetically at Stevie, he said, "I wouldn't expect to get back in the car the rest of this year."

I sat up, wincing. "The rest of the year? I've gotta be in the car next *week*!"

"You don't understand," he said, and he went through the list of my injuries again.

"No, no, *you* don't understand," I protested. "I've gotta be in Pocono next week. I only have to make one lap. I don't have to do anything else. I'll get in the car and make one lap to get the points, and then I'll get out."

"Well, there's no way you're going to do that," the doctor said. "Not in the condition you're in. No way."

"*Yes* way," I insisted. "We've *gotta* figure out a way."

My brother Bobby was in Daytona with us, and I knew that one of our show cars was parked inside a mall nearby. "Here's what we're going to do," I told the doctor. "Bobby is going to take you over to the mall and show you how we get in and out of the car. There's no door, you understand. We climb in through the window. I want you to get into the car yourself so you can see what I'm talking about. Then come back here so we can talk about it."

The doctor shook his head.

"Please," I said. "Just look at the car."

Dr. Gillespie sighed and hung the chart on the end of my bed. "Okay," he said. "I'll look at the car."

*   *   *

When Bobby and Dr. Gillespie returned to the hospital, the doctor had a grim expression on his face. "The problem I see is that there's no way to get you in the car without twisting your leg," he said. "And if you twist your leg, you'll break the screws and pop the plate off. We can't let that happen."

"So?" I said. "What could we do to keep that from happening?"

"You could stay out of the car."

"Let's think of something else," I said.

Dr. Gillespie thought. "You know," he said, "I had a meeting last week with some guys from Jacksonville who are building removable casts. I'm going to call them and see if I can set up a meeting."

The following day a team of technicians made a plaster mold of my leg. They returned a couple of days later with a removable cast that went around my foot and up my leg and bolted on at my waist. I could bend my knee a little with the cast on, but I couldn't twist my foot. Dr. Gillespie looked the cast over and said, "If we can figure out a way to keep your leg stable and get you in that car, I might go along with it."

On Sunday, a week and a day after the accident, I checked out of Halifax Hospital with my removable cast. We flew back to Nashville in my King Air, then went directly to the Baptist Hospital Sports Medicine Facility, where David Stringfield had arranged for me to begin physical therapy. Stevie got me into a wheelchair and pushed me into the building, where I met the doctors and was introduced to my trainer, a very nice guy named Nick.

"Let's go on down to the training room and start your evaluation," Nick said. When we got to the room, he pointed to an Airdyne exercise bike. "I want you to get up on that bike and see how long you can ride it."

"Piece of cake," I said.

I was feeling wobbly, but with Nick and Stevie's help I got up onto the bike. I placed my broken leg on a peg, got my good foot on a pedal, grasped the handlebars, and started to pedal. I was winded almost immediately. I had barely eaten anything since the accident and had lost about 25 pounds. I was weak and feeling awful, but I had a goal. I was determined to be in Pocono on Friday with a letter from the doctor releasing me to drive the car.

On Wednesday Nick flew with me to Charlotte, where we spent the afternoon at the shop, practicing getting in and out of the car. On Friday the doctor looked me over and gave me a letter clearing me to drive, and we headed for the airport. Nick accompanied me again, along with Stevie and Joe Carver, my business manager. My pilot, Jerry Vanderflutz, had the King Air ready to go.

Stevie hobbled onto the airplane. Her knee was bothering her, and she was finding it difficult to walk. A doctor had prescribed naproxen for the pain, but she hadn't taken any yet.

The flight was excruciatingly long because the weather was foul. Jerry had to keep flying around thunderstorms. The plane bounced and jolted, and I struggled to keep my leg straight. By the time we landed in Pocono I would have gladly taken a bullet to end my misery.

We finally got to the Holiday Inn at about ten o'clock that night. All I wanted to do was lie down. Nick and Stevie got me up into the room, and I fell into bed. Stevie's knee was throbbing, so she took a pill before climbing into bed and kissing me good-night.

About an hour later, Stevie poked me. "I don't feel good," she said.

"What's wrong?"

"I feel really dizzy and I just don't feel good."

I thought, *If you think you don't feel good, you ought to be over here where I am.* I reached over and turned on the light, then looked at Stevie and yelped. Her face had puffed up like a basketball; her eyes were almost swollen shut, and her lips were huge. I grabbed the phone and told Joe Carver to come up right away. Joe hustled Stevie out the door and rushed her to the emergency room. They were gone for hours, while I lay awake, worrying. When they returned at about 4 a.m., the swelling in Stevie's face had started to go down, but she still looked like she had gone 12 rounds with Muhammad Ali. "She had a severe allergic reaction to the naproxen," Joe explained. "It could have been fatal, but they gave her an antidote at the hospital and she'll be okay."

We were scheduled to be at the racetrack at ten o'clock in the morning for a press conference. We dragged ourselves into the media room a few minutes after ten, me on crutches and Stevie looking like a victim of domestic violence, and the reporters went into a frenzy.

"Are you really going to drive?" somebody shouted.

"Yeah, I'm going to make a lap." Shutters clicked, and Stevie did her best to smile.

"Are you sure you can make a lap?"

"I'm sure. I don't have to carry the car—I just have to drive it."

I made the required practice lap on Friday, then turned the car over to Jimmy Horton for qualifying. Jimmy qualified somewhere in the middle of the field.

On Sunday morning I was sitting in the car in front of the grandstand when Dick Beatty, NASCAR's director of competition, came over to talk to me. He was plainly nervous about my presence in the race. "Here's what I want you to do, Darrell," Dick said. "Drop to the back of the field. Drop way back, let everybody else in front of you, and do not pass anyone. Make your lap, then get your butt on pit road and out of that car. Understand?"

"Got it," I said.

We came around the track for the start, the green flag dropped, and I dropped to the rear of the pack. Then I called Jeff Hammond on the radio. "I'm going to try to stay out until the first caution," I said. Staying out made sense. If we could change drivers while the race was under caution, we wouldn't have to hurry during the driver change and we wouldn't lose a lap.

On the back straightaway I came up on five or six cars that were straggling along behind the pack. I swung around them and went on into the second turn, and when I came off turn 3, the yellow flag was out and I was being black-flagged. I pulled into the pits congratulating myself on my strategy and foresight. The guys dragged me out of the car and put Jimmy Horton in it, just as a NASCAR inspector walked over and stood in front of the car. The officials had decided to penalize me two laps for failing to follow the NASCAR directive not to pass any cars. Jimmy spent the rest of the day two laps down, and we finished in 20th place. It would have been better for the team if I had just stayed home.

On Monday morning I called Jeff Hammond and said, "You'll have to find someone else to drive while I recuperate. That was the dumbest thing I've ever done in my life. It almost killed me."

I didn't know it at the time, but the Tide guys had already decided that they wanted another driver. After I got hurt, they started pressuring Rick Hendrick to give my ride to Ricky Rudd. Rick wouldn't do it. "That's Darrell's car for the rest of the year," Rick told them. "If he can recover and wants to drive it, the car is his. We'll make the change next year." Meanwhile Rick settled on Greg Sacks as my temporary replacement.

I went to the gym fanatically, spending three hours every day working my legs and arms, building up my stamina. My injured leg was healing nicely, far better than anyone expected. Soon I was hustling the Airdyne pretty well with both legs. Meanwhile the morale of the team was flagging. They couldn't win a race, and Greg wasn't clicking with the crew. The same guys who had wanted to kill me in February were now calling every week to ask "How much longer? When can you come back?"

In September I went to Darlington to watch the Labor Day race. I was on crutches, but I was feeling pretty good. Greg Sacks drove into the wall during qualifying, completely destroying our car and forcing the crew to get out a backup car. "I think I'm good enough to get back in the car next week," I said. The crew grinned.

The following week, at Richmond, I chased Dale Earnhardt for the entire race and almost caught him. I finished third—pretty good for my first day back.

It was autumn now, and I was trying to negotiate a deal to buy the equipment in the shop from Rick Hendrick. Rick had put the head of his race company, a guy named Jimmy Johnson, in charge of the negotiations, and Johnson and I were miles apart on price. I figured the equipment was worth about a million bucks, and Johnson valued it at about four times that amount.

I was also trying to find a sponsor for my new team. I came close to signing a sponsorship deal with Mellow Yellow in September, but that deal fell through at the last minute when the marketing people decided they preferred a young driver—Kyle Petty, who drove for Felix Sabates—to a 40-year-old with a broken leg. A couple of other sponsor prospects faded too.

When the Western Auto people came to see me at the race shop in October, everybody in the building knew that it was crunch time. The year was rapidly coming to a close, and we still did not have a backer for the upcoming season. I had hidden my crutches and was seated casually behind my desk when John Barlow, the president of Western Auto, arrived with a couple of his executives. I liked them immediately. Western Auto was a family-owned company with a small-town focus, and I was a small-town guy with a family-owned business.

"You can do whatever you want if you're our sponsor," I told them. "You can put a Western Auto front on this building, you can put Western Auto on everything we do. We'll answer the phone 'This is Western Auto Race Team.' You'll own this place. Whatever you want, it's yours."

John Barlow liked my pitch, but he wasn't ready to commit. "We've got another meeting this afternoon," he said. "We're going to go over and talk to Felix Sabates. We'll get back to you."

I sat alone in my office for the next few hours making contingency plans. Felix Sabates was a world-class salesman, a successful entrepreneur with vast resources, and I figured he would dazzle the guys from Western Auto. Late in the afternoon a rental car pulled into our lot and John Barlow and his guys got out of it. John was smiling when he came through the door. "You've got a deal," he said, extending his hand.

I was in high spirits the next time I spoke with Jimmy Johnson about the shop equipment I was trying to buy from Rick Hendrick. Johnson was still insisting on a big price, far more than I thought the stuff was worth. Finally I said, "I'll tell you what to do—just come get all your stuff." I knew that Hendrick Motorsports was already well-equipped; they certainly didn't need the used tools and equipment in my shop. I figured that after he added up the costs of moving and storing and liquidating all that stuff, Johnson would do the sensible thing and come back to me with a reasonable counteroffer. Meanwhile I had a race to prepare for. There were only two events left in the season, and we had to get ready for the Checker 500 in Phoenix.

Dale Earnhardt was trailing Mark Martin by 45 points going into Phoenix, and he won the race to take a 6-point lead in the chase for the championship. We finished fourth, another solid performance, but a call from the shop instantly dampened our spirits. "You're not going to believe what happened," my shop manager told me when he got me on the phone. "The Hendrick people came in here and took absolutely everything. There is nothing left. They took it all."

When we got back to Charlotte, the guys took one look at the empty shop and went ballistic. It wasn't just the expensive equipment that was missing, the dynamometers and lifts and things like that—*everything* was gone. The guys' tools and toolboxes, which every man regarded as his own even though they technically belonged to the company, had all been taken. Special jigs that the guys had built had been hauled away as well. The Hendrick crew had unbolted racks from the walls, leaving nothing but holes.

This was my fault, and I knew it. Hendrick had told me to negotiate with Jimmy Johnson, and I had told Johnson to come and take Hendrick's stuff. I had expected a little more time, but Johnson had obviously taken me literally and had wasted no time at all.

"What are we gonna do, Darrell?" the guys asked. "How are we going to get our stuff back?"

"We're not going to get that stuff back," I said. "All that stuff belonged to Rick. We're going to have to get stuff of our own." I looked around at the 15 guys who had been working together all year. "I believe in you guys," I said. "I believe you can do anything you set your mind to. And if you decide to build a whole new racing company in twelve weeks, I believe you can do it."

"Let's do it," the guys said unanimously. "Where do we start?"

CHAPTER THIRTEEN

THE OWNER-DRIVER YEARS

Other teams relaxed after the 1990 season, but our team worked night and day through the Thanksgiving and Christmas holidays and on into the new year. In less than 90 days we outfitted the shop with new tools and equipment, purchased and outfitted a hauler, and built four new race cars from scratch. In February our Western Auto Race Team showed up at Daytona ready to compete.

I might have notched my second consecutive victory in the Daytona 500 if circumstances hadn't intervened. I was leading the race with only 12 laps to go, and I'd saved enough fuel to reach the finish line. Since everybody else would have to pit for gas, we would win the race on fuel mileage unless a caution gave the other guys a chance to refuel. Sure enough, the caution lights came on. Two laps later we were bunched up on the restart, going into the third turn, when Rusty Wallace came up from the apron and hit Kyle Petty, knocking Kyle into me and causing all three of us to wreck.

It didn't matter. We left Daytona knowing that we had looked like a race team, we had functioned like a race team, and we were competitive. Our sponsor was delighted, and our morale was sky-high. As the owner of an underdog team, I was having more fun than I'd had in years.

We were competitive all year, finishing 17 times in the top ten. We won at Wilkesboro, making 1991 the first year since 1964 that the first seven races of the season were won by seven different drivers. We won at Pocono, where a caution flag came out because a chicken tried to cross the track. Dale Earnhardt won the championship in 1991, the fifth championship of his career. We ended the season eighth in the points, a solid showing for a first-year team.

On Christmas morning Stevie gave me a love poem she had composed. It was a beautiful expression of affection, sketched on fine paper in her perfect handwriting, and it made me wish I had written something for her.

"Well?" Stevie looked at me expectantly as I laid the poem down.

"I love you too," I said.

Stevie looked disappointed, so I picked the poem up again to see what I had missed. "This line, here," I said, pointing to the paper, "*You'll become the father of two in 1992.* You're talking about the Daytona 500, right? I'm going to win again?"

"No, you dolt," Stevie said, snatching the paper out of my hand. "I'm pregnant! You're going to be a father again!"

I was floored. After Jessica was born in 1987, the doctor told us that there was virtually no chance that we would ever have another child. The possibility that I might become a father again had never even entered my mind. "Are you sure?" I asked.

Stevie nodded. "Absolutely. I'm due in August."

I kissed Stevie and held her tight, my mind whirling. I would be the father of *two* kids now, a bona fide family guy, an average American dad. The implications of that responsibility were sobering.

The birth of Sarah Kaitlin on August 25, 1992, was the high point in another great year for the Waltrips. I won three races in 1992 and finished the season ninth in the points. The Western Auto team was starting to hit on all cylinders.

The last race of the 1992 season was the finale for one legendary NASCAR Cup career and the beginning of another. Richard Petty piloted his #43 Pontiac around the Atlanta Motor Speedway for the very last time, finishing four places behind a dark-haired 21-year-old Californian named Jeff Gordon, who was driving for Hendrick Motorsports. In the years ahead Gordon would become Dale Earnhardt's new nemesis.

Earnhardt finished 12th in the points in 1992, only the second time since 1979 that he had finished out of the top ten.

After five wins in my first two years as an owner-driver, I was confident about my prospects for 1993. "I can't believe I waited so long to go out on my own," I told Stevie. "I should have been doing this all along."

Determined to become even more competitive, I looked around for another way to take charge of my own destiny. I decided to start my own engine program.

I had been leasing my engines from Rick Hendrick, paying him $1 million a year for motors that would never belong to me. Starting my own engine program would be expensive, I knew. The equipment alone would cost about $1 million, and I would need to hire a team of six expert engine builders. Then I would have to buy parts and pieces for the 20 or 30 engines we would need for a whole year. I ended up spending $2.5 million just to get the engine program started, and that took a big bite out of what I had to spend for the year.

In my eagerness to become self-sufficient, I had neglected to consider a couple of important facts about starting an engine program. First, no new program is going to be as good as one that has been running for a while. It takes time to get the kinks worked out, and we did not have any time. We needed these engines immediately. Second, when it came time to order parts for repair, our little operation did not carry the clout of a big-time engine builder. Hendrick Motorsports was ordering 100 camshafts or cylinder heads at a time, while we were ordering three. As a result suppliers tended to put our order at the bottom of the list.

Our first engines were reliable enough, but they had no power, so although I finished 13th in the points, I didn't win a single race in 1993. As the season wore on I could tell that some of my crew members were getting discouraged. I assured them that if we would just keep focused on improving our engines we would soon be winning again, but my guys had been working their hearts out for two solid years and some of them were tired. Predictably a few of my key people left in 1993, accepting offers from more successful teams.

Jeff Gordon, who won no races in 1993 but finished 11 times in the top ten, was named Rookie of the Year. Dale Earnhardt won the championship, his sixth, by an 80-point margin over Rusty Wallace.

On February 11, 1994, during the first practice session for the Daytona 500, Neil Bonnett's car blew a tire in the fourth turn at the Daytona International Speedway. The car abruptly swerved and slammed into the wall head-on, killing Bonnett instantly.

Neil had been my teammate during the championship season of 1985, and he was also one of Dale Earnhardt's closest friends; the two blue-collar drivers often fished and hunted together. Bonnett had become a television commentator in 1991, after a horrifying crash at Darlington forced him to retire from racing, but he never lost his desire to drive. Earnhardt had hired Neil to test cars for him in 1992, and when Bonnett was finally cleared to race again in 1993, Dale persuaded Richard Childress to give him a ride at Talladega. Neil had wrecked spectacularly in that race, going airborne and almost breaching the spectator fence, but his performance was good enough to win him a sponsor for at least six races in the 1994 season.

Now, suddenly, the affable Bonnett was gone. All of NASCAR was stunned by his death, but no one was more devastated than Dale. When Stevie and I met the Earnhardts at the private memorial service two days after the accident, Dale was more subdued than I had ever seen him.

The next day the Daytona International Speedway claimed another life. Rodney Orr, the reigning Goody's Dash series champion, was making a mock qualifying run for the upcoming race when his Ford Thunderbird spun and went airborne, smashing into the retaining wall and catch-fence in turn 2 roof-first at more than 175 miles per hour. Orr succumbed to massive chest and head injuries.

The mood was somber on the morning of the Daytona 500 when Stevie walked onto pit road before the race to give me my scripture. This was a ritual she had been following for several years. She prayed faithfully for me every morning during her personal devotions, and she was always on the lookout for a Bible verse that seemed especially appropriate for the week. When she found that special verse, she would copy it onto a 3-by-5 card and give it to me on Sunday morning. On this morning Earnhardt came walking toward my car just as Stevie was taping the card onto the dashboard.

"What's that?" Dale asked, pointing to the card.

"A scripture," Stevie said, pulling the card out and holding it up so Dale could see it. "I give one of these to Darrell every week."

"Where's mine?"

Stevie smiled tentatively. "Really?"

"Really."

"You want one?"

"I want one."

"I'll be right back." Stevie rushed back to her purse, retrieved her little Bible, and flipped through the pages while praying for inspiration. A verse quickly caught her eye. She didn't have another card, so she wrote the scripture on a piece of duct tape and ran back to pit road.

Dale was waiting beside his car when Stevie arrived. He took the tape and read what she had written on it, then nodded. "Thanks," he said, and reached inside the car to place it on the dash. Then he gave Stevie a hug and hoisted himself through the window.

That scene would be repeated week after week throughout the 1994 season, and in every year that followed. For the rest of his career Dale Earnhardt would not leave pit road until my wife had brought him his verse.

*   *   *

I did not win a single race in 1994, but I still managed to finish ninth in the points, right behind Jeff Gordon. Gordon won his first race, the Coca-Cola 600, at the Charlotte Motor Speedway on May 29, 1994, and was so overcome by the enormity of the accomplishment that he broke down and cried in Victory Circle. Earnhardt, who won his seventh and last championship that year, mocked Gordon's open display of emotion. He started referring to the young media darling as "Wonder Boy," and at the awards banquet in New York at the end of the year he toasted Gordon with a bottle of milk.

Since he had captured four championships in the previous five years, Dale Earnhardt was heavily favored to win again in 1995. One man stood between him and the all-time record for total championships: Jeff Gordon. There were other stories in NASCAR in 1995, of course, but the battle between Earnhardt and Gordon turned out to be the most compelling of the year.

In May I found myself in the middle of the battle. We were at the Winston, the Saturday-night all-star race at the Charlotte Motor Speedway. The race is run in three segments. I finished third in the first segment and second in the second segment, almost catching Gordon at the end. When the field was set for the final segment, the ten-lap shootout, Gordon had the pole position, I was on the outside pole, and Earnhardt was in the third position, right behind Gordon. I knew my car was at least as fast as Gordon's. Passing would be difficult, but if I could jump in front of him when the green flag fell I could outrun him and win the race.

As we came around for the start of the sprint, I anticipated the flag and got a little break, jumping in front of Gordon and beating him to the first turn. I held my breath, hoping that the officials would not order a restart. But they did. The caution lights came on, and the field was set again. If I jumped the start a second time, I would be sent to the rear.

I was careful on the restart, and Gordon and I went into the

174

first turn side by side. We came out of turn 2 together and surged down the back straightaway door to door, battling for advantage. As we approached the third turn, I suddenly caught a glimpse of Earnhardt out of the corner of my eye. Behind the wheel of the car I called the Silver Bullet, Earnhardt was barreling down the inside, sparks flying. Gordon and I were still neck-and-neck, me on the outside, and I knew there was no way that Earnhardt, Gordon, and I could make it through the corner three abreast. I figured I was in a pretty good position. If I sailed the outside, Gordon would probably drop down to block Dale, allowing me to take the lead.

Gordon, however, was smart enough to see a different scenario, and when we got to the corner, he checked up. I went into the turn about a mile over my head, and Dale went into the corner a mile over his head too because he was trying to clear Gordon. Dale lost control of his car and came up the track, body-slamming me and driving my car into the fence. It was one of the hardest licks I had ever taken in my life. My car spun down the front straightaway, finally coming to rest in the infield in front of the grandstand. The breath had been knocked out of me, and I was so angry that I didn't realize I was hurt. I wanted to kill Earnhardt.

When I recovered my breath, I went looking for Dale. "What the hell were you thinking?" I shouted, when I found him.

"Go away and leave me alone," Dale said. "I'm wrecked, you're wrecked, and Wonder Boy won the race." That was a common exchange for Dale and me. We'd both rather wreck each other than see the other one win.

I had left the track and was on my way back to the shop when I realized that something was wrong. My right arm was numb. I couldn't lift it, and my ribs were hurting.

On Monday morning I went to see a doctor. The doctor told me to exercise my arm. He gave me a rubber band and showed me how to hook it over my foot and pull. I couldn't do it. The next day I went over to the big hospital in Charlotte for an MRI. The scan showed that I had three broken ribs under my collarbone. The fractures were in the back, under my shoulder blade—one of the most painful injuries you can get.

On Wednesday I went to the track to practice. I got into the car and cranked the engine, but when I reached over to push the shifter down to slip it into reverse, I couldn't move it. I took both hands and pushed the shifter down, then tried to turn the wheel with my right hand. I couldn't even lift my arm. Undeterred, I got the car into first gear and drove out onto the track. I got up to speed and went into the first turn and almost blacked out. The pain was excruciating. I almost hit the wall.

I managed to make it back to the garage, where Jeff Hammond was looking concerned. "What's wrong?" he asked.

"I can't drive the car," I said. "I'm hurt."

Hammond was furious. "Why did you wait until now to tell me you can't drive the car?" he demanded.

"Well, I didn't know I couldn't drive the car until just now."

"I'm going to get Doc Brewer," Hammond said.

Tom "Doc" Brewer is a medical doctor who also raced in NASCAR's Baby Grand series, and Doc often helped drivers with various medical issues. He soon arrived with his uniform tied around his waist and a wad of chewing tobacco under his lip. He looked me over and said, "I know what to do. Stay here. I'll be back."

Doc got into his rental car and drove to a nearby hospital for a syringe and some numbing medicine. He almost got arrested by security, but he was finally able to convince the hospital staff that he was a doctor. When he returned, he was carrying a huge needle. He pulled my shoulder up, stuck the needle in, and emptied the syringe. In a few minutes I could move my arm well enough to drive. I went out and qualified seventh.

On Sunday night I drove until the first caution, then turned the car over to Jimmy Hensley, who finished 18th. The next week we went to Dover, where Jimmy relieved me again and finished 20th. I was out of the car for the next couple of weeks before crashing again in Michigan, aggravating my injury.

Race teams are fragile; they run on emotion. In racing, the

highs are never as high as the lows are low. When you hit the skids, people naturally start looking for explanations. The talk on the track was that I was hurt and scared, that I didn't want to drive and would never be the same again. My crew members were starting to look for other jobs.

During this trying period I got a lot of encouragement from Max Helton, the pastor who headed up Motor Racing Outreach. In the years since 1987, when Stevie and I had been instrumental in getting the ministry going, MRO had developed into a traveling "home church" for a lot of drivers and their families. Max was a dynamic personality and a cool guy, a former go-kart racer from California, and he slipped easily into our lives. I could see some symmetry in Max's arrival. I had lost my first spiritual mentor when Dr. Cooper had moved to California to start a new church. I had felt that loss acutely, but then Max Helton had come from California to fill the void.

In October 1995 I was on the last lap at Rockingham, running in sixth place, when Ricky Craven, a hotshot rookie from Maine, bumped me in the fourth turn, sending me up the track and into the wall, hard. I sat in my ruined car, dazed, and watched Craven cross the finish line. I couldn't believe it—that stupid Yankee had wrecked me to finish *sixth*!

When I finally caught my breath, I unstrapped all my gear, threw my helmet down, and started running down the track after Ricky Craven. The cars were lined up to go into the garage area, and Craven could see me coming. When I reached his car, I jerked the window net down, grabbed him by his helmet, spun him around, and wheezed, "Don't get out of that car, because as soon as I catch my breath I'm going to whip your ass!" Several bystanders restrained me, and my crew dragged me over to my truck to cool down.

Fifteen minutes later I was in the front of my hauler, in the driver's lounge, changing my clothes and getting hotter by the minute. That idiot Craven had wrecked my car and cost me the finish! Who did he think he was? I decided I would go back and finish the job.

I had pulled on my shoes and was just about to leave the hauler when Max Helton stepped inside and closed the door. "I can't let you do this," Max said. "You're making a fool of yourself."

"Get out of my way, Max," I said. "I've made up my mind. I'm going to defend myself and my team."

Max stood in the doorway. "Think about it for a minute. Is it a good testimony for you to be running around in the garage area looking for somebody to whoop up on?"

"Out of my way," I repeated, moving toward the door. "This is something I have to do."

Max raised both arms. He stood in the doorway like he was hanging on a cross. "If you've gotta hit somebody," he said, "hit me. Just go ahead and knock the fire out of me right now if that'll make you feel better."

I stood there for a moment, my fists knotted, while Max braced for the blow. Suddenly the whole scene struck me as ridiculous, and Max's invitation—"If you've gotta hit somebody, *hit me*"— seemed like the funniest thing I had ever heard. I cracked up, and soon Max was laughing too. We howled until we were both gasping for breath.

"You're right," I said, wiping the tears from my eyes. "That would be a stupid thing to do. Thanks for stopping me."

"You're welcome," Max said. "Any time."

The next race, in Phoenix, was the second-to-last race of the season. On Sunday morning I went to the drivers' meeting with my crew, and when the meeting ended I stayed behind for the chapel service. Many of the other drivers stayed too, along with wives and crew members. The service, led by Max, had become an important part of our Sunday-morning routine.

Max started every service by asking a driver to come to the front and pray. My brother Michael was supposed to pray that morning, but when it came time to start the meeting, Michael still hadn't shown up. Max walked over to where I was sitting and whispered in my ear. "It looks like your brother isn't going to make it," he said. "Would you mind doing the opening prayer?"

"I'd be happy to," I said.

When Max called my name, I walked to the front and turned to face the crowd. There were about 100 people in the room, maybe more, but one face immediately caught my attention. Ricky Craven was sitting in the front row, and he was looking at me with an expression that said I was the biggest hypocrite in the world.

I stood there for a second, considering what I should do. Praying like nothing had happened just didn't seem right. "I've gotta do something before I pray," I said. "Ricky, will you come up here please?"

Ricky looked at me warily and reluctantly rose to his feet. When he got to the front, I put my arm around him and looked him in the eye. "I'm sorry about what happened last week," I said. "Will you forgive me?"

Ricky hugged me. "I will," he said. "You've always been my hero, and I'm sorry about what happened too."

Afterward I felt like God had orchestrated that whole scene. I hadn't expected to pray that morning, and I certainly hadn't known that Ricky Craven would be sitting in the front row when I did. God had set it up, giving me a chance to make amends for a serious mistake.

Jeff Gordon won the season championship in 1995, despite a late-season charge from Dale Earnhardt. At the awards banquet at the end of the year, Gordon toasted Earnhardt with a flute of milk.

I don't know exactly what happened, but sometime between the 1995 season and the 1996 season somebody flipped a switch. Overnight, it seemed, the cost of fielding a NASCAR team tripled. What had cost $3 million in 1995 suddenly cost $9 million. Salaries shot way up, and all the best people began to drift toward deep-pocket owners like Rick Hendrick and Jack Roush and Richard Childress. A little guy like me couldn't keep up.

Dale Earnhardt was still keeping up, but on July 28, 1996, he slammed into the wall at Talladega during the Diehard 500, cracking his sternum and breaking his clavicle. Two weeks later he climbed behind the wheel at Watkins Glen and astonished the world by capturing the pole for the Watkins Glen International road race.

The day after the Watkins Glen event, I flew to Michigan, along with Dale and Teresa Earnhardt, to compete in an International Race of Champions race. Dale and I both owned King Air turboprops at the time, but on this occasion we were traveling on a NASCAR airplane. After we had taken off, Teresa turned to Dale and said, "This plane sounds completely different from ours."

"That's because it's a jet," Dale said.

"I like this sound better," Teresa said. "Let's get one of these." Within weeks Dale had purchased a Lear jet.

Dale had arranged for a massage therapist to help him with rehab on his cracked sternum. When we got to the drivers' lounge at the Michigan International Speedway, the therapist was there with her chair. She worked on Dale, and when she had finished Dale pointed at me. "Now work on him," he said.

I didn't know Becky, and she didn't know me. She had been referred to Dale by an orthopedic doctor; she didn't know anything about racing. I told her that a couple of my ribs were hurting, so she got me up in the chair and manipulated them back into place. Boy, did that feel good!

From then on, Dale had Becky come to every race. After she'd worked on him, she would work on me. Word spread, and she eventually wound up treating several drivers every weekend. Today she's a regular member of the NASCAR family, married to Tony Stewart's spotter, Bob Jeffries.

When we sent out invitations to a dinner and press conference to be held at a downtown Charlotte hotel in January, the people who received our mysterious invitation naturally assumed I was planning to announce my retirement, and when the appointed date arrived they came to Charlotte in droves to show their support. Looking out over the ballroom on the night of the dinner, it seemed to me that all of NASCAR's luminaries had shown up. Bill France was there, along with Humpy Wheeler, Bruton Smith, David Pearson, and a host of others. Cameramen were standing shoulder-to-shoulder along the walls, and there were satellite trucks in the parking lot.

When the meal was over I went to the stage to make my announcement. There were two cars on the stage, both of them shrouded. In my best ringmaster voice I ordered the first car to be unveiled. It was the Mercury Cyclone I had driven in 1972, and the crowd responded to the sight of it with a warm round of applause. Then, to a drum roll, I unveiled the second car: the Darrell Waltrip Silver Anniversary Special, a Monte Carlo Elite that was *all chrome*! I expected some oohs and ahhs, since nobody had ever seen an all-chrome car before, but a dead silence fell across the room instead, as the crowd suddenly realized that Darrell Waltrip was *not* retiring. The TV people lowered their cameras. Folks shook their heads and got up to leave. That evening may have been the biggest let-down in the history of the sport. Looking back, I think I missed a great opportunity to retire.

With 12 laps to go, Dale Earnhardt was locked in a four-way battle for the lead in the 1997 Daytona 500 when he made contact with Ernie Irvan on the backstretch. Earnhardt's car nosed into the wall, then flipped and went tumbling down the track. After the wreck Earnhardt refused to be taken to the infield care center. He got back into his crumpled car, which had landed upright on all four tires, and drove it to the garage for repairs. He then returned to the track and completed the race, finishing in 31st place. Jeff Gordon took the checkered flag to become the youngest winner in the history of the Daytona 500.

That year would turn out to be another disappointing season on the track for our team, but at least it would be profitable.

Sales of souvenirs such as die-cast cars, collectible books and videos, limited-edition posters, playing cards, and even a commemorative Winchester rifle were brisk. We made enough money on merchandise that year to keep the team going. It was the final year of my sponsorship deal, and toward the end of the season Western Auto let me know that they would not be coming back. I would have to find a new sponsor.

Our search for a new sponsor went into high gear. Pennzoil expressed serious interest, and we spent a lot of time and money painting a car with Pennzoil graphics. Suddenly, however, our negotiations stalled. When the Pennzoil executives canceled a meeting we had scheduled to finalize the deal, I got suspicious. It turned out that Earnhardt had invited them out for the day on his boat, *Sunday Money*. Earnhardt got that deal.

The marketing company we were working with told us that the television show *America's Most Wanted* was interested in sponsoring a car, so we painted up a car with *America's Most Wanted* graphics, shipped it to New York, and parked it in front of the building where the show was being shot. It turned out that none of the show's decision makers had ever heard about the NASCAR idea, much less endorsed it, and they were definitely not interested.

At the final hour Speed Block showed up. Nobody seemed to know much about this company, except that they were based in Cincinnati and were introducing a new way to build homes quickly and cheaply with a proprietary concrete block system that had been developed in Europe. As it was described to me, the company would be selling turnkey homes through top home-builders and major building-supply retailers such as Builder's Square and Home Depot. Speed Block was guaranteeing me only $2 million a year, but they were promising a commission on every sale, making the deal potentially worth $10 million a year. It was risky, but at least it was a deal. I signed.

The NASCAR media tour was scheduled to come to our shop in January. As we did every year, we would put on a breakfast for the media, unveil the car, talk about the upcoming season, and make a pitch for our sponsor. I hadn't received any money from the new sponsor yet, but we painted up the cars and hauler with Speed Block graphics and ordered new uniforms for the team. I wanted to make sure we looked first-class.

On the morning of the event the owner of Speed Block walked into our shop for the first time, followed by a couple of his cronies. I had never met the guy before, and the moment we shook hands I sensed that we were in trouble. The guy obviously didn't know a thing about racing, and when he talked about his company I couldn't shake the feeling that he wasn't telling the whole truth. It was too late to back out of the deal, though. We were the Speed Block team now, for better or worse, and the cameras were rolling.

I expected the owner of Speed Block to bring a check to the breakfast, since the terms of our contract required his company to pay us $500,000 before the season started, but he never produced an envelope. I raised the subject as he was leaving, and he snapped his fingers. "We'll mail it," he said.

Weeks passed. No check. On the first of February, as we were leaving for Speedweeks, we called Speed Block to inquire about the money. "We'll send it to Daytona," they promised. For the next two weeks we watched the mail every day, but no check arrived. Finally, on the Friday before the Daytona 500, Speed Block answered one of my phone calls. "We're cutting the check right now," they said. "We're sending it by FedEx. You'll have it in the morning."

The check arrived on Saturday morning as promised, but when I opened the envelope I found that the check was made out for $50,000, not $500,000. Also, since the check had arrived after the banks had closed for the weekend, I would not be able to deposit it until the Monday after the race.

Dale Earnhardt had won 30 races at the Daytona International Speedway over the span of his 20-year career, more than any other driver, but he had never won the Daytona 500. This year he led the race for 107 laps. With less than two laps to go, he was fending off a late charge by pole-sitter Bobby Labonte when an accident farther back in the field caused the race to end under caution. Dale had won! Mike Joy called it "the most anticipated victory in the history of NASCAR," and as Dale rolled toward Victory Circle, every member of every team came out onto pit road to congratulate him.

I had finished the race in 33rd place, four laps down, earning $82,005 in prize money. On Monday morning we took the $50,000 check from Speed Block to the bank, only to be told that it was worthless. There was no money in the account.

This was bad. When I got home from Daytona I took another look at our books and confirmed that I was spending $600,000 a month to keep the team going. That staggering sum was coming out of my own pocket, where supplies were extremely limited. I continued to fund the team through the next three races, while trying without success to force Speed Block to honor their contract.

I was between a rock and a hard place, and I was scared. In just four months I had spent about $2.5 million of my own money—*my own money*—and things had only gotten worse. For the first time in my life a business venture I had launched was in serious trouble. I could see bankruptcy on the horizon. Other owner-drivers I knew had gone broke: Bobby Allison, Cale Yarborough, and Buddy Baker, to name just three. Even if I managed to retain my current assets, the value of those assets was declining by the day. NASCAR had just approved a new small-block Chevrolet engine, thereby making the 40 SB-2 engines in my shop obsolete. The cost of the engine upgrade alone would be about $1.5 million, and it would not be enough to keep us competitive. My cars were outdated too. I needed new cars *and* new engines, and I didn't have the money for either.

The next race was Darlington. I still had not received a dime from Speed Block, and my attorney, Ed Silva, advised me that racing at Darlington without the Speed Block logo on my car would violate the contract and give the sponsor an excuse never to pay me. "Yeah, but they're not paying me anyway," I said. I had come up with a better idea.

Stevie and I had become close friends with one of NASCAR's old-time drivers, Tim Flock, and his wife, Frances. Tim had competed in NASCAR's very first Strictly Stock event back in 1949, finishing fifth, and had gone on to win the Grand National Championship in 1952 and 1955. In fact Tim had won 21 percent of the races in which he competed, the highest winning percentage of any driver in NASCAR history. A natural showman, he drove his Fabulous Hudson Hornet to victory at the Hickory Motor Speedway in 1952 with a codriver, a Rhesus monkey named Jocko Flocko. Now Tim was in the hospital, fighting a losing battle with lung and liver cancer, and Frances was in dire financial straits. She was facing the loss of her husband, and she had no insurance to cover the mounting medical expenses. Our troubles were serious, certainly, but her problems were worse, and I wanted to help her.

Since it made absolutely no sense to continue advertising for a sponsor who would never pay me, I decided to run my last race as a tribute to Tim Flock. We painted the car white, with "Tim Flock Special" in red lettering on the sides, and we arranged to give proceeds from the sale of a die-cast souvenir version of the car to Frances. I wanted the car to carry the number 300, but Bill France would not allow a three-digit number on the track, so I entered the Tim Flock Special at Darlington carrying #17 instead. I finished 30th in my final race as an owner-driver, and sales of the #300 die-cast version of the car netted Frances a tidy sum. I was done, but at least I'd helped someone else in the end.

On the Monday morning after Darlington, I called Rick Hendrick to ask whether he knew anybody who wanted to buy a race team. Rick laughed and said, "In this economy? Are you kidding?" I told him I was as serious as a heart attack. Rick listened sympathetically as I described my dilemma, and then he said, "Let me think about it."

Later that afternoon Rick called back. "I was talking to the guys," he said, "and they remembered somebody who has talked about wanting to own a race team or get involved with one. His name is Tim Beverly. He's an airplane dealer from Tyler, Texas. Would you like me to call him?"

"Heck, yeah," I said. "Call him up!"

Rick phoned back a few minutes later. "Beverly's interested," he said. "When I told him that Darrell Waltrip wants to sell his team, he said he'd fly up in the morning to meet you. I suggest you show him around your shop, then bring him over to my place so we can talk."

Tim Beverly's Falcon 20 business jet landed at the Concord airport the next morning, and the Texan strode across the tarmac in his calfskin boots and Stetson to shake my hand. Beverly told me that his company, Tyler Jet, was the biggest purveyor of business aircraft in the world. His specialty was refurbishing planes and reselling them. It was clear to me that he didn't know anything about racing, but he nodded approvingly when he saw my immaculate shop, the well-kept inventory of cars and engines, our gleaming and perfectly organized hauler. Afterward I drove him over to Rick's house, and Rick sat down to explain the costs and demands of racing to him.

When we were back in the car, Tim suddenly turned to me said, "So what do you want for your deal?"

I kept my eyes on the road. "Four-point-eight million," I said.

Beverly punched me on the shoulder, stuck out his hand and said, "You've got a deal!" I instantly wished I'd said $6.8 million, but it was too late.

"How soon do you want to make the transfer?" Beverly asked.

"Tomorrow would be fine with me."

We went back to my shop and worked out the terms of the deal. Beverly's new racing company, Tyler Jet Motorsports, would take ownership of my company, DarWal, Inc., assuming our debt and paying me the balance of our agreed purchase price in cash. I would drive for Tyler Jet Motorsports for the rest of the year.

As I signed the letter of intent, I felt an enormous weight lift from my shoulders. Stevie and I would not be going bankrupt after all. Becoming an owner in 1991 had been the biggest blunder of my career, but I'd learned the lesson, and it was over.

CHAPTER FOURTEEN

TOWARD THE FINISH LINE

On the Monday after Darlington, I received a phone call from the Bahamas. My brother Michael had flown down there with Earnhardt after the race to go fishing, and he was calling to alert me that my name had come up in a conversation he'd just had with Dale.

Although Earnhardt still drove for Richard Childress, he had started his own Winston Cup team, with Pennzoil as the sponsor and Steve Park as the driver. Park, a rookie, had crashed during testing in Atlanta, breaking a leg. He would be out of commission for several months. As Earnhardt and my brother relaxed together on the deck of his boat, Earnhardt had asked Michael what I was planning to do now that I'd sold my team. "I need somebody to drive my car," Dale had said. "If I asked Darrell, I guarantee he wouldn't do it."

"Look," Michael whispered on the telephone, "if Dale called and asked you to drive his car, you wouldn't be stupid enough to tell him no, would you?"

"I guess not," I said. "But what makes you think he's going to do that?"

"He's going to call you in the morning. Act like you're surprised, and just say yes."

The next morning about 50 guys were gathered in the garage below my office for a Bible study, a meeting I had hosted every Tuesday morning for years. I asked them to pray for me. I explained to the guys that I had promised to finish out the year driving for my old team, but I was facing a potential conflict:

another owner might be interested in hiring me. Two owners might want me, but I could drive for only one of them.

As I was talking, Stevie came halfway down the stairs and called my name. "Darrell! Tim Beverly's on the phone."

"I've got something I need to talk to you about," Beverly said when I picked up the receiver in my office. "We've done an inventory here in Charlotte, looked the place over, and we've decided that we're not ready to race. We need to shut this thing down for about three or four months, rebuild everything, and start all over. How would you feel about that?"

"Oh, I don't know, Tim," I said. Not driving would mean no points or purse money, and I was starting to doubt that Earnhardt would actually call.

"I'll still pay you, of course," Beverly said. "We just don't need to go to the track with what we've got. Is that okay?"

I paused. "I'll think about it and call you back," I said.

I went back downstairs and told the guys what had happened. A few minutes later Stevie hollered down again. This time it was Dale on the phone.

"I've got a problem," Dale said. "I need your help."

That simple statement stunned me. I had expected that if Dale approached me at all with the offer of a job, he would be casual about it, or even condescending.

"I need you to drive my car for three or four months while Steve Park gets well," Dale said. "Would you be interested in doing it?"

"Yes I would," I replied. "I'd be honored."

"Good. One problem, though. Bristol's coming up, and my inventory is pretty thin. My car is not really a good short-track car."

"I think I know where I can get one," I said.

I called Tim Beverly back and told him I could accept a layoff because I had been offered a temporary job with another team. Then I reminded him that his new team had already prepared a car for the Bristol race. I suggested that since he'd decided not to enter the race himself, he should think about leasing that car to Dale. Tim liked the idea, so I gave him Earnhardt's number and they worked out the deal. I wound up driving my old car at Bristol, but with Earnhardt's paint scheme and the Pennzoil logo on it.

Years later, Ty Norris, who was the general manager of Dale Earnhardt Inc. (DEI) when Dale Earnhardt hired me, explained the rationale behind Dale's decision. Earnhardt's fledgling team was in trouble. They had missed a few races, and were ranked 32nd in the points. Their sponsor, Pennzoil, was very unhappy, and Dale was afraid that his sponsorship deal might unravel. When Dale announced that his temporary driver would be three-time champion Darrell Waltrip, the sponsor responded enthusiastically, and his team got a new lease on life. The irony of this situation was not lost on Earnhardt. During the helicopter ride from his home in Concord to the racetrack in Bristol, Tennessee, Dale turned to Ty and said, "Can you believe it? I spent half my life trying to wreck that son-of-a-bitch, and now he's driving my car!"

Dale had assembled a cast of talented professionals for his start-up team, including Philippe Lopez as crew chief and Derrick Finley as engineer. Kevin "Bono" Manion, who would later become the crew chief for Jamie McMurray at DEI, was on the crew, as was Chad Knaus, who would go on to become famous as Jimmy Johnson's crew chief. Working with this team revitalized me. Lots of people had written me off as too old, too scared, too hurt, or too complacent to compete again, but Earnhardt and his boys were happy to have me on board, and they let me know that they still believed in me. I drove in 14 races for DEI and almost won three of them. Then August arrived, and it was time to turn the Pennzoil car back over to Steve Park and fulfill my commitment to finish out the year with Tim Beverly.

Beverly had signed a sponsorship deal with Tabasco, a relationship that would end quickly in a flurry of lawsuits, with allegations that Beverly and his associates had billed the sponsor for fraudulent racing expenses. Beverly himself would become the focus of a massive federal investigation, and would eventually plead guilty to charges of fraud and money-laundering in connection with his airplane business. In 2005 he was sentenced to six years in prison and ordered to pay more than $18 million in restitution to banks for airplane improvements that were never made.

One day in mid-September Dale called me at home, bursting with news. He had just signed the biggest sponsorship contract of his career. "Budweiser's payin' us ten million a year for five years!" Dale crowed. "That's fifty million damn dollars! Can you believe it?"

"Unbelievable!" I said. "Who's going to drive the car?"

"They want Junior. That's the deal. The kid'll run five Cup races next year and a full schedule after that."

I was not surprised. In his first full year on the Busch circuit, Dale Earnhardt Jr. was on his way to winning the series championship, a feat he would repeat the following year. I felt a twinge of nostalgia, remembering my own days as a hotshot young talent. "Well, if you ever need a backup driver, I'm available," I said.

Dale's voice grew sharp. "Why are you still doing this?" he demanded.

"Doing what?"

"You know what I'm talkin' about. Going out there every week and takin' chances, competin' against kids half your age. And for what? What are you tryin' to prove? Retire before you— aw hell, before something happens. Get on with the rest of your life."

Bill France Jr. had been saying much the same thing every time he saw me. "Get your ass out of that race car and up in the television booth, Darrell," he would say. "That's where we need you. That's where you can help."

When the 1998 season ended, NASCAR ran an exhibition race in Motegi, Japan, a nonpoints Winston Cup event called the Coca-Cola 500. A number of American drivers, including Jeff Gordon, Dale Earnhardt, and Dale Earnhardt Jr., were scheduled to compete against some of Japan's finest drivers in this race. The

Motegi event would be Junior's first Winston Cup race, and it would also be his first chance to compete head-to-head against his father. The media were fascinated by the match-up.

Dale Jarrett, who had finished third overall in the Cup standings in 1998 in a car owned by Robert Yates, was scheduled to compete at Motegi too, but he wound up undergoing gallbladder surgery. Yates had been my friend for years—we had worked together for both DiGard and Junior Johnson—and when he called to ask whether I would like to drive his car, I naively assumed he was offering me a permanent ride. "What are you going to do with Jarrett?" I asked. "How's he going to feel about it?"

"One race, Darrell," Robert said gently. "I'm hiring you for one race."

The course at Motegi is a mile and a half long, a low-banked oval that is oddly egg-shaped, making turns 3 and 4 much tighter than turns 1 and 2. The Yates #88 car was fast—I qualified third—and I was running well during the race when Bobby Hamilton made a tactical error that knocked us both out of contention. Bobby got a run on me on the back straightaway, then dove into the third turn beneath me going way too fast. Unable to hold the line, he came up the track and slammed into me, knocking me into the wall. Mike Skinner wound up winning that race, his first of the year, edging out Jeff Gordon with the help of a late caution. Dale Earnhardt Jr. and his father finished sixth and eighth, respectively.

After the race Shorty Edwards, one of Jimmy Spencer's crew members, asked me whether I had heard about the Kmart deal. I hadn't heard anything about it. "Travis Carter just signed a sponsorship deal with Kmart," Shorty said. "Travis hasn't named a driver yet. I heard he was considering Rick Mast, but that's only a rumor. You should call him."

I had known Travis Carter since the 1970s, when he had worked as a crew chief for Benny Parsons and Cale Yarborough during their championship seasons. Travis had started his own team in 1990 and had seen spotty success. I called him from the plane.

"I heard you've got a deal with Kmart and you might be looking for a driver," I said, coming straight to the point. "If that's true, I'm interested."

"It's not my deal, exactly," Travis replied. "Carl Haas has the connection with Kmart, but he's never been in NASCAR before, so we're working together. We're going to use my shop, my people, and my cars. I'll manage the team, but the Kmart deal really belongs to Carl. He'll make the final decision about the driver."

I had met Haas a couple of times. An iconic Indy car owner known for the unlit eight-inch Honduran cigar that was perpetually clenched in his teeth, Haas had hoisted trophy after trophy with legendary Formula One drivers like Jackie Stewart and Mario Andretti. His most famous business partner was Paul Newman. Now, it seemed, Haas would be stepping into NASCAR with a new partner, Travis Carter.

When I got home from Japan, I called Carter again. "I'm all for hiring you," Travis told me this time, "but Carl is a little skeptical. You need to call him."

I called the number Travis gave me and spoke with Mr. Haas for several minutes. I told him how much I'd like to drive his car and assured him that I would do a bang-up job. Suddenly Haas interrupted me. "Who the hell is this?" he asked.

"Darrell Waltrip."

Haas grunted. "Darrell? I thought *Michael* was the one who wanted to drive the car."

"No," I said. "It's me. My brother already has a ride. He'll be driving for Jim Mattei next year."

"Well, all right," Haas said. "Darrell Waltrip. That's all right." He grunted again and hung up.

I spent the last two years of my career driving the #66 Kmart Ford for Carter-Haas Motorsports. On a rainy Thursday morning in Indianapolis in early August 1999 I called a press conference to announce that I would make a farewell tour in 2000, then retire. Nobody was surprised.

My plan for 2000 was simple: say good-bye to the fans and sell a boatload of souvenirs at Kmart's thousands of stores. The first part of the plan went swimmingly; at race after race I basked in the affection and best wishes of my loyal fans. The second part of the plan didn't turn out so well, however. Unbeknown to me, our huge sponsor was teetering on the brink of bankruptcy. The merchandise deal I had negotiated with Kmart's racing division suddenly died one day when, in one of those abrupt reorganizations that seems to precede any bankruptcy, all of the Kmart people I'd been dealing with were fired. What I'd hoped would be the Blue Light Special suddenly became the Red Light Special, and I was left holding an empty Kmart bag.

At the end of the 1999 season NASCAR announced an astonishing deal: they had sold the broadcast rights to Fox, NBC, and TBS in a six-year contract worth $467 *million per year*. That staggering figure, more than four times the amount NASCAR had been collecting each year from ESPN, illustrated the rising popularity of the sport. Fox and its cable affiliate FX would broadcast the first half of each season beginning in 2001; NBC and TBS would broadcast the second half. If I were going to make the jump to television, I would have to work for one of these networks.

A few months later I received a phone call from an NBC executive in New York, asking for an appointment. The guy wanted to come down to Tennessee and talk to me about going to work for his network. When I picked him up at the airport, the fellow was wearing sharply pressed jeans and cowboy boots. The jeans looked new, and the boots did too. I liked the guy, but it looked to me like he had dressed up for a visit to a dude ranch.

We rode around Nashville for a while, exchanging pleasantries while I showed him a few of the sights. Then I brought him to the house, where Stevie served us a nice lunch. The fellow was very friendly, and he said highly complimentary things about everything I showed him, but he never raised the subject of a job until we were back in the car, headed for the airport and his four o'clock flight. "Well," he said at last, "I've had a great day. I've enjoyed being with you, but we haven't talked at all about a contract."

"I know," I said. "I thought that's what you came for."

"It is." The guy smiled broadly. "I really like what I've seen today, and I want to make it official. We'd love for you to come to work for us at NBC. So tell me, what would it take? Can you give me a ballpark figure?"

I had been anticipating this question ever since the first phone call, and I had asked a few of my friends in the TV business, including Ken Squier and Terry Bradshaw, for advice. Keeping my eyes on the road, I told him how much I'd like to make. The fellow flinched and grew pale. "There are people at NBC who have been in this business for ten years and don't make that kind of money," he said.

"Well, I feel sorry for those people. I just feel like that's a good place for me to start."

"Most people with your experience would be lucky to start at *half* that."

"Well, that's my number."

We drove the rest of the way to the airport in strained silence. When I pulled up to the curb at Departures, the fellow reached over, shook my hand, and said, "We'll be in touch."

Weeks went by without a word from NBC, and I started to get nervous. What if nobody hired me? I wanted to stay involved with auto racing—that much I knew for sure—and I also knew I didn't have the resources to do so as an owner. Broadcasting would be ideal, but it looked like I had blown my chance to work in that field by overestimating my value to a network that was genuinely interested in me. I debated calling NBC back, but decided against it. Stevie and I continued to pray and wait.

One Monday afternoon Stevie and I were relaxing at the house when the phone rang. A guy with an Australian accent said he was calling from Fox Sports. He wanted to know whether I had made any commitments for the following year. I told him I hadn't. "We should meet," he said. "Why don't you come up to New York so we can talk?"

I was not eager to spend one of my days off on a trip to New York City. The memory of my last such trip to Manhattan, that expensive and fruitless effort to secure a sponsorship from *America's Most Wanted* in 1997, was still fresh in my mind. "I can't," I said. "My plane is in the shop getting painted, so I don't have any way to get there."

"Have you lost your mind?" Stevie said when I hung up the phone. "You need a job, buddy. Call that man back right now and tell him we're coming."

We flew commercial to New York, and David Hill picked us up at LaGuardia in a taxi. The head of Fox Sports turned out to be an ebullient ringmaster with a quick wit and an unparalleled gift for profanity. He greeted me with a crushing handshake, bowed gallantly to Stevie, and said, "I'm going to take you to one of the nicest restaurants in New York, one of my favorites. You'll love it!"

Hill gave the cabbie an address on Fifth Avenue, and when we arrived at the building he ushered us through the doors, across the cavernous lobby, and onto an elevator, where he pressed a top button. When the door opened, a thick wave of smoke billowed toward us, and I heard Stevie stifle a cough. "It's Arnold Schwarzenegger's cigar bar!" Hill said. Before us was a dark-paneled clubroom with arched doorways and a spectacular view of the Manhattan skyline. The place was packed, and every member of the sophisticated clientele, men and women alike, was drinking and smoking a cigar. *Holy crap,* I thought, looking quickly at my teetotaling, nonsmoking wife. *Stevie is not going to go for this at all.*

Hill secured a table at the back of the bar and called for menus, then proceeded to regale Stevie and me with stories about television and his boss, Rupert Murdoch. The more David talked, the more I liked him. By the time dessert arrived, I had decided that David Hill was the Junior Johnson of television, a canny competitor and coach who could take any aspiring talent, Darrell Waltrip included, to the next level of excellence. This man wanted me to work for him, and I realized that I desperately wanted to do it.

Hill spoke directly to Stevie. "I don't want you to think this will be just a Sunday job for Darrell," he said. "Our contract with NASCAR" (he pronounced it NAS-CAH) "is for the first half of the season, so it's only a six-month schedule, but during those six months Darrell will be very busy. We're going to build a team around him. We will expect a lot from your husband, and the job will require a great deal of his time."

I winced. Stevie had made it clear that, whatever I did in retirement, she did not want me to be gone all the time. Hill reached into his pocket, pulled out a couple of folded sheets of paper, and laid them on the table. "Take this home with you," he said. "Read it over, talk about it, and let me know what you think."

I picked up the papers and, before slipping them into my pocket, opened them up and peeked at the bottom of the first page. There was a number there, and it made me smile.

Stevie was delighted. She had liked David Hill too, and, although she understood that the job would demand a lot from me for six months each year, she liked the idea of a six-month off-season. When we got back home I called David Hill and told him that I'd love to work for Fox Sports.

"Who else should we hire?" Hill asked, as soon as the papers were signed. "Who would you like to work with?" I knew exactly who I preferred: Mike Joy to call the races, Larry McReynolds and Jeff Hammond for color. For coverage in the pits, Steve Byrnes, Matt Yocum, and Dick Berggren would be top-notch. Larry was making good money with Richard Childress, serving as Mike Skinner's crew chief. When Larry made it clear that he could not take a pay cut, Fox stepped up and hired him. They did the same for Jeff Hammond, who was working as a crew chief for Roush Racing. Every person I said we needed to hire, David

Hill hired. The only one he signed without asking my opinion was Chris Myers, and that was a no-brainer.

By October 2000 Bobby Labonte was close to clinching the season championship, and Dale Earnhardt was battling Jeff Burton and Dale Jarrett for second place. Earnhardt electrified the fans at Talladega on October 15, surging from 16th place to capture the checkered flag in one of the most memorable victories of his career. That victory would prove to be his last. Earnhardt would end the year as runner-up in the championship race, and Dale Jr. would be named Rookie of the Year.

The skies above the Atlanta Motor Speedway were overcast on the morning of November 20, 2000, as I rolled onto pit road for the last race of my career. Rain spattered across the track, and we waited. Noon passed, and we continued to wait.

I kept an eye on Dale Earnhardt. If NASCAR decided to call the race, Earnhardt would be the first to know. If Dale headed for the exit, all the other drivers would start packing up too.

At around one o'clock Dale sauntered over to my car. "They're callin' the race," he said, "but you can't leave yet. Meet us in the media center."

Dale was in the media room when I arrived, along with Rusty Wallace, Jeff Gordon, and several of the other drivers. The country music singer Billy Ray Cyrus was there too. In a brief ceremony before the television cameras, Jeff presented me with a steering wheel, and some of the other drivers stepped forward with mementos of their own. Dale, with a mischievous grin, gave me a rocking chair.

When the green flag finally waved on the NAPA 500 the following morning, the stands were mostly empty. I finished the race in 34th place. When it was over, all of the teams came out onto pit road and saluted me as I went by.

Afterward I sat in the car, reluctant to climb out of it for the last time. I stayed there for 20 minutes or more, running my fingers across the dash and touching every familiar component in the cockpit while I fought a rising tide of tears. I had expected to feel a certain amount of relief at this moment, but what I felt instead was an aching sense of loss. Racing had been the great joy of my life, the one thing at which I truly excelled. Life on the racetrack had tested and formed me, making me into the man I had become. Who would I be without it?

Stevie reached through the window and touched my arm. "Darrell? The guys want to load the car now."

In the privacy of the drivers' lounge, I removed my uniform and got dressed in my street clothes. I placed my helmet in its bag for the last time, pulled the zipper closed, and then sat down on the sofa and looked at it a while.

The door opened, and Stevie poked her head inside. "You ready, honey?"

I drew a deep breath and rose to my feet.

"Ready as I'll ever be," I said.

More than two weeks had passed since my retirement, and I was depressed. I certainly did not want to travel to New York to attend the annual NASCAR awards banquet, as Stevie and my business manager, Van Colley, were urging me to do. What would be the point? I had finished the season 36th in the points, more than 3,000 points behind Bobby Labonte, and, oh yes, I had *retired*. I was done. Finished. That meant I could stay home, didn't it? Stevie and Van were insistent, however, and I finally relented.

Seated in the sumptuous Grand Ballroom of the Waldorf Astoria Hotel, I was shocked when Bill France Jr. arrived. The aging head of NASCAR had been out of the public eye for months, undergoing treatment for lung cancer. I'd last seen him shortly after he was diagnosed, when I'd made a special trip to Daytona Beach to visit him because I'd been told he might have only days to live. That had been a tender moment. Lying against a pillow in Halifax Hospital, a frail France had told me he was proud of me, and he'd urged me again to move from the driver's seat to the broadcast booth. He'd held my hand as I prayed with him. That visit had felt like good-bye, but here he was in New York City, sitting alertly in a wheelchair, as Mike Helton, the new president of NASCAR, took the stage.

As it turned out, Bill France had traveled to New York because he wanted to witness the presentation of a special award, the prestigious Bill France Award of Excellence. This award was given from time to time to recognize a superior contribution to motor racing, and tonight it was being presented to me. I looked at Stevie, momentarily confused. Could I have heard correctly? She was beaming, and Van was grinning and motioning toward the stage. The room echoed with roars of approval as I rose to my feet and stumbled through the standing crowd to the platform. Dale Earnhardt clapped me on the shoulder as I went by.

A fresh wave of applause broke across the room as I accepted the award. When the ovation had finally died away, I looked out at the faces of friends and former rivals, and I realized that these people had actually become my family. We were a fractious and competitive family, to be sure, but we were family nonetheless, and our mutual affection was real. Suddenly I was at a loss for words.

CHAPTER FIFTEEN

THE UNTHINKABLE

If you've ever been in a bad wreck, you probably have a hole in your memory, a blank spot that begins right before impact and ends when you wake up on the ground or in the hospital. I know I do. Witnesses could describe my wrecks to me afterward, and if cameras were running when the accident occurred (as they usually were) I could review the pictures days later, but my own brain would refuse to yield a coherent independent memory, almost as though it was trying to protect me from the trauma. Come to think of it, Stevie experienced the same thing after childbirth. She couldn't remember the worst parts, so she was willing to go through it again.

Millions of race fans around the world still remember the day Dale Earnhardt died; they can tell you exactly where they were and what they were doing when it happened. Dale's death was a pivotal point in history that arrived out of the clear blue, taking everyone by surprise. For those of us who were connected to him in a personal way, the shock of his death jarred our ability to remember exactly what transpired immediately before and after the accident. Even now, more than a decade after it happened, the subject is so painful that we usually avoid it, but on the rare occasions when we talk about the day Dale died, we find that our memories are fractured and incomplete, even contradictory. It's almost as though we experienced his death separately, each of us in our own world or on our own plane of reality, and the details of the day have slipped through our fingers, leaving only fragmentary images behind.

*   *   *

My memories of the 2001 Daytona 500 begin two weeks before the big race, when I showed up at the Daytona International Speedway in my new role as the lead analyst for Fox Sports. On that day I felt like a rookie all over again. I'd been given this new ride because I'd performed well in smaller venues; I had sometimes shared the microphone with veterans like Ken Squier, Eli Gold, and Buddy Baker during Saturday races on cable television, and I'd been able to hold my own there. The distance from that experience to this new job, however, was enormous. I felt like a freshly commissioned pilot stepping from a flight simulator into the cockpit of a sold-out jumbo jet for the very first time. The kid from Owensboro, Kentucky, would be helping to carry the Daytona 500, the Super Bowl of stock car racing, to hundreds of millions of viewers around the world. Just thinking about that audience made me giddy and a little nauseous.

I wasn't the only one feeling nervous. Neither Larry McReynolds nor Jeff Hammond had ever worked at this level before, and I could tell that they were as jumpy as I was. Fortunately Larry and I would be working with Mike Joy, who had narrated countless races over the years, and Jeff was teamed with Chris Myers and the legendary Voice of NASCAR, Ken Squier. With these veterans beside us and David Hill as our executive producer, I figured the show would turn out well no matter what mistakes we made.

The multiple events of Speedweeks gave us all a chance to work together prior to the big race. Our live coverage began eight days before the Daytona 500, with a show devoted to the ritual of qualifying. The following day, the Sunday before the 500, we covered the Budweiser Shootout (Tony Stewart edged out Dale Earnhardt to win the 70-lap nonpoints race), and on the next day we showed practice. By Thursday, when we geared up again to cover the Gatorade 125s, I was no longer apprehensive about the upcoming broadcast of the Great American Race. I just wanted to get the show over with.

*   *   *

Dale Earnhardt, universally acclaimed as the virtuoso of the Daytona International Speedway, had been in high spirits all week. Relaxed and playful, he had just returned from whirling Terry Bradshaw around the track on a ride-along. Now he sat in the media center, his face wreathed in smiles, as technicians adjusted lights and tested microphones. A few feet away, J. R. Rhodes, his public relations man, nervously consulted his watch. I had been granted 15 minutes for an interview.

I opened by asking Dale about the open-faced helmet he continued to wear, even though everyone else had switched to full-face helmets, and about the persistent rumor that he drafted so well on the track because he could actually see the currents in the air.

> DW: *"Seein' the air"—Explain that to me. Do you think you can see the air? I mean, do you really?*
>
> Dale: *No. It's nothing but practice, and practice, and practice.*
>
> DW: *Do you think the open-face helmet has anything to do with it?*
>
> Dale: *This is how I got it figured: I know where the air is supposed to be.*
>
> DW: *How do you know?*
>
> Dale: *Well, you just know where the air is on the race car. You figure where the air is.*
>
> DW: *So, like, you go to the wind tunnel and stand there and watch?*
>
> Dale: *No. How many times have you drove a race car? How many times have I drove, how many times has Buddy Baker or David Pearson or Richard Petty or you and me raced at Talladega and Daytona and got beat or beat somebody by drafting by or getting drafted by? And how many times have you raced around these cars and listened? The open-face hel-*

*met lets you hear better and feel more in the open
than the full-face helmet does—and I also think it's
safer in a head-on collision. It doesn't break your
neck.*

I asked Dale to describe his feelings about being back at Daytona.

Dale: *Daytona is a unique racetrack. It's a unique place, a
magical place. You come here the first time and it's
so big and so intimidating, and then you learn to
drive the track, and you learn to understand it, and
then you like the racetrack, and then all of a sudden
it's good to you. The first time I drove down here in
seventy-nine as a rookie I got my butt chewed out on
pit road by Bobby and Donnie and Richard and all
those guys about the way I was driving the car. And
you probably wanted to too, but the crowd was too
big around me, you couldn't get to me. But Donnie
and Bobby really helped me, because I was listening.
Everybody chewed me out, everybody was getting on
me, and I learned quick. You had to learn quick. I felt
like if I didn't learn and establish myself I would be
out of a job. After all, you fired me once. I drove one
race and I was out of a job!*

DW: *Well, you got even. You fired me too.*

Dale: *(smiling) I didn't really fire you, Darrell. We had an
agreement and that's the way it went.*

Shifting the conversation to DEI, I asked Dale about his plans
for the company.

Dale: *The plan was to have a race team, and then all of
a sudden it became a Winston Cup team, and then
it was two, and now it's three. I'm pretty comfortable where we're at, and I feel like when I get out*

of the race car in three, four, five, ten years down the road, whenever it is, I will have a good business to look after. Dale Jr. and I can be involved with it, and hopefully Park and Michael will still be there, and all our sponsors too, because I like a long-term commitment out of myself and out of our sponsors. I want to be a Winston Cup owner for years down the road. I mean, you got to do something. You can't just stop driving and not do anything. I got to have something going on, and I think we can do it and do it well and have a good business and be competitive and be a part of NASCAR and be a part of the business.

I felt it was time to get personal. Dale radiated confidence, and I wondered whether he ever wrestled with fear or insecurity.

DW: *What are you afraid of?*

Dale: *Oh, my wife. (laughter) I'm not really afraid of her, I just don't want to disappoint her.*

DW: *That's a real good answer.*

Dale: *I don't know. I've never really been afraid of anything in a race car. The fact of fire is always there, but that's not a fear, it's a concern. The safety aspect of racing that I worry about is fire. I've really never been scared or nervous when I got in a race car. I was scared when Tim Richmond was running across the racetrack like he was going to kill me after we wrecked in Pocono (laughing), and after you and I got into it at Richmond I thought somebody was going to kill me then. I thought Stevie was going to get me.*

Out of the corner of my eye I could see activity among Dale's assistants. J. R. Rhodes had risen to his feet. We were running out of time.

DW: *How do you see yourself? How do you feel about Dale Earnhardt?*

Dale: *A lot better today than I did several years ago, because of family, and because I think I'm a better person than I used to be. I got a great wife, a great family. I'm proud of my kids, all of them. I've really got it all right now. I'm racing and enjoying it. I win, I'm competitive—and my family, everything is great there. I have some good race teams too. My kids win races. Kerry, my oldest son, is there with us. I've got grandkids. I mean, I'm having a great time! I've got it all right now, Darrell, I've got it all!*

DW: *You really do.*

Dale: *I'm a lucky man. I have it all.*

"Do you think Dale will want his verse today?" Stevie asked. We were sharing breakfast in our motor coach, which was parked in its customary #17 spot in the fenced driver-owner lot on the infield.

"I'm sure he will," I said. "You remember that race in Wilkesboro a few years back, don't you, when you didn't give him one? As soon as he realized it was missing, he unbuckled and climbed out of the car and came looking for you. He wasn't going to start that race without his verse."

"Do you think they'll let me onto pit road so I can give it to him? I mean, now that you're not driving . . . "

"You've been on pit road every week for more than twenty-five years, honey. You're a fixture down there. I'm sure nobody is going to stop you today. By the way, what verse are you going to give him?"

"I don't know yet. Believe it or not, I haven't opened my Bible all week." Her confession made me smile. It wasn't at all like Stevie to neglect her morning devotions. She must have been feeling the disruption in our routine as keenly as I was to have gone an entire week without her daily reading.

Stevie laid her Bible on the table and closed her eyes for a moment. "Since it's February eighteenth, I think I'll start with Proverbs eighteen," she said. "Maybe that will send me in the right direction." A few moments later she said, "What do you think of this one? 'The name of the Lord is a strong tower; the righteous man runs into it and is safe.' That's Proverbs eighteen-ten."

"No, I don't think so. That doesn't sound like a very good verse for the Daytona 500."

Stevie kept reading for a long time, flipping from one section of the Bible to another. Finally she sighed and picked up a card and a pen. "No, that's the one," she said. "Proverbs eighteen-ten is the right one for today."

The pneumatic door on the motor coach hissed and I heard Smitty, our driver, call my name. "We'd better get moving if you're going to make it to that production meeting," he said.

I kissed Stevie good-bye. "I'll meet you and the girls back at the condo right after the race. We'll be going straight home. Unless Mikey wins, that is. If Mikey wins, we'll be staying another night."

David Hill had been omnipresent in Daytona for the previous two weeks, enthusiastically overseeing the same elite team of camera operators, sound and light specialists, directors, and technicians that produced the network's innovative broadcasts of NFL football. During our shows leading up the Daytona 500, David had studied the monitors with Ed Goren, Richie Zyontz, and Artie Kempner, analyzing and critiquing everything we did. Their suggestions, transmitted to our headsets, had been gentle and encouraging. I expected this morning's production meeting to be much the same.

Larry, Mike, and I were standing in the broadcast booth, reviewing a photocopied outline for the day, when our boss burst through the door carrying a folded piece of paper. "I'm tired of this sh*t," David said, waving the paper. "I'm f***ing tired of hearing you tell me that this happened, that happened, something else happened. I have eyes! I never watched a f***ing race before in my life and I don't even know anything about this f***ing sport, and even I can recognize that some bloke just passed another bloke on the back straightaway, or some bloke on a pit stop just took two tires. For God's sake, stop telling me what's happening. What I want you to tell me today . . ." He opened the piece of paper, on which he had written the letters W-H-Y with a heavy black marker, and taped it to the window. "Tell me *why*," he said. Then he left.

The strains of a pre-race concert rolled across the stands as Big Andy, the sheriff's deputy, escorted Stevie around the Goodyear tower and past the gas pumps, toward pit road. When they reached the gate, Andy said, "You know, I think this is the first time in ten years that I've gone out onto pit road without Darrell next to me." He looked over at Stevie. "You're much better looking."

Stevie laughed and glanced upward, toward the broadcast booth atop the grandstand. She knew I was up there somewhere, even though she couldn't see me through the glass, and she knew that I had missed the chapel service that morning. A local worship group had led the singing for the service. Dale Beaver, the chaplain, had spoken briefly about how a Savior who is worthy of worship is worthy of trust, and the youth pastor, Lonnie, had spoken to the kids, including my daughters and Taylor Earnhardt, about the brevity of our lives. Altogether it had been the most powerful chapel service Stevie could remember, a true worship experience right in the middle of the Daytona International Speedway. She was sorry I had missed it.

Out on pit road, the drivers and crews were waiting for the race to start. Back in the 1970s, when we were just getting started in NASCAR, pit road had been a solely masculine domain; women were not allowed in the pits when a race was in progress. Stevie had been the first. I had designated her the team owner, giving her the right to enter the pits, and my beautiful redhead had taken responsibility for counting laps and calculating fuel consumption during every race. For Stevie, reducing the race to numbers and keeping track of those numbers until the race was over was a constructive way to handle her anxiety. The numbers kept her mind occupied, preventing her from imagining the unthinkable as her husband hurtled around the track at nearly 200 miles per hour.

Today, as she passed the crews and cars on pit road, Stevie caught the eyes of several other drivers' wives. The women hugged and exchanged knowing glances, saying little. Stevie understood what these women were feeling, and she also knew that they would not speak their fear aloud. Saying it, just saying it, might be enough to make it happen.

Near the front of the column of cars Stevie was surprised to see Teresa Earnhardt in the crowd around Dale's black Chevy. The intensely private Teresa rarely lingered on pit road, but today she was staying close to her husband, who was surrounded by a sea of media and fans. From the opposite side of the car, Stevie held up the card for Teresa to see. Teresa smiled, tapped Dale on the arm, and pointed. Dale motioned Stevie over, and she handed him the scripture.

Earnhardt seemed to retreat inward as he read what Stevie had written. The moment passed, and Dale nodded. "Thank you," he said. He reached inside the car and instructed a crew member to mount the card on the dash, then turned to give Stevie a hug.

"Love you," Stevie said into Dale's ear.

"Love you too."

Stevie gave Teresa's wrist a warm squeeze, then watched as Dale wrapped his wife in a final embrace. The Earnhardts were kissing as Stevie turned to leave. It was time to get off pit road, Stevie thought. The race was about to start, and she didn't work there anymore.

I took a deep breath and smiled at the camera. Mike, Larry, and I were standing side by side in the booth, the racetrack visible through the glass behind us, as the unseen director counted down to the opening of the broadcast. "Three, two, . . ."

On the monitor to my left I could see the jittery images and swirling graphics of the opening montage: Dale Earnhardt walking down pit road with my brother, cars flashing under a blurred flag, Jeff Gordon swiveling toward the camera, cars tumbling, fans rising to their feet, Dale Earnhardt with one arm around his son's neck and the other around his wife's. Above a background of wailing guitars, the movie-trailer voice of the announcer dramatically intoned, "Fox Sports, your new home for NASCAR, presents . . ."

Mike Joy welcomed the viewers to Daytona, and we delivered our introduction to the race. After two weeks of working together, we were starting to find our roles. I would describe what was going through the mind of the driver, and Larry would explain the thinking of the crew chief. Mike Joy, in addition to his role as ringmaster, would represent the owner.

Mike tossed the broadcast to Dick Berggren on pit road for the first human-interest story of the day. A ponytailed Kyle Petty, whose grandfather Lee had won the first Daytona 500 in 1959 and whose father, Richard, had won the race a record seven times, was buckled into the #45 Dodge. This was his son Adam's car, and Kyle was driving it in memory of the 19-year-old boy who had been killed the previous May. Adam had died of a basilar skull fracture caused by a head-snapping collision with the concrete wall in Loudon, New Hampshire. It was the same injury that had taken the life of Kenny Irwin Jr. two weeks later.

Today Kyle was wearing the HANS device, a carbon-filament shoulder harness to which the sides of his helmet could be tethered. This head and neck support prevented a driver's head from snapping forward in the event of a sudden stop. It had been invented in the early 1980s and was well known in NASCAR, but most drivers resisted it. Dale Earnhardt, who showed his contempt for safety innovations by continuing to drive in his open-face helmet and racing goggles, had dismissed the HANS device as "that damn noose." Kyle wore the device without comment, and we cut back to a boy band singing the national anthem without mentioning it.

It soon became apparent that this would be a very special race, the most exciting Daytona 500 we had seen in years. In the previous year's race, only seven drivers had ever been in contention, and they had exchanged the lead only nine times. This race, by contrast, would see 48 lead changes involving 14 drivers. The Dodges were strong, as we'd expected them to be, with Sterling Marlin taking the lead for 40 laps and Ward Burton for 53, but the Chevys driven by Earnhardt and the DEI team were consistently near the front of the field.

Dale Earnhardt was in classic form, bullying his way around the track. Never far from the front, he drove aggressively in the early going, pushing and bumping and retaliating against any driver foolish enough to challenge him. I could tell that he was enjoying himself. On the 77th lap, after receiving a nudge from the rookie Kurt Busch, Earnhardt responded with a jarring bump that nearly drove Busch from the track, then sailed past the rookie with his left hand extended out the window in a one-fingered salute. Earnhardt's crew members watched the exchange with delight, howling at the old man's schoolyard antics.

Early that morning Dale had called Dale Jr. and Michael into his hauler, where he had laid out their strategy for the race. Michael should hang back for the first half of the race, he said, then begin his move toward the front. Dale choreographed the team's moves, predicting what the other teams would try to do and prescribing countermeasures. When it came down to the end of the race, Dale said, they would finish together: one, two, three.

When my brother moved to the front of the lead pack on lap 171, I felt my first twinge of hope that he might actually win the race. Then, two laps later, the Big One happened. As Tony Stewart was trying to evade contact between Robby Gordon and Ward Burton, his car got turned around, and the sudden change in aerodynamics lifted the car into the air and sent it flipping and tumbling through oncoming traffic, pieces flying in all directions, as other cars collected and collided behind it in a massive, smoking pileup. The race was stopped as a rescue team pulled the dazed Stewart from his demolished car and helped him into the ambulance for a trip to nearby Halifax Hospital. Then, after all 18 cars that had been caught up in the colossal crash had either limped from the track or been towed away and the debris has been cleared, the race was restarted with 22 laps to go—and Michael was in the lead!

As the race unwound, Mike Joy started to suspect that this Daytona 500 would come down to a duel between Michael Waltrip and the younger Earnhardt, and that the elder Earnhardt would likely play some role in it. Sensing my personal connection to the unfolding drama, Mike and Larry allowed me to speak as though I were talking directly to my brother.

"Mikey," I said at one point, "that's two Earnhardts up there. I think you're odd man out, buddy."

My concern escalated on lap 182, when Dale Earnhardt tried to pass Michael for the lead. "Michael's in a bind," I said. "If he lets Earnhardt by, I'm gonna kick his butt, and if he don't let Earnhardt by, *Earnhardt's* going to kick his butt. So he's in trouble!"

I was worried about more than the ever-treacherous Dale Earnhardt. The Dodges driven by Sterling Marlin and Kenny Schrader were faster than the Chevys my brother and the Earnhardts were driving, and Marlin and Schrader were running right behind Dale. If they ever got past him, they could team up and blow past Dale Jr. and Michael to win the race. My heart was in my throat as I urged my little brother to hang on.

Michael, you're in the best place you've ever been. Hold 'er there.

Just don't get overconfident, Mikey.

Seven laps to go in the biggest race in the world!

Keep it low, Mikey. Keep it low. Don't let 'em under ya. Take that back straightaway wide, buddy. Get all over the place! Don't let 'em run up on ya! C'mon man! Watch that mirror, watch 'im!

He's going to make a run inside. Block him! Block him! Attaboy! You got 'im, Mikey! You got 'im!

I was so absorbed in the drama of my brother's improbable quest that I barely registered the crash in turn 4 when it happened, but Mike Joy watched with alarm as Earnhardt's car wobbled, swerved, and shot up the track and into the concrete retaining wall at a 45-degree angle. Mike and Larry continued to watch Dale's car as it drifted back down toward the infield and I celebrated my brother's victory. Their concern deepened when they could see no activity inside Dale's car. Kenny Schrader, whose car had ridden Earnhardt's Chevy into the wall, ran to the side of Dale's car and pulled down the window net, then recoiled and began motioning frantically for the rescue crew. Seeing Schrader's reaction to whatever he had seen inside Earhnardt's car, Mike's mind grasped for an explanation. Perhaps Earnhardt had suffered a superficial face wound and was bleeding profusely. Maybe he was unconscious. Or maybe—and Mike was chilled by the thought—maybe it was much worse.

By now I knew that something was wrong. The control room was not giving us any information, but they supplied a slow-motion replay of the wreck that we reviewed for the audience at home. Watching it, I felt a cold dread settle in the pit of my stomach. This crash might not look bad to the untrained eye, but I knew better, and I tried to explain the physics of it to the audience. Tony Stewart's spectacular somersaulting wreck 30 minutes earlier had actually been far less dangerous to the driver than Dale's, because the kinetic energy Tony's car had carried was gradually dispersed with every twist and tumble and with every piece of metal that tore away from the car. Dale's car, by contrast, had been stopped instantly by an immovable concrete wall, the g-forces imposed upon the driver actually multiplied by the added load of Schrader's car against it. Dale had been subjected to all the stresses produced by that instant loss of momentum. The difference between Tony's wreck and Dale's was huge, equivalent to the difference between a dropped hammer and the impact of a hammer swung by an expert, and the results were bound to be shattering.

Big Andy had expected to accompany me to Victory Circle at the end of the race, where I would interview the winner in the closing minutes of the broadcast. In all his years at the track, Andy had never been to Victory Circle, and he relished the prospect. Now, however, as the safety crew worked feverishly to remove Earnhardt from his car and our broadcast team continued to analyze the limited footage of the crash that we'd been given, Andy recognized that plans would change.

The producers arranged for me to communicate with my jubilant brother from the booth, and I managed to control my rising panic long enough to congratulate him. Michael was delirious, hoarse with happiness, and I could not bring myself to cast a shadow on his celebration.

During the final commercial break I asked for details about Dale's condition. What was happening? What were we going to tell the audience? "We can't confirm anything," came the reply over our headsets. "We can't say anything." Our broadcast closed with a long, wavering camera shot from the blimp, following the ambulance down Route 92 toward Halifax Hospital. The slow pace of the ambulance down the empty street was an ominous indication of what was going on inside.

Afterward, when Mike, Larry, and I had taken off our headsets, we joined hands there in the booth and said a prayer for Dale Earnhardt.

Meanwhile Big Andy was on the phone with his wife, Maryann. Maryann was a trauma nurse, on duty that day at Halifax Hospital. "Is he there yet?" Andy asked.

"No. He's on his way, but he's gone."

Andy was stunned. "Gone? How can he be gone?"

"I have to go," Maryann said, and hung up.

Andy quickly phoned one of his motor buddies on the police force. "I need an escort," he said. "I'm taking Darrell Waltrip to the trauma center at Halifax Hospital, and I need an escort right away. Meet me outside the communication tower." Andy closed his phone, wiped his eyes with the back of his hand, and went to give me the news.

When we jumped into Big Andy's Chevy Tahoe and followed a patrol motorcycle with flashing lights out onto Fentress Boulevard, the street was already jammed with departing fans still unaware of Dale's death. Our progress was slow, and we were headed in the wrong direction. "Where the hell is he taking us?" I said. "This ain't the way to the hospital!"

Our escort led us onto a rough dirt road, past idling buses and throngs of pedestrians trudging toward their distant cars. The crowd flowed around us. Occasionally someone would recognize me and shout my name, but I was too distraught to acknowledge anyone. Suddenly the police motorcycle stopped, blocking our way. Fans pressed against the truck, rocking it. "That guy has lost his chain," Andy said. "He's not going anywhere." Spinning the wheel and laying on the horn, Andy abandoned the road and bumped across a field toward a narrow dirt lane. When we reached Dunn Avenue, where traffic was relatively light, he gunned the engine and raced to White Street, then cut into the parking lot for the emergency room, stopping in a spot reserved for police vehicles.

A uniformed cop was posted outside the door to the emergency room. "No entry," he said, raising a hand. "You can't come in this way."

"This is Darrell Waltrip," Andy protested. "We were told to come over."

The officer shook his head. "We're not letting anybody in. I'm sorry, but those are my orders."

Behind him, another figure exited the building. It was Kenneth Small, the chief of police, and he recognized us. "It's okay," Chief Small said to the officer guarding the door. He waved us toward the building. "C'mon in, guys."

Suddenly Dale Earnhardt Jr. rushed out of the emergency

room, followed by Dale Beaver, the chaplain from Motor Racing Outreach. Junior's face was pale and expressionless. He accepted a quick hug from me, then pushed away, wordlessly, and bolted toward the parking lot. "He's gotta go tell the team," the chaplain explained.

When we rounded the corner of the waiting area we found Teresa Earnhardt sitting beside her driver, Jimbo Diggs, her head in her hands. A stunned Richard Childress was sitting a few feet away, and Mike Helton was standing helplessly nearby. There were others in the room too, but all these years later I can no longer see their faces or remember their names. What I remember most clearly is this: Teresa looking up in anguish and saying, "Will somebody please tell me what to do?"

"You want to see him?" Teresa asked, her voice flat.

I nodded numbly. *I want to see him alive,* I thought. *I want Dale to pop up with a devilish grin and roar with delight at the joke he just pulled on all of us.*

Maryann ushered us into the room where Dale's body lay on a table, covered from the neck down by a sheet. The sight was surreal. Teresa gently ran her fingers over her husband's face, smoothing his mustache. Except for an abrasion on his chin— "From his chin-strap," Maryann explained softly—Dale's features were unmarked. He looked peaceful in repose.

"The medical examiner will be here soon," another nurse said. "He'll be taking . . . the body. Would you like us to remove his jewelry?" Teresa shook her head. "Leave his rings on him," she said. "You can take his watch, but leave his rings."

Teresa was talking on the phone with Taylor, her 12-year-old daughter. "You just stay with Mammaw and Pawpaw a little longer, honey," she said. "I'll be home in a while. Daddy's been in a bit of an accident."

A wheelchair was passing through the hallway, pushed by

an orderly, and I turned to see Tony Stewart's smiling face. The young driver had survived his spectacular crash without serious injury and was being discharged. Tony noticed Teresa and Richard Childress, and his expression changed to alarm. "What's wrong?" he asked. "Did something happen to Dale?"

"He's gone," I said. "He was in a bad wreck, and he's gone." A look of incomprehension crossed Tony's face, and he moaned and crumpled in his wheelchair.

Rusty Wallace arrived, out of breath. The policeman had blocked the door of the emergency room, so Rusty had run to the opposite side of the building and found another way inside. "How is he?" Rusty asked. "Is he going to be okay?"

I shook my head, unable to speak, and Big Andy told him what had happened. Rusty swayed and started crying. Andy caught the driver and steadied him against a wall, while I cried too.

Richard Childress was sitting at a table in the corner, talking to nobody in particular. "It's my fault," he said through clenched teeth. "Dale wanted to quit a year ago because we weren't winning, but I talked him out of it. I told him that the problem was the cars, not him. It was the cars that weren't competitive, but we'd get them right, and as soon as we did he'd be right back in the thick of things. If I had let him retire, this never would have happened." Tears were running down Richard's face.

"It's not your fault," Bill France Jr. said gently. He and his wife had arrived moments earlier, silent and somber. NASCAR's powerful owner and his most successful driver had formed a close friendship in recent years, and it was obvious that Dale's death had shaken Bill deeply. He looked at the red-faced Childress with concern. "Are you okay, Richard?" he asked.

"I don't feel so good," Richard said weakly.

Bill called for a nurse, and Maryann rushed to examine him. "We need to get this man into a room," she said, her fingers against Richard's neck. "We need a room *now*."

Richard Childress spent the night in the hospital, and was discharged the next day.

We stayed at the hospital for an hour and a half. Outside, police cordoned off an area around the emergency-room entrance where reporters and photographers had gathered. When the coroner's transport van arrived, Maryann draped the space between the van and the exit with a large sheet in order to prevent cameras from capturing the image of Dale's shrouded body leaving the building.

People were leaving the emergency room now. Mike Helton sighed and said, "I'm going back to the track to give a press conference, if any of you want to participate." Nobody responded.

As we walked out of the building, Big Andy positioned himself between me and a knot of reporters who were hollering my name. Andy hustled me into the truck, waved away the reporters, and locked the doors. Then he took off toward I-95 and the condo at Spruce Creek where Stevie and the girls were waiting for me.

I managed to maintain my composure for most of the 20-minute ride to Spruce Creek, but the moment I stepped inside the door of the condominium and met Stevie's eyes I broke down completely. We sank onto the sofa and held each other, sobbing uncontrollably, while Big Andy stood crying in the doorway and our daughters watched in despair.

"What about Michael?" Stevie asked suddenly, wiping the tears from her eyes. "How's your brother taking this?"

"I haven't seen him," I said. "I talked to Mikey from the booth right after the race, but I haven't seen him or heard from his since. I'm sure he got trapped in Victory Circle or the media center. He's gotta be devastated."

"We need to go check on him," Stevie said. She quickly arranged for someone to watch the girls, and we headed for the car.

By the time we reached the speedway, dazed fans had already started to gather along the spectator fence at the north end of the track. We drove slowly toward the tunnel, threading our way through the growing crowd of stunned men, sunburned women, and mute teenagers, their tear-stained faces turned toward the point where the fatal crash had occurred.

We found Michael and his wife, Buffy, in their motor coach in the owner-driver lot, stunned and distraught. Michael, looking exhausted, set a drink aside and rose to give me a mechanical hug.

"I'm so sorry, buddy," I said.

"Yeah," Michael said, looking at me bleakly, his eyes red.

"You okay?"

Tears welled in Michael's eyes, and he shook his head. "This is the worst day of my life." That broke my heart. Michael had been allowed to enjoy the happiness of a Daytona victory for only about 15 minutes before it was snatched away, along with the life of his hero and friend. How would he ever put this experience behind him?

"Have you eaten anything?" I asked after a while. "Do you want to go get dinner somewhere?"

Michael shook his head. "I'm not hungry."

"We'll be all right," Buffy said, caressing her husband's hair. "Thanks so much for coming over, really. I think we're going to stay here tonight, just us."

As we left, Michael was pouring himself another drink.

The following week was a maelstrom. My phone rang constantly from the moment we left the speedway, and when Stevie and I finally got home to Franklin there were satellite trucks in our driveway. As the news of Dale's death spread around the globe, so many requests for interviews and tributes poured in that Van Colley, my business manager, could barely keep track of them. By Wednesday afternoon I was starting to fade. "That's it," I told Van when he called to relay yet another stack of requests. "No more media. I'm done."

Stevie and I flew to Charlotte for the invitation-only memorial service on Thursday, where thousands of grieving fans stood respectfully outside barricades the police had erected around Calvary Church to protect the privacy of the family. Randy Owen of Alabama sang "Angels Among Us" during the 25-minute service, and Dale Beaver delivered an emotional eulogy. By the time it was over, I was completely drained.

After the memorial service I kissed Stevie good-bye and walked through the rain to my car. The Rockingham Speedway was a 90-minute drive away, and I was scheduled to be there that afternoon to begin preparing for our coverage of the next race. I turned on the windshield wipers, switched off the radio, and drove alone into the bleak North Carolina countryside.

This world, the rolling hills where Dale Earnhardt had grown up and built a life, seemed to have lost all color. Under the dull sky, the silence broken only by the hiss of my tires on the wet pavement, I felt my inner sadness start to dissipate, my sorrow replaced by a gathering fury. Why in hell had this happened? Suddenly I was angry with Dale, my bullheaded friend, for his refusal to wear the HANS device. I was angry with myself for not grasping the gravity of the threat and doing something, anything, to prevent Dale's death. I was angry with NASCAR. I was angry with God.

I thought again of my conversation with Dale only days earlier. I could see the happiness on his face as he savored his good fortune. "I've got it *all* right now, Darrell, I've got it all! I'm a lucky man. I've got it all." Dale Earnhardt had planned a wonderful future with his family and friends, a future neither he nor they would ever see. This was not fair, and it certainly was not right. I pounded the steering wheel as I thought of what lay ahead for Teresa, now that her husband was gone, and for Kerry and Kelley, Dale Jr. and Taylor, as they faced a life without their father.

By the time I arrived at the Rockingham racetrack, Smitty had already parked my motor coach in its assigned spot in the owner-driver lot, the same spot it occupied every year, right beside Dale's. Dale had always insisted that we park side by side in Rockingham, both of our coaches drawing power from the Goodyear building so that Dale's sleep would not be disturbed by the noise of a generator. Today, however, a simple wreath lay in the place where his coach should be parked. At the sight of that wreath, the awful reality of Dale's death struck me full in the chest again, even harder than before. Suddenly I wanted to turn around and drive away, go home, forget about racing for a while—maybe forever. At that moment I could not imagine a future without Dale Earnhardt. His loss had changed NASCAR forever. Sundays would never be the same.

They asked me to give the invocation before the race at Rockingham, and I agreed to do it. Under a threatening sky Teresa Earnhardt and Dale Jr. stood on the front straightaway as I took the microphone. Drivers and thousands of fans bowed their heads, and I did my best to pray. For a fleeting moment the speedway felt like a church.

Our broadcast team had already planned to go silent for the entire third lap of every race for the rest of the season in tribute to #3, but on this day the drama started even earlier. On the very first lap Dale Jr. was running high in the fourth turn when an inadvertant bump from Ron Hornaday sent him hard into the wall. The cruel irony of that wreck silenced the crowd. Fans stood hushed, craning anxiously for signs of movement inside the cockpit of Dale Jr's car. When the young man finally climbed from the crumpled car and limped down the banked track, a wave of relieved applause swept across the stands.

Then the rain came, forcing a suspension of the race. When it was completed the following day, Steve Park would drive #1, owned by Dale Earnhardt, Inc. to victory, flashing across the start/finish line a scant 0.138 seconds ahead of Bobby Labonte as fans wept and waved black pennants toward the sky.

Already the world was awash in speculation about the cause

of Dale Earnhardt's death. Many rumors centered on his seat belt or his open-face helmet, but my attention had been drawn elsewhere. I knew that Samuel J. Gualardo, president of the American Society of Safety Engineers, had written a letter to Mike Helton at the beginning of the season, urging NASCAR to accelerate its safety efforts following the deaths of Adam Petty, Kenny Irwin Jr., and Tony Roper. I knew that Dr. Robert Melvin, a biomedical research scientist who worked for GM, had tried during Speedweeks to persuade Earnhardt to endorse the HANS device, believing that if Dale would agree to use it the other drivers would follow his example. Dale had refused, and I knew why. I'd tried the apparatus myself, and I hadn't liked it at all. The device was primitive and uncomfortable; it inhibited the movement of my head and restricted my field of vision. I wouldn't have worn it voluntarily either if I were still competing on the track, but now I had a new job and a new responsibility. I was an analyst, charged with finding and explaining the objective truth about racing, and I knew two things for sure. I knew that many drivers would not wear the device unless they were forced to do so, and I knew that in a crash like Dale Earnhardt's, the device could save a driver's life.

I interviewed Mike Helton during a pre-race segment at Rockingham, and I asked him specifically about the HANS device, demanding to know whether NASCAR would make it mandatory. Mike shook his head. While he agreed that the use of head restraints should be encouraged, he continued to defend NASCAR's historic approach to driver safety. A driver was in charge of his own environment, Helton said. He pointed out the reasons that some drivers objected to the HANS device, and he said that NASCAR would not make its use compulsory. NASCAR's intransigence on the subject irritated me and inflamed my determination to see things change. Two weeks later I demonstrated the device during our broadcast of the Atlanta race, showing our huge television audience how it could prevent the head-whip and the resulting basilar skull fracture that had killed Adam, Kenny, Tony, and Dale.

My passionate argument for mandating the HANS device, together with my implicit criticism of NASCAR's failure to do so, strained my relationships with Mike Helton and Bill France considerably, but I didn't care. I was on a mission. I knew that the NASCAR executives had many factors to consider, but only one factor mattered to me. It was too late to save Dale Earnhardt, but it was not too late to save the drivers who would follow him. If those drivers would not adopt the HANS device voluntarily, then NASCAR must make it mandatory, without delay, before another life was lost.

There were no more deaths in NASCAR that year, but in early October a 25-year-old racer named Blaise Alexander Jr. made contact with Kerry Earnhardt, Dale's oldest son, during an ARCA-sanctioned race at the Lowe's Motor Speedway in Charlotte. Alexander's car slammed into the outside wall at an angle eerily similar to the accident that had taken Dale's life. According to the coroner, Blaise Alexander died instantly of a basilar skull fracture. Within days of his funeral, NASCAR announced a change in its safety requirements. Drivers would now be required to wear approved head and neck supports in all NASCAR events.

EPILOGUE

On June 14, 2011, Stevie and I took our seats in the front row of the Great Hall in the NASCAR Hall of Fame and waited for the press conference to begin. We'd been here before. Two years earlier, when the Hall of Fame opened its doors for the first time, we had applauded the announcement of its inaugural class: Bill France Sr., Bill France Jr., Junior Johnson, Richard Petty, and Dale Earnhardt. That had been a glorious day. When we returned to the Hall the following year, I halfway expected my name to be among the next five inductees to be announced; after all, every member of the voting panel with whom I'd spoken prior to the ceremony had made a point of telling me they'd voted for me. But my name had not been called. Stevie and I had helped to celebrate the well-deserved inductions of Bobby Allison, Ned Jarrett, Lee Petty, David Pearson, and Bud Moore as members of the Hall of Fame's second class.

Did I want to be named to the Hall of Fame today? To be honest, yes—who wouldn't? But I told myself for the thousandth time that I *didn't need it,* and I mentally reviewed the long list of people on the voting panel I had offended over the years. During my best years in the sport I had antagonized many with my quick tongue and superior attitude, and in later years, after I had passed my prime, I had lingered too long at the edge of the limelight, reluctant to make a graceful exit.

Even after I retired from racing and took up my new life as an analyst, my lack of diplomacy had sometimes caused heartburn in NASCAR's executive offices. After NASCAR made the HANS

device mandatory, for example, I spoke rashly at a press conference in Nashville. "If NASCAR had acted sooner," I said, "Dale
Earnhardt and Adam Petty and Kenny Irwin Jr. would still be
with us." Bill France Jr. was deeply wounded by that statement.
When he arrived in Nashville a few days later for the ceremonial
opening of a road named in his honor, NASCAR'S owner had
looked at me and shaken his head. "That hurt, Darrell," he said.
"That really hurt."

There was no doubt that Earnhardt's death had provoked a
sweeping wave of change in NASCAR. In a radical departure
from its historical reactive approach to safety changes on its
tracks, NASCAR had taken a proactive and aggressive stance on
safety, opening a new safety research facility in Charlotte in 2002
and spending millions of dollars to review every facet of the sport
with the driver in mind. In 2004 NASCAR began installing a new
barrier system on its tracks in order to prevent drivers from colliding directly with the concrete wall. This barrier, a sandwich
of extruded aluminum and high-density foam, was capable of
absorbing up to 60 percent of the energy from a direct impact.
Three years later NASCAR introduced the Car of Tomorrow, a
vehicle completely redesigned to protect the driver. The new car
featured an enlarged cockpit, with the driver repositioned closer
to the center of the car and surrounded by "crumple zones" to
absorb the energy from a crash. The new car's larger windows
provided improved visiblity and easier escape for the driver, and
its aerodynamics and lower center of gravity made the car more
resistant to rollover.

The payoff for all this work had been dramatic. In the ten years
since since Dale Earnhardt's death, no other driver had lost his
life in a NASCAR-sanctioned race. The wrecks continued—1,320
crashes on the NASCAR Cup circuit between 2001 and 2006
alone, according to *USA Today*—but not a single driver had died
as a result. This was an extraordinary turnaround, and it bore the
imprint of the immortal Dale Earnhardt.

Dale was gone, but his influence was not. As big as Dale had
been in life—and he had been very big indeed—he had become

even bigger in death. His memory was everywhere, and the tragedy of his passing had forced virtually everyone in the racing world to change. Not all of those changes had been welcomed, but they had worked together for good. Our lives and our sport had improved, and in some mysterious way Dale Earnhardt had been responsible.

As I waited for the press conference to begin, I found myself wishing again that Dale were here to enjoy the life he had dreamed about. I had been fortunate; I had survived, and I had thrived in retirement. My new career in television had allowed me to stay close to the sport I loved, and as the years passed, other doors of opportunity had opened for me as well. I had helped to design and promote the new Kentucky Speedway, which would soon bring NASCAR Cup racing to my home state. I had worked in movies, and now I was often approached by children who knew me only as Darrell Cartrip from the animated film *Cars*. I had been named to the Motorsports Hall of Fame of America and the International Motorsports Hall of Fame. I had visited the White House, flown on Air Force One, and had even sat at the President's desk.

Most important, I had enjoyed my family. It had been my privilege to walk a beaming Jessica down the aisle on her wedding day and hug my younger daughter, Sarah, at her high school graduation. Stevie and I were as much in love as we had ever been. Reflecting on all these blessings, I concluded again that *I did not need to be in the Hall of Fame*. The selection panel could pass me over year after year, and I would be just fine.

The press conference was about to start. As Brian France took the stage and approached the lectern, the fans who ringed the circular gallery fell silent. Stevie squeezed my arm.

I don't need this.

Brian France accepted an envelope, then turned to face the cameras and the seated crowd.

"He won three championships—"

I don't need this.

"—in a row."

I exhaled, and joined the audience in applauding Cale Yarborough's induction into the Hall of Fame. A highlight video of Cale's career played on a huge screen above the stage.

When the video ended, Brian stepped to the microphone again. "He won eighty-four races and three championships," Brian began.

Stevie gasped, and my heart skipped a beat.

"Please welcome Darrell Waltrip to the stage."

Yesss!

As the room erupted in applause, I leaped to my feet and bounded onto the platform. Brian extended a congratulatory hand, but I wrapped him in a hug instead, then planted a big kiss on his cheek. Grinning uncontrollably, I returned to my seat, where Stevie, Jeff Hammond, my sister, Carolyn, and a cluster of others were waiting to celebrate with me. Bud Moore was the first to shake my hand.

Afterward an interviewer asked me what I thought Dale Earnhardt would say about my induction into the Hall of Fame. "That's easy," I replied. "He'd say 'I got there first.'"

Truth be told, I did want to be in the NASCAR Hall of Fame, not just for myself, but for all the people who helped me get there. As I see it, my place in the Hall is a fitting tribute to the pit crews and crew chiefs, the owners and mechanics, the family, friends, and fans who believed in me, supported me, forgave me, and worked so hard to turn my dreams to reality. It is an honor I owe to many more people than I could possibly name in a book like this one, and it is to all those people that I dedicate these pages.

You know who you are.

Thank you.

Darrell Waltrip
Franklin, Tennessee
July 24, 2011

ACKNOWLEDGMENTS

I'd like to thank everybody who had a hand in making this book a reality, and I would do exactly that if only I could remember them all. In addition to the people whose names and contributions I'll suddenly recall as soon as this manuscript has gone to the printer, let me acknowledge the following:

Matt Ruff, who provided invaluable technical support and whose tenacity brought author, writer, and agent together.

Nate Larkin, the brilliant writer whose peerless work included this sentence.

David Dunham, our wise and persistent literary agent.

My sister **Carolyn Waltrip,** the heart of Darwal, Inc.

Van Colley, my business manager and curator of the photographs that appear in this book.

Mike Joy, whose career has paralleled mine and whose memories enrich this story.

Ty Norris, who graciously lent recollections from his colorful life in NASCAR.

Big Andy, whose big memory filled gaps in my own.

Ed Silva, my trusted advisor through thick and thin.

Eric Rayman, for his careful reading of the manuscript.

Dominick Anfuso, my editor at Free Press, who saw the value of this project and whose guidance brought the story into sharper focus.

Maura O'Brien and **Sydney Tanigawa,** and all the other members of the team at Free Press. Working with them has been a joy.

Most of all, I want to thank my beautiful wife, Stephanie (or, as most of you know her, Stevie). From the very beginning of our marriage some 42 years ago she has been my biggest fan and an incredible source of strength in my life and career. If not for her and the encouragement she gave me in tough times, I would never have had the success I've had. My faith I owe to her, my career I owe to her, my success I owe to her . . . I could go on, but you get the picture. She held me together when I was falling apart. It's not easy living on the road and raising two girls on the road, but she did it, and she did it without complaining. As a matter of fact, she homeschooled both girls all the way through high school.

Stephanie is truly a remarkable lady and a model of what a man wants in a wife. She's a good friend, a good mother, a good homemaker, and most of all she's been unfailingly loyal to me. She honestly married me for better or worse. I really do get my inspiration from her, and she possess all the qualities I admire. Her faith is strong, her commitment is endless, and her support for me and is girls is unshakeable.

When I meet Stevie in Owensboro, Kentucky, back in the '60s, God whispered in my ear and told me "I've sent you an angel. Don't let her get away." Thank God I was listening. She's been my best friend, and I love getting hugs from my best friend. When you read the stories in this book and wonder how in the heck I accomplished what I did, just know it wasn't because of Darrell Waltrip. It was because of Stephanie Rader Waltrip. She's the real star in the Waltrip family.

PS: my mom and dad and my two sisters and two brothers contributed and sacrificed a lot for me to do what I've done as well. My family and I have been blessed beyond our wildest dreams. They say "Dream big." I'm glad we did.

INDEX

ABC, 89
Adkins, Grover, 121
Alabama Gang, 59
Alexander, Blaise, Jr., 223
Alexander, Dave, 102
Allison, Bobby, 2, 13, 59, 61, 65,
    71, 72, 94–95, 97, 99, 110,
    113, 116, 119, 120, 184,
    204
  in Hall of Fame, 225
  singing career of, 79–81
  Waltrip's relationship with,
    54–56, 88–89, 98, 111, 128,
    140–42
Allison, Clifford, 142
Allison, Davey, 142
Allison, Donnie, 81, 89, 90, 94–95,
    204
Allison, Judy, 56, 128
Allman, Bill, 107–8
American Automobile Association,
    16–17
American Society of Safety
    Engineers, 222
America's Most Wanted, 182, 195
Amick, George, 18
Anderson, M. C., 100, 110
Andretti, Mario, 64, 192
Arrington, Buddy, 96
Atlanta Journal 500, 135
Atlanta Motor Speedway, 79, 146,

148–49, 151, 155, 170,
    197–98, 222
Automobile Club, U.S., 76
Automobile Racing Club of
    America (ARCA), 52, 66–67

Baby Grand series, 176
Bahari Racing, 135
Baker, Buddy, 76, 79–81, 93, 94,
    184, 202, 203
Balough, Gary, 94
Banner, 58
Barlow, John, 165
Barrett, Charles, 75, 76
Beatty, Dick, 141, 142, 163
Beaver, Dale, 208, 216
Becky (therapist), 10
Benfield, Henry, 101
Berggren, Dick, 196, 210
Beverly, Tim, 186, 188–90
Bible, Lee, 15–16
Big Andy, 11, 208, 214–15, 217,
    218
Bill (body man), 49
Bill France Award of Excellence,
    199
Billmyer, Jack, 121
Bluebird V, 16
Bodine, Geoffrey, 139, 144
Bonnett, Neil, 6, 121, 132, 172
Bradley, Jerry, 80

Bradshaw, Terry, 7, 194, 203
Brady, Bo, 65
Brasington, Harold, 17
Brewer, Tim, 107, 109, 110, 137, 176
Bristol, 72, 79, 109, 117, 131, 189
Brooks, Dick, 88, 114, 115, 121
Bruckheimer, Jerry, 154
Budweiser, 135, 137, 190
Budweiser Shootout, 2, 105, 202
Buford, Flookie, 59
Builder's Square, 182
Burton, Jeff, 197
Burton, Ward, 8, 211
Busch, Kurt, 211
Busch circuit, 190
Busch Grand National series, 2, 6, 61
Busch series car, 90–91, 136
Byrnes, Steve, 196

Caldwell, Joe, 58
camber, 55
Campbell, Malcolm, 16
Cardiges, Jim, 122
Car of Tomorrow, 226
Carolina 500, 116
Cars (film), 155, 227
Carter, Travis, 191–92
Carver, Joe, 58, 59, 162
CBS, 92, 93–94
Championship 400, 3
Charleston (South Carolina) Post and Courier, 5–6
Charlie (friend), 62
Charlie Brown (dog), 65, 116
Charlotte, N.C., 87–88
Charlotte Motor Speedway, 83, 84, 112, 113, 123, 125–26, 127, 152, 153, 156, 162, 163–64, 174
Checker 500, 166
Chevrolet, 6, 51–52, 114, 133

Childress, Richard, 3, 127, 131, 172, 179, 196, 216, 217–18
Coca-Cola 500, 190–91
Coca-Cola World 600, 123, 125–26, 152, 174
Colley, Van, 198, 199, 219
Compton, Stacy, 5
Cooper, Cortez, 117, 119, 177
Craftsman Truck series, 2
Craven, Ricky, 177, 179
cross-member, 70–71
Crowell, P. B., 53, 61, 62, 64, 65, 69, 81
Cruise, Tom, 154
Cruz, Darrell, 91
CSX, 63
Cyrus, Billy Ray, 197

Dale Earnhardt Inc. (DEI), 189, 204, 211, 221
Darlington Raceway, 17, 74, 78, 79, 83, 88–89, 96–97, 99, 109, 117, 126, 127, 164, 172, 184, 185, 187
Darrell Waltrip Silver Anniversary Special, 181
DarWal, Inc., 186
Days of Thunder (film), 154–55
Daytona 500:
   of 1965, 13, 22–23, 52
   of 1967, 64
   of 1973, 72
   of 1974, 79
   of 1976, 87
   of 1977, 100
   of 1979, 93–95
   of 1981, 108–9
   of 1982, 111
   of 1983, 114
   of 1986, 128
   of 1987, 136
   of 1989, 2, 143, 144–46, 151, 155

of 1990, 155, 169
of 1992, 170
of 1993, 3
of 1994, 172–73
of 1997, 181
of 1998, 183–84
of 2001, 1–11, 202–13, 219
history of, 14–18
Daytona Beach Road Course,
    16–17, 18
Daytona International Speedway,
    1, 6, 13, 17–18, 19, 66, 67,
    81, 83, 112, 118, 157,
    172–73, 183, 202, 203,
    204, 208
    banks at, 21–22
    Days of Thunder shot at,
    154–55
Daytona Land Speed Trials, 16
DeWitt, L. G., 78
Diehard 500, 180
DiGard Motorsports, 81–83, 87,
    92, 93, 101, 103–5, 113,
    120, 191
DiProspero, Mike, 81
Dodge, 5
Don Moore Chevrolet, 30, 38, 45
Donoho, Bill, 58, 79, 80–81
Donoho, Jim, 79, 80
Dorton, Randy, 155
Dover Downs, 78, 87, 110, 112
Duvall, Robert, 154

Earnhardt, Dale, 13, 93, 114–15,
    116, 127, 131, 138, 145,
    158, 164, 170, 171, 173,
    174–75, 180, 182, 187,
    210–11, 228
    accidents of, 10–11, 60, 101,
    129–30, 144, 148–49, 153,
    175, 180, 181
    aggressiveness of, 84
    as awkward with media, 128

Busch series car finished by,
    90–91
car trouble of, 115
championships won by, 170,
    172, 174
in Charlotte race, 84–85
as controversial driver, 153
Daytona 500 won by, 183–84
death of, 10–11, 201, 213–23,
    226–27
earnings of, 143
in Hall of Fame, 225
injury of, 180
in Japanese event, 190–91
last race of, 3–5, 8–11
NASCAR's fining and
    penalizing of, 130, 139,
    141
#3 Chevy of, 7, 144
pass in the grass of, 138–39
Rookie of the Year won by, 99,
    101
Stevie's verses for, 173, 206–7
Waltrip as driver for, 188–89
Waltrip's first meeting with, 68,
    136
Waltrip's rivalry with, 4, 60,
    128–30, 189
Earnhardt, Dale, Jr., 3, 5, 9, 10,
    179, 190, 205, 211, 212,
    215–16, 220, 221
    in Japanese event, 190–91
    as Rookie of the Year, 197
Earnhardt, Kelly, 220
Earnhardt, Kerry, 220, 223
Earnhardt, Taylor, 208, 216,
    220
Earnhardt, Teresa, 180, 209,
    216, 217, 220, 221
Economaki, Chris, 89
Edwards, Shorty, 191
Elder, Suitcase Jake, 67–68, 69–71,
    72–73, 76, 92–93

Elliot, Bill, 5, 8, 143
  quick car of, 126–27, 131,
    138–39
Elliot, Harold, 107, 110
Ellis Speedway, 84
Elmer, Mr., 63–64
Entertainment Tonight, 157–58
ESPN, 109, 193
Evernham, Ray, 5, 77

Fabulous Hudson Hornet, 18, 185
Fairgrounds racetrack (Nashville),
    53, 54, 58, 79, 87, 91
Farmer, Red, 61
FBI, 152
Finley, Derrick, 189
Firecracker 400, 81, 118
"fireproof suit," 21
Fishel, Herb, 114
Flock, Francis, 185
Flock, Tim, 185
Follmer, George, 76
Ford, '58, 14, 18–19
  inspection of, 19–20
  work on, 13–14, 20–21
Formula One, 192
Fox, Ray, Jr., 76
Fox Sports, 3, 149, 193, 194–97,
    202, 210
Foyt, A. J., 158
France, Bill, Jr., 17, 18, 77–78, 98,
    181, 185, 190, 198–99, 217,
    223, 225, 226
France, Bill, Sr., 67, 225
France, Brian, 227–28
Franklin, Ky., 53–54, 121–22
Frank Rader, 63
Freels, Paul, 14
FX, 193

Gant, Harry, 124–25, 126
Gardner, Bill, 81, 87–88, 99–100,
    101, 103, 104–5

Gardner, Jim, 82
Gatorade 125s, 202
Gatorade car, 87
Gatorade Duels, 2
Gee, Jake, 83
Gee, Robert, 67–68, 69, 73, 76–77,
    83, 84, 136
Gillespie, Albert, 159–61
GM, 222
GM Goodwrench car, 153
Gold, Eli, 202
Golden Arrow, 15
Goodyear, 71–72, 208, 221
Gordon, Jeff, 6, 60, 77, 170, 172,
    174–75, 197, 210
  championship won by, 179
  Daytona 500 won by, 181
  as Earnhardt's nemesis, 170
  in Japanese event, 190, 191
  Rookie of the Year won by,
    172
Gordon, Robby, 8, 211
Goren, Ed, 207
Grand National Championship,
    110, 113–14, 120, 185
Grand Prix, 76
Great Depression, 16–17
GTO, '69, 45–51
Gualardo, Samuel J., 222

Haas, Carl, 192
Hamilton, Bobby, 191
Hammond, Jeff, 5, 112, 113,
    125–26, 132, 136, 137, 142,
    145, 158, 163, 164, 176,
    228
  hired by Fox, 196, 202
Hamner, Bill, 71
HANS device, 210–11, 220,
    222–23, 225–26
Helton, Max, 177–79
Helton, Mike, 199, 216, 218, 222,
    223

Hendrick, Rick, 122, 127, 132–34, 136, 137, 156–57, 164, 167, 171, 179, 185–86
Hendrick Motorsport, 133, 136, 144, 156, 170, 171
Hensley, Jimmy, 176
Hickory Motor Speedway, 185
Hill, David, 195–97, 207–8
Hill, Mike, 111
Hillin, Bobby, 141
Hillin, Kim, 141
Hines, Hope, 59
Hodgson, Warner W., 132
Holman-Moody, 14
Holmer, Phil, 98
Honda, 121–22, 132
Hornaday, Ron, 221
Horton, Jimmy, 164
Hurd, Mr., 70
Hutchinson, Dick, 69–70
Hutchinson-Pagan, 69–70
Hyde, Harry, 67, 77
Hylton, Jim, 71, 72

Iff, David, 89, 96
Indianapolis 500, 123
International Motorsports Hall of Fame, 227
International Race of Champions, 180
Irvan, Ernie, 181
Irwin, Kenny, 6, 210, 222, 226
Isaac, Bobby, 73
Isaacs, Ann, 117
Isaacs, Leonard, 117

Jarrett, Dale, 3, 191, 197
Jarrett, Ned, 3, 13, 225
Jeffries, Bob, 180
Jocko Flocko (monkey), 185
Johnny (friend), 31, 32–33
Johnson, Flossie, 159
Johnson, Jimmy, 165

Johnson, Junior, 13, 79, 83, 104, 107, 111–12, 117, 120, 122–24, 125–26, 127, 129, 159, 189, 191, 225
  in Hall of Fame, 225
  and Hendrick's offer to Waltrip, 133–34
  loss of crew by, 110, 111
  special engines built by, 123, 125, 131–32
  Waltrip's deal with, 100–101
  Waltrip threatened by, 109
Jordanaires, 80
Joy, Michael, 4, 196, 202, 207, 209–10, 212, 213

Keech, Ray, 15
Keller, Pete, 19–20
Kempner, Artie, 207
Kentucky Electronics, 52
Kentucky Speedway, 227
King, Wayne, 73
King Air turboprop, 162, 180
Kmart, 191–92, 193
Knaus, Chad, 189
Kukler, Len, 74–75
Kulwicki, Alan, 135, 145

Labonte, Bobby, 197, 198, 221
Labonte, Terry, 112, 137, 138
Late Model Sportsman series race, 13, 53, 58, 61, 62, 65, 77–78, 93
Lockhart, Frank, 15
Lonnie (pastor), 208
Lopez, Philippe, 189
Lowe's Motor Speedway, 223

McCoy, Charlie, 80
McDuffie, J. D., 88
McMurray, Jamie, 189
McReynolds, Larry, 196, 202, 207, 209–10, 213

Madden, John, 92
Maggiacomo, Jocko, 142
Manion, Kevin "Bono," 189
Marcis, Dave, 93, 158
Marcum, John, 67
Marion, Milt, 17
Marlin, Coo-Coo, 59, 60
Marlin, Sterling, 5, 8, 10, 59, 211, 212
Martin, Mark, 166
Martinsville Speedway, 79, 83, 87, 113, 117, 118, 131, 138, 151, 153
Maryann (nurse), 11, 214, 216, 217, 218
Mast, Rick, 191
Mattei, Jim, 192
Mellow Yellow, 165
Melvin, Robert, 222
Mercury Cyclone, 64, 67, 69–71, 181
    cross-member problem of, 70
    engine problem of, 72
    tires of, 71–72
Michigan International Speedway, 3, 87, 142, 176, 180
Miller Beer, 141
Miller High Life 400, 128–29
Monte Carlo, 114, 118
Monte Carlo Elite, 181
Montegi, Japan, 190–91
Moore, Bud, 73, 76, 225, 228
Motor 500, 146, 148–49
Motor Racing Outreach, 177, 216
Motorsports Hall of Fame of America, 227
Mountain Dew, 104, 135
Murdoch, Rupert, 195
Music City Motorplex, 13
Myers, Chris, 5, 197, 202

Nab, Herb, 111
NAPA 500, 197

NASCAR:
    annual awards banquet of, 143, 174, 179, 198
    birth of, 13, 17
    deaths in, 6, 10–11, 18, 20, 172–73, 201, 210, 213–23, 226
    as mainstream, 95
    media tour of, 182–83
    point system of, 98
    safety issues in, 6–7, 17, 210–11, 220, 222–23, 226
    on television, 91–92, 93–94
NASCAR Goes Country, 79–81
NASCAR Hall of Fame, 142, 225, 227–28
Nashville, Tenn., 72
Nashville Fairgrounds Speedway, 53, 54, 58, 79, 87, 91
National 500, 113
Nationwide series, 61, 123
NBC, 193, 194
Newman, Paul, 154, 192
New York Times, 95
Nick (trainer), 161–62
nitrous oxide, 81
Norris, Ty, 189

Ontario, 98–99
Orr, Rodney, 6, 172–73
Osterlund, Rod, 92–93, 111
Owens, Slick, 14

Pabst Blue Ribbon, 135
Park, Steve, 3, 5, 187, 189, 205, 221
Parrot, Buddy, 89, 96
Parsons, Benny, 89, 90, 97, 191
Parsons, Phil, 118
pass in the grass, 138–39
Patrick, 45–51
Pearson, David, 13, 69, 71, 76,

79–81, 88, 94, 181, 203, 225
Pedley, Harry, 45, 49
Pennzoil, 182, 187, 189
Pepsi, 104
Pepsi 400, 157
Petty, Adam, 6, 210, 222, 226
Petty, Kyle, 129, 165, 169, 210–11
Petty, Lee, 210, 225
Petty, Richard, 6, 59, 71, 76, 79–81, 88, 95, 99, 110, 113, 128, 129, 203, 204, 210
    in Hall of Fame, 225
    retirement of, 170
Phillips, Lee, 29, 30
Phoenix International Raceway, 166, 178
Pit Stop (TV show), 59
Pocono, 141, 159, 160, 162, 205
Presidents' Day Blizzard, 94
Procter & Gamble, 134–35, 144, 154, 155–56

race cars, science of, 55–56, 111
Rader, Carol, 35, 41
Rader, Mr., 35, 41–43, 51, 52, 62–63, 65, 78, 102, 104
Rader, Mrs., 36, 51
Rader, Stevie, *see* Waltrip, Stevie Rader
Ranier, Harry, 131
RC Cola, 76
Reagan, Larry, 76
Rebel 500, 88–89
restrictor plates, 6
Rhodes, J. R., 205
Richert, Doug, 111
Richmond, 72, 78, 83, 109, 110, 111, 116, 128–29, 130, 136, 155, 164
Richmond, Tim, 205

Riddle, John, 78
Ridley, Jody, 144
Riverside International Raceway, 75, 87, 100, 112, 113, 127, 131, 140–41
R. J. Reynolds, 122, 123, 126
Rob, 35–37
Robbins, Marty, 79, 80
Roberts, Fireball, 20
Robinson, T. Wayne, 122–23
Rockingham Speedway, 78, 79, 109, 116, 127, 155, 177, 220, 221
Roger, 117–18
Roper, Tony, 222
Rossi, Mario, 81, 87
Roush, Jack, 179
Roush Racing, 196
Rudd, Ricky, 113, 118, 164
Ruttman, Joe, 114

Sabates, Felix, 165
Sacks, Greg, 164
safety, 6–7, 17, 210–11, 220, 222–23, 226
Salem, Ind., 13, 51
Salem Speedway, 51–52, 62–64
Sanders, Ed, 14
Sawyer, Paul, 78
Schrader, Kenny, 144, 145, 159, 212, 213
Schwarzenegger, Arnold, 195
Seagraves, Ralph, 122–23
Segrave, H. O. D., 15
Silva, Ed, 102–3, 184
Simpson, Don, 154
Skillman, Ray, 14, 18–19, 20
Skillman Auto Sales, 14
Skinner, Mike, 191
Small, Chief, 215
Smith, Bruton, 181
Smitty (driver), 207, 220–21
Snow, Les, 52

Southern Methodist University, 35, 43
Speed Block, 182, 183, 184
Speedweeks, 1–2, 3, 5, 6, 66–67, 93, 105, 143, 183, 202, 222
Spencer, Jimmy, 5–6, 191
Sports Illustrated, 100
Squier, Ken, 91, 92, 95, 194, 201, 202
Sterling Beer, 62, 135
Steve (friend), 29, 30
Stewart, Jackie, 192
Stewart, Tony, 8, 180, 202, 211–12, 213–14, 217
stock car racing, rules of, 17
Streamline Hotel, 17
Strictly Stock, 185
Stringfield, David, 159, 161
Sunday Money, 182

Tabasco, 189
Talladega Superspeedway, 6, 69–72, 73, 79, 83, 87, 89–90, 91, 118, 126, 131, 142, 172, 197, 203
Taylor, Bernie, 18
TBS, 193
Teague, Marshall, 18
Tennessean, 58
Terminal Transport, 66, 69, 76, 79
Texas Gas, 35, 42–43, 63, 66
Texas Motor Speedway, 65, 109
Thomas, Ronnie, 94
Thompson, Bobby, 80
Tide, 135, 136, 151, 155–56, 157
Trammel, Dr., 159
Traub, Charles, 16
tunnel vision, 7
21 team, 121
Twin 125, 4–5

Twin 125s, 2
Tyler Jet Motorsports, 186

USA Today, 226

Vanderflutz, Jerry, 162

Wallace, Rusty, 141, 151–52, 153, 169, 172, 197, 217
Waltrip, Bobby, 160
Waltrip, Buffy, 219
Waltrip, Carolyn, 228
Waltrip, Darrell:
    acting by, 154–55, 227
    Allison's relationship with, 54–56, 88–89, 98, 111, 128, 140–42
    autowork of, 14, 21
    barnstorming by, 61
    Bill France Award of Excellence won by, 199
    broadcasting career of, 2–4, 7, 9–11, 149, 190, 193–97, 199, 202–6, 207–8, 209–10, 212–15
    chrome car press conference of, 180–81
    contract of, 101–5
    in deal with Kmart, 191–92
    in dispute with Craven, 177, 179
    in dispute with Rusty Wallace, 151–52
    Earnhardt's first meeting with, 68, 136
    Earnhardt's rivalry with, 4, 60, 128–30, 189
    engagement of, 42–43
    engine program started by, 171
    engines in cars of, 123, 125, 131–32
    equipment problems of, 165–67

fan dislike of, 78, 110, 153
in first trip to Daytona, 13,
    18–19
growing reputation and fanbase
    of, 90, 110, 128, 130, 152,
    153, 228
hair dying by, 143–44, 146–47,
    149
Hendrick's offer to, 132–34
Honda dealership of, 121–22,
    132
inducted in Hall of Fame,
    225–28
International Race of
    Champions, 180
interviews of, 59, 78, 128
Junior Johnson's deal with,
    100–101
Junior Johnson's threat to,
    109
marriage of, 51
in meeting with CBS, 92
money troubles of, 51–52,
    77–78, 79, 81, 82, 131
Most Popular Driver won by,
    153
NASCAR's penalizing of, 152
in newspapers, 61
outdated cars of, 184
parents of, 25, 79
personality of, 57, 60, 78–79,
    100, 107, 111
in physical therapy, 161
pit crews of, 61–62, 67–68,
    69–71, 76–77, 99, 111–13,
    145, 156–58, 165–67, 169,
    171–72, 228
plane of, 180, 195
rebelliousness of, 25, 26, 27–28,
    74–75
religious faith of, 117–20,
    127, 135, 173, 177, 178–79,
    187

retirement of, 192–93, 196,
    197–98, 225
science of cars learned by,
    55–56, 111
sense of humor of, 57–58
singing career of, 79–81
souvenirs of, 182
sponsors of, 134–35, 144, 154,
    155–56, 182, 192
and Stevie's pregnancies, 135,
    137, 170
team sold by, 185–86
team started by, 156–57, 169,
    186
track run by, 25–28
trash talk by, 4, 61
in trouble with police, 28–30,
    31–33, 39–42, 45–51,
    65–66
on TV special, 91
winnings and earnings of, 72,
    82, 127, 132, 133, 143, 153,
    181–82
Waltrip, Darrell, races of:
    accidents in, 60, 114–16, 118,
        129–30, 151–52, 158–59,
        175–76, 191, 201
    all-star race, 151–52
    Atlanta, 79, 146, 148–49, 151,
        155, 197–98
    black flag of, 98
    Bristol, 79, 109, 131, 189
    car troubles in, 76, 79, 83, 87,
        109, 112, 116, 124–25, 141,
        164
    championships won by, 110,
        113–14, 127
    Charlotte, 83, 112, 113, 123,
        125–26, 127, 152, 162,
        163–64
    Checker 500, 166
    Coca-Cola World 600, 123,
        125–26, 152

Waltrip, Darrell, races of: (*cont.*)
  crowd's reaction to, 60
  Darlington, 74, 78, 79, 83,
    88–89, 96–97, 99, 109, 117,
    184, 185, 187
  Daytona 500, 3, 22–23, 52, 72,
    79, 87, 93–95, 100, 108–9,
    111, 114, 128, 136, 143,
    144, 169, 170, 172–73, 181,
    183–84
  Daytona 500 won by, 2,
    145–46, 151, 155
  Dover Downs, 78, 87, 110,
    112
  as driver for Earnhardt,
    188–89
  fight after, 152
  injuries of, 114–16, 158–64,
    175–76
  International Race of
    Champions, 180
  Japanese event, 191
  Martinsville, 79, 83, 87, 113,
    117, 118, 131, 138, 151,
    153
  Michigan, 87, 176, 180
  Motorcraft 500, 146, 148–49
  Nashville Speedway, 53, 54,
    79, 87, 91
  Pocono, 169–70
  popularity of, 58–59, 61
  at Richmond, 72, 83, 109,
    110, 111, 116, 128–29,
    130, 136, 155, 164
  Riverside, 87, 100, 112, 113,
    127, 131, 140–41
  Rockingham, 79, 109, 116,
    127, 155, 177
  strategy of, 27, 145
  Talladega, 69–72, 79, 83, 87,
    89–90, 91, 118, 126, 131
  victories of, 2, 13, 53, 83, 87,
    88–89, 90, 100, 109, 113,
      124–25, 126, 131, 145–46,
      149, 151, 153, 155, 169–70
  Wilkesboro, 74, 79, 87, 97–98,
    99, 117, 127, 131, 136, 169
  Winston, 151–52, 174–76
  Winston Cup, 79
  Winston Western 500, 93, 110,
    113, 118
Waltrip, Jessica, 137–38, 170, 227
Waltrip, Michael, 3, 5, 8–10, 52,
  79, 135, 142, 178, 187, 192,
  205, 207, 211–13, 218, 219
Waltrip, Sarah Kaitlin, 170, 227
Waltrip, Stevie Rader, 35–43, 52,
  53, 56, 65, 68, 69, 79, 81–83,
  84–85, 104, 105, 114, 121,
  128, 144, 145, 148, 156,
  160, 172, 177, 188, 193,
  195–96, 198, 199, 205,
  208–9, 218–19, 225, 228
  marriage of, 51
  medical problems of, 162–63
  pregnancies and childbirth of,
    135, 137, 170, 201
  religious faith of, 117, 119,
    173, 206–7
Watkins Glen International, 180
Western Auto Race Team, 165,
  169, 170, 182
Wheeler, Humpy, 181
Whitesville speedway, 28, 53, 84, 91
White Triplex, 15–16
Wilkesboro, 74, 79, 87, 97–98, 99,
  117, 127, 128, 129, 131,
  136, 153, 169, 206
Williamson Country Bank, 73
Wilson, Waddell, 131, 136
Winner's Circle, 77
Winston, 123–25, 151–52
Winston All-Star Race, 138–39
Winston Cup Grand National
  Championship, 2, 3, 6,
  71–72, 79, 93, 99, 100, 127,

129, 135, 151, 174–75, 187, 190, 191, 204
Winston Million, 126
Winston Western 500, 93, 110, 113, 118
Witlock, Joe, 98
Woody, Larry, 58
World 600, 20
World War II, 17
Wrangler Jeans car, 153

Yarborough, Cale, 59, 71, 72–73, 76, 89, 90, 94–95, 107, 110, 114–15, 128, 184, 191, 228

accident of, 114
Honda dealership offered to, 121
Junior Johnson left by, 100–101
singing career of, 79–81
versatility of, 111
victories of, 100
Yates, Robert, 83, 87, 88
Yeiser, Jim, 14, 18–19, 20
Yocum, Matt, 196

Zelasko, Jeannie, 4
Zyontz, Richie, 207

ABOUT THE AUTHORS

Darrell Waltrip is a three-time NASCAR Cup Series champion and three-time runner-up, the winner of the 1989 Daytona 500, and five-time winner of the Coca-Cola 600. He has won 84 Cup Series races—the most by any driver in the modern era and tied for third on the all-time list. He is a two-time winner of NASCAR's Most Popular Driver Award and was named as "NASCAR's Driver of the Decade" in the 1980s. Waltrip was honored as one of NASCAR's 50 Greatest Drivers in 1998, and was inducted into the NASCAR Hall of Fame in 2012.

Darrell is the author of two previous books, *DW: A Lifetime Going Around in Circles* and *Darrell Waltrip One-on-One: The Faith That Took Him to the Finish Line.* Now the lead NASCAR analyst for Fox Sports, he owns auto dealerships in Franklin, Tennessee, where he lives with his wife, Stevie, and their two daughters.

Nate Larkin is a popular speaker and writer best known for his inspirational book for men, *Samson and the Pirate Monks: Calling Men to Authentic Brotherhood.* A graduate of Princeton Theological Seminary, Larkin is the founder of the Samson Society. He lives in Franklin, Tennessee, with his wife, Allie.